W9-CHP-463

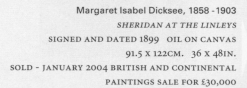

Carlos Nadal
SAINT TROPEZ
SIGNED, TITLED AND STAMPED WITH THE ATELIER
MARK ON THE REVERSE   OIL ON PAPER
LAID DOWN ON CANVAS   27.5 BY 35.5CM.
SOLD – MARCH 2004 IMPRESSIONIST SALE
FOR £13,800

Margaret Isabel Dicksee, 1858 - 1903
SHERIDAN AT THE LINLEYS
SIGNED AND DATED 1899   OIL ON CANVAS
91.5 X 122CM.   36 X 48IN.
SOLD – JANUARY 2004 BRITISH AND CONTINENTAL
PAINTINGS SALE FOR £30,000

After Tiziano Vecellio, called Titian
THE VENUS OF URBINO
OIL ON CANVAS
SOLD – DECEMBER 2003 OLD MASTER PAINTINGS SALE
FOR £44,400

Richard Eurich
HARBOUR SCENE, PENZANCE
OIL ON PANEL
SOLD – FEBRUARY 2004 MODERN BRITISH & IRISH
PAINTINGS SALE FOR £11,400

Paintings Department at Sotheby's Olympia

At Sotheby's Olympia we hold a selection of Painting sales throughout the year. These range from earlier works in our Old Master Paintings and British and Continental Picture sales through to the more recent period with Modern British and Irish Paintings and Contemporary and Impressionist Art.

For more information about buying or selling paintings at Sotheby's Olympia please call the department on 020 7293 6435

Sotheby's EST. 1744

MILLER'S

pictures

MILLER'S PICTURES PRICE GUIDE 2005

Created and designed by
Miller's
The Cellars, High Street
Tenterden, Kent, TN30 6BN
Tel: 01580 766411
Fax: 01580 766100

General Editor: Hugh St. Clair
Managing Editor: Valerie Lewis
Project Co-ordinator: Melinda Williams
Editorial Co-ordinator: Deborah Wanstall
Picture Researcher: Léonie Sidgwick
Editorial Assistants: Melissa Hall, Joanna Hill, Maureen Horner, Jo Wood
Production Assistants: June Barling, Ethne Tragett
Advertising Executives: Emma Gillingham, Jill Jackson
Design: Philip Hannath
Production: Sarah Rogers, Faizah Malik
Advertisement Designer: Simon Cook
Additional photography: Justin Piperger
Jacket Design: Alexa Brommer

First published in Great Britain in 2004
by Miller's, a division of Mitchell Beazley,
imprints of Octopus Publishing Group Ltd,
2–4 Heron Quays, London E14 4JP

© 2004 Octopus Publishing Group Ltd

A CIP catalogue record for this book is
available from the British Library

ISBN 1 84000 957 8

Colour origination by 1.13, Whitstable, Kent
Printed and bound by Toppan Printing Company, China

Miller's is a registered trademark of
Octopus Publishing Group Ltd

Front cover illustrations:

Molly M. Latham British (1900–87)
Foxhunter
Signed and dated 1952, oil on canvas
25 x 30in (63.4 x 76cm)
£1,100–1,300 / €1,600–1,900 / $ 2,000–2,350 ⌘ G(L)

Nelson Mandela South African (b1918)
The Guard Tower
Signed, limited edition, lithograph
25½ x 19¾in (65 x 50cm)
£3,600–4,000 / €5,200–5,800 / $6,500–7,300 ⊞ Bel

Jenny Pockley British (b1973)
Ghost
Oil and graphite on gesso
48 x 54in (122 x 137cm)
£2,950–3,500 €4,300–5,100 / $5,400–6,400 ⊞ SMy

Rachel Deacon British (20thC)
Woman Reclining with Pot
Oil on canvas
39½ x 47¼in (100.5 x 120cm)
£1,250–1,400 / €1,800–2,000 / $2,300–2,600 ⊞ CAMB

Contents page illustration:

Stuart Stanley British (20thC)
Evening Friday Street
Oil on canvas, 16 x 30in (40.5 x 76cm)
£360–400 / €520–580 / $660–730 ⊞ ST

MILLER'S

pictures

HUGH ST. CLAIR *General Editor*

Contents

How to use this book

It is our aim to make this book easy to use. In order to find works by a particular artist, consult the index which starts on page 237. If you are looking for the special features consult the contents list on page 5.

◀ Francis Bacon
British (1909–92)
Untitled
Signed and numbered 74/100, lithograph
19¼ x 14¼in (49 x 36cm)
£2,450–2,950 / €3,600-4,300
$4,450–5,300 ➤ DORO

▶ Qi Baishi
Chinese (1864–1957)
Chrysanthemum and Crabs
Signed and dated, artist's seal, ink and colour on paper
41½ x 13½in (105.5 x 34.5cm)
£17,000–20,400 / €25,000–30,000
$31,000–37,000 ➤ S(HK)

▼ For further information
see Botanical & Flower Painting (pages 32–35)

A good provenance can make a huge difference to the price of a picture. Collectors like something new to the market; a good picture that has been in a family for generations will fetch more than a picture that has been in and out of auction houses.

Charles Thomas Bale
British (d1875)
Still life with game and fruit
Signed, oil on canvas
20 x 30in (51 x 76cm)
£900–1,050 / €1,300–1,550
$1,600–1,900 ➤ B(Kn)

Margaret Ballantyne (20thC)

Margaret Ballantyne paints decorative still lifes in oil and landscapes in mixed media – oil, charcoal and acrylic. Many of her pictures have been reproduced as greeting cards and therefore the original familiar image will always be collectable. She studied at the Glasgow School of Art and is now a member of the Glasgow Society of Women Artists and the Paisley Art Institute. She is based on the west coast of Scotland but travels frequently to Europe where she seeks out picturesque villages in France, Spain and Italy to commit to canvas.

◀ Margaret Ballantyne
British (20thC)
Arrochar, Islay
Oil on canvas
26in (66cm) square
£2,350–2,600
€3,450–3,800
$4,300–4,750
⊞ CFAG

◀ Margaret Ballantyne
Scottish (20thC)
Farm Steading, Through Trees, Renfrewshire
Oil on canvas
18 x 22in (45.5 x 56cm)
£1,450–1,650 / €2,100–2,400
$2,650–3,000 ⊞ WrG

▶ Margaret Ballantyne
British (20thC)
St Ives, Cornwall
Oil on canvas
24in (61cm) square
£2,050–2,300 / €3,000–3,350
$3,700–4,200 ⊞ CFAG

Running head
this refers to the first or last artist appearing alphabetically on a left or right hand page.

For further information box
directs the reader to related topics elsewhere in the book.

Information box
covers relevant information on artists, care and restoration, and insuring your pictures.

Price guide
this is based on actual prices realized. Remember that Miller's is a price guide not a price list and prices are affected by many variables such as location, condition, desirability and so on. Don't forget that if you are selling it is quite likely you will be offered less than the price range. Price ranges for items sold at auction tend to include the buyer's premium and VAT if applicable.
The exchange rate used in this edition is 1.46 for € and 1.82 for $.

Artist profile
provides further information on an artist's life and work together with a sample(s) of their work.

Caption
includes the artist's name, dates and country of birth, title of the work, medium, year it was produced and size.

Source code
refers to the Key to Illustrations on page 234 that lists the details of where the item was offered for sale. The ➤ icon indicates the item was sold at auction. The ⊞ icon indicates the item originated from a gallery.

Acknowledgments

The publishers would like to acknowledge the great assistance given by all galleries, auction houses and their press offices, in particular:

BONHAMS AUCTION HOUSES
We would like to acknowledge the
help supplied by all staff at branches
of Bonhams Auction Houses.

MATTHEW FLORIS
Sotheby's,
34–35 New Bond Street,
London W1A 2AA

HAUSER & WIRTH
196a Piccadilly,
London W1J 9DJ

TONY HAYNES
Haynes Fine Art of Broadway,
Picton House Galleries, 42 High Street, Broadway,
Worcestershire WR12 7DT

LAURA HUNTER
Belgravia Gallery, 59 Ebury Street,
London SW1W 0NZ

PETER JOHNSON
Ackerman & Johnson Ltd,
27 Lowndes Street,
London SW1X 9HY

We would also like to acknowledge the help given by the following Fairs & Publications:

Maine Antiques Digest USA

The 20/21 British Art Fair London

Affordable Art Fair London

Affordable Art Fair New York

The Art on Paper Fair London

Frieze Art Fair London

Introduction

Welcome to the third edition of *Miller's Pictures Price Guide*. As in previous editions we have included a representative and interesting cross section of oil paintings, watercolours, drawings and prints sold worldwide during the past 12 months. Although you may not find work by the particular artist that you are interested in, they might appear in a previous *Miller's Pictures Price Guide* or, indeed, in a future edition.

These books are intended to be collected annually to form a comprehensive art price library and we rarely include a work if a similar example by that artist has been featured in previous books. However, works by one artist can differ in price depending on subject matter and size. If the price of a work by a particular artist differs enormously this year compared to similar examples in a previous edition, the artist will appear in more than one volume. In this edition we have shown some price comparisons. For example, it is possible to buy a small pen-and-ink drawing for £3,500 / €5,100 / $6,400 by world-famous artist Edouard Vuillard who was the subject of a blockbuster show at London's Royal Academy and whose large pictures can fetch six-figure sums. The dateline for this book is from 1700 onwards, although some artists born before then are included because of their huge and important influence on subsequent painters.

Pictures continue to be a good investment and there is more choice than ever, thanks to the proliferation of new art fairs – including Bristol, Sydney, Melbourne, New York and London. The new Frieze Art Fair in London, run by the excellent *Frieze* magazine, was launched in 2003. An extremely high example of work was on show and the fair was well attended. However, this does not necessarily mean that the quality of art has gone up. Before you buy, check the artist's provenance – where they have exhibited or where they studied. Ultimately, investing in contemporary art is a gamble but if you find a picture that you like and can afford, it will certainly bring you pleasure.

When Charles Saatchi, famous collector of a group known as Young British Artists (YBA) – Damien Hirst, Tracy Emin etc – opened a new contemporary art gallery in London, he declared that the panelled rooms of the former County Hall, built in the 1920s, were a better backdrop for modern art than stark white spaces. Not all contemporary artists agreed with him, however, and Damien Hirst bought back his own pictures from Saatchi because he did not feel they were properly displayed. Saatchi, of course, made money on the deal; Hirst had to pay more than he had sold them for.

Although serious collectors don't like to admit it, interior design trends do influence picture tastes. The stark minimalist interior is losing ground to the warmer, colourful one and installation art, now so copied and devalued by scores of imitators of the masters, is no longer as exciting as it once was. Paintings on canvas are becoming fashionable again, and Americans continue to pay high prices for home-grown art in these politically and economically uncertain times. Russian art, too, is making record prices due to the country's new wealth.

The special features in this book reflect a return to simple but more homely tastes. Take floral art, for instance. This year saw the sale of a painting by Jan van Huysum, who is considered to be one of the very best flower painters and who was paid more than Rembrandt in his time. I have written about the development of flower painting through the ages. Pictures of flowers do brighten up a home but some of the works we have chosen have greater depth – they are not just pretty pictures.

Equestrian art, another special subject, will always be collectable and of value as long as the close relationship between humans and horses continues. Simple, smart and with such a lightness of touch, 18th-century paintings of horses will always appeal. Equally, there are some very talented equestrian artists working today whose work could well increase in value. They are collected by the same kind of patrons who in centuries past would have bought Wootton or Munnings.

Art based around the theatre is another fascinating and popular subject and this is a good area to start collecting. Paintings that evoke memories are becoming increasingly popular. Urban landscapes of London and New York are a special feature this year.

Canadian artists are included as another special subject and their work certainly costs less than their contemporary European Impressionists and Expressionists. As many of us live in suburbs a Canadian landscape of the great wilderness can give us a longed-for sense of freedom.

Our desire for celebrity gossip continues unabated. Quite a few stars from the world of stage and screen manage to find time to paint, but is a painting worth more because of its celebrity provenance? Find out in the special section on Celebrity Art.

I hope you find this latest edition of *Miller's Pictures Price Guide* informative and enjoyable. If there are particular artists you would like us to include, or areas of art you would like to see, please do let us know.

Hugh Gillan

Artists A–Z

Ilmari Aalto
Finnish (1891–1934)
Storm Clouds
Oil
15¾ x 19¾in (40 x 50cm)
£690–830 / €1,000–1,200
$1,250–1,500 ⚵ BUK

Ilmari Aalto was on the one hand a pure Expressionist and on the other a bold Cubist experimenter. Aalto's graduation from art school in 1908 coincided with eventful times in Finnish art. In that year the Finns had received provocative criticism from the French, which resulted in a re-evaluation of their art. Edvard Munch's exhibition at the Atheneum in the following year had a profound effect on Aalto, as it did on everybody interested in Expressionism. Rumours of the new European art movements, Cubism and Expressionism, gradually reached Finland and the first exhibition of Cubists and Expressionists to be held in Finland was in 1914.

▶ **Ian Abdulla**
Australian (b1947)
Untitled
Signed and inscribed, synthetic polymer paint on paper
22 x 30in (56 x 76cm)
£2,450–2,950 / €3,600–4,300
$4,500–5,400 ⚵ SHSY

The artist has recorded a period in rural Aboriginal histories referred to as the Depression of the 1950s, when Aboriginal families such as Abdulla's sought an independent life away from the mission.

Veikko Aaltona
Finnish (1910–90)
Valoa Ikkunassa
Oil
37 x 47¼in (94 x 120cm)
£960–1,150 / €1,400–1,650
$1,750–2,100 ⚵ BUK

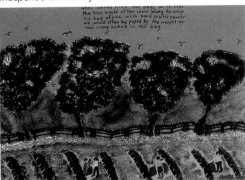

Ian Abdulla
Australian (b1947)
Untitled
Signed and inscribed, synthetic polymer paint on paper
22 x 30in (56 x 76cm)
£1,950–2,350 / €2,850–3,400
$3,550–4,250 ⚵ SHSY

▶ **Benno Adam**
German (1819–92)
Landscape
Signed, oil on paper laid down on canvas
10¼ x 14½in (26 x 37cm)
£2,650–3,150
€3,850–4,650
$4,800–5,750
⚵ S(NY)

Patrick William Adam, RSA
British (1854–1929)
In the Garden, the Knoll, North Berwick
Signed and inscribed, oil on canvas
19¾ x 26½in (50 x 67.5cm)
£2,500–3,000 / €3,600–4,300
$4,550–5,400 ⚖ B(Ed)

Louis Emile Adan
French (1839–1937)
Elegant ladies at rest beside a pond
Signed, oil on canvas
30¾ x 48in (78 x 122cm)
£6,500–7,800 / €9,500–11,400
$11,80–14,200 ⚖ B

Taisto Ahtola
Finnish (1917–2000)
Esiintymiseen Keskittyminen
Signed, oil
9½ x 7½in (24 x 19cm)
£1,000–1,200 / €1,500–1,800
$1,800–2,150 ⚖ BUK

Watercolours
When framing your
watercolours insist on
mounting the picture on
acid free boards. Poor
mounting and the wrong
adhesives can cause works
on paper to deteriorate.

► **Federico Aguilar Alcuaz**
Spanish (b1932)
Yellow Still Life
Signed, titled and dated 1963,
oil on canvas
36¼ x 28¾in (92 x 73cm)
£2,350–2,800 / €3,400–4,100
$4,250–5,100 ⚖ S(SI)

► **Cecil Charles Windsor Aldin**
British (1870–1935)
Exhausted Companions
Signed, watercolour and ink
on ivorine
3¾ x 4½in (9.5 x 11.5cm)
£1,400–1,650 / €2,050–2,450
$2,550–3,050 ⚖ B(Kn)

Douglas Alexander
Irish (1871–1945)
Sun Burst, West of Ireland
Signed, oil on canvas
30 x 36in (76 x 91.5cm)
£3,850–4,650 / €5,600–6,700
$7,000–8,400 ⚒ WA

John Aldridge, RA
British (1905–83)
Landscape, May 1949
Inscribed, oil on board
20¾ x 24¾in (52.5 x 63cm)
£1,400–1,650 / €2,050–2,450
$2,500–3,000 ⚒ B(Nor)

Mary Allen
American (1888–1974)
Floral Still Life
Signed, oil on board
9 x 12in (23 x 30.5cm)
£175–210
€250–300
$320–380 ⚒ JAA

▶ **Robert C. G. Allen**
British (20thC)
Pekingese 'Jero's
Pu Zin'
Signed, pastel
on paper
22½ x 15¼in
(57 x 38.5cm)
£500–600
€730–880
$900–1,100 ⚒ DNY

David Alison, RSA, RP
British (1882–1955)
Summer
Signed and inscribed, oil on canvas
24 x 20in (61 x 51cm)
£1,200–1,450 / €1,750–2,100
$2,200–2,600 ⚒ B(Ed)

Helen Allingham (1848–1929)

Helen and her husband, poet and diarist William Allingham were at the centre of Victorian cultural and intellectual life. They were Tennyson groupies and in the summer of 1880 rented a house in Surrey near Tennyson's home. In exchange for one of Helen's pretty watercolours the poet agreed to sit for her. Helen's cottage scenes continue to be as popular now as they were during her lifetime, and have increased in value. Many prints have been taken from the the book *Cottage Homes of England* which was first published in 1909.

Helen Allingham, RWS
British (1848–1929)
Parsonage Row at West Tawing, near Worthing
Signed, watercolour
18¼ x 14¾in (46.5 x 37.5cm)
£36,000–40,000 / €52,000–58,000
$65,000–73,000 ⊞ HFA

Helen Allingham, RWS
British (1848–1929)
A Wiltshire cottage
Signed, watercolour
10 x 13in (25.5 x 33cm)
£23,000–27,000
€34,000–40,000
$42,000–49,000 ⚒ B

► **Helen Allingham, RWS**
British (1848–1929)
Portrait of Alfred,
Lord Tennyson
Signed, inscribed and dated
1880, watercolour
7¾ x 6¼in (19.5 x 16cm)
£4,000–4,800
€5,800–7,000
$7,300–8,700 ⚒ B
Smaller pictures generally fetch less than larger pictures by the same artists.

Attributed to Jean Altamuras
Greek (1852–78)
After the storm
Signed, oil on canvas
15 x 21½in (38 x 54.5cm)
£5,200–6,200 / €7,600–9,100
$9,400–11,300 ⚒ B

Robin Christian Andersen
Austrian (1890–1969)
Still life with apples, pears and a jug
Signed and dated 1913, oil on board
19¼ x 27¼in (49 x 69cm)
£5,100–6,100 / €7,500–9,000
$9,300–11,100 ⚒ DORO

Anders Andersen-Lundby
Danish (1840–1923)
Sailing ships off the coast
Signed, oil on board
13¾ x 24¾in (35 x 63cm)
£2,450–2,950 / €3,600–4,300
$4,400–5,300 ↗ DORO

Charles Anderson, DA
Scottish (b1936)
Highland Township, Midwinter
Acrylic
24in (61cm) square
£1,700–1,900 / €2,450–2,750
$3,100–3,450 ⊞ WrG

*Charles Anderson trained at Glasgow School
of Art, graduating with a Diploma in 1959.
He has worked as a professional artist for
the past 30 years on major art and design
projects throughout the UK. Since early 1997
he has exhibited at the Royal Glasgow
Institute, the Royal Scottish Society of
Painters in Watercolours and at several mixed
exhibitions in Burford, Oxfordshire.*

◄ **John MacVicar Anderson**
British (19thC)
Columbia Market
Signed, inscribed and dated 1870,
oil on canvas
21¾ x 36in (55.5 x 91.5cm)
£3,500–4,200 / €5,100–6,100
$6,400–7,600 ↗ B

◄ **Raúl Anguiano**
Mexican (b1915)
Woman carrying a platter of fruit
Pastel on paper
12¾ x 9½in (32.5 x 24cm)
£1,750–2,100 / €2,550–3,050
$3,150–3,750 ↗ LCM

*Raúl Anguiano was born in
Guadalajara, Jalisco in 1915.
After studying in his native city,
he went to Mexico City, where
he formed part of the Group of
the 30s. He took part in the
foundation of the Popular Painting
Establishment in 1938 and later
moved to New York where he
continued his studies. His works
have been shown in the USA,
Cuba and Mexico.*

Richard Ansdell
British (1815–85)
Bloodhound in an interior
Signed and dated 1847, oil on canvas laid to masonite
12 x 16in (30.5 x 40.5cm)
£4,400–5,200 / €6,400–7,600
$8,000–9,600 ↗ DNY

Fred Aris
British (20thC)
The Merry-go-round
Signed, oil on board
22 x 26in (56 x 66cm)
£400–480 / €580–690
$730–870 B(Kn)

Erling Ärlingsson
Swedish (1904–82)
Horses Grazing
Signed and dated 1968, card panel
15½ x 19¾in (39.5 x 50cm)
£1,200–1,400 / €1,750–2,050
$2,200–2,550 BUK

Mary Armour, RSA, RSW
British (1902–2000)
Gourds on a Plate
Signed and dated 1959, ink,
watercolour and gouache
20½ x 25½in (52 x 65cm)
£1,450–1,750
€2,100–2,500
$2,650–3,150 B(Ed)

Alejandro Aróstegui
Nicaraguan (b1935)
Nocturne with Two Figures
Signed and dated 1997,
mixed media on collage
51¼ x 70½in (130 x 179cm)
£420–500 / €610–730
$760–910 LCM

Will Ashton
British (1881–1963)
In the Luxembourg Gardens, Paris
Signed, inscribed and dated 1926,
oil on canvas
17¼ x 23½in (44 x 59.5cm)
£2,850–3,400
€4,150–4,950
$5,200–6,200 LJ

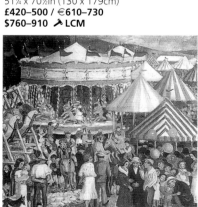

◄ **Evelyn Winifred
Aston**
British (1924–75)
The Fairground
Oil on board
21 x 23in
(53.5 x 58.5cm)
£2,650–2,950
€3,850–4,300
$4,800–5,300 JN

William Edward Atkins
British (1842–1910)
Portsmouth Harbour
Signed and dated 1865, watercolour
10¾ x 17¾in (27.5 x 45cm)
£950–1,100 / €1,350–1,600
$1,700–2,000 Bea
*This scene shows the ironclads HMS Royal Sovereign and HMS
Resistance with HMS Victory in the foreground.*

George Mounsey Wheatley Atkinson
Irish (1806–84)
The entrance to Rio de Janeiro, Brazil
Signed, oil on canvas
27¼ x 40½in (69 x 102cm)
£4,000–4,800 / €5,900–7,000
$7,300–8,700 ⚖ B

*Atkinson spent his early life at sea as a ship's carpenter and later
became Government Surveyor of Shipping and Emigrants at
Queenstown, New Zealand. He exhibited 21 marine subjects at the
RHA, mainly depicting scenes around Ireland.*

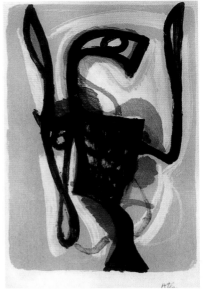

► **Jean Michel Atlan**
French (1913–60)
Astarte
Signed and
numbered 48/220,
lithograph
19 x 13in (48 x 33cm)
£410–490
€600–720
$750–890 ⚖ BUK

◄ **Felix Auguste**
French (fl1850–70)
Two hat designs
Watercolour
4 x 4½in (10 x 11.5cm)
£200–240 / €290–350
$360–430 ⚖ B(Kn)

*The fashion designer Felix
Auguste worked for the firm of
Poirier in Paris and also had
connections with Worth. He
produced witty and exquisite hat
designs for society ladies.*

James Aumonier
British (1832–1911)
Brighton
Signed, inscribed and dated 1896, watercolour
6¾ x 9½in (17 x 24cm)
£700–840 / €1,000–1,200
$1,250–1,500 ⚖ B(Kn)

Milton Avery
American (1885–1965)
Owl
Signed and dated 1955,
oil on board
9 x 5¼in (23 x 13.5cm)
£24,700–29,600
€36,000–43,200
$44,900–53,900 ⚖ S(NY)

Milton Avery
American (1885–1965)
Lone Chicken
Signed and dated 1954, oil on board
8¾ x 8½in (22 x 21.5cm)
£43,000–51,000 / €63,000–75,000
$78,000–93,000 ⚖ S(NY)

**Paul Ayshford (Lord Methuen), RA, RWS, PRWA,
RBA, NEAC**
British (1886–1974)
Nude in a blue hat
Oil on canvas
20 x 28in (51 x 71cm)
£5,300–5,900 / €7,800–8,600
$9,700–10,800 ⊞ JN

◄ **Francis Bacon**
British (1909–92)
Untitled
Signed and numbered 74/100, lithograph
19¼ x 14¼in (49 x 36cm)
£2,450–2,950 / €3,600-4,300
$4,450–5,300 ➚ DORO

▶ **Qi Baishi**
Chinese (1864–1957)
Chrysanthemum and Crabs
Signed and dated, artist's seal, ink and colour on paper
41½ x 13½in (105.5 x 34.5cm)
£17,000–20,400 / €25,000–30,000
$31,000–37,000 ➚ S(HK)

A good provenance can make a huge difference to the price of a picture. Collectors like something new to the market; a good picture that has been in a family for generations will fetch more than a picture that has been in and out of auction houses.

Charles Thomas Bale
British (d1875)
Still life with game and fruit
Signed, oil on canvas
20 x 30in (51 x 76cm)
£900–1,050 / €1,300–1,550
$1,600–1,900 ➚ B(Kn)

Margaret Ballantyne (20thC)

Margaret Ballantyne paints decorative still lifes in oil and landscapes in mixed media – oil, charcoal and acrylic. Many of her pictures have been reproduced as greeting cards and therefore the original familiar image will always be collectable. She studied at the Glasgow School of Art and is now a member of the Glasgow Society of Women Artists and the Paisley Art Institute. She is based on the west coast of Scotland but travels frequently to Europe where she seeks out picturesque villages in France, Spain and Italy to commit to canvas.

◄ **Margaret Ballantyne**
British (20thC)
Arrochar, Islay
Oil on canvas
26in (66cm) square
£2,350–2,600
€3,450–3,800
$4,300–4,750
⊞ CFAG

◄ **Margaret Ballantyne**
Scottish (20thC)
Farm Steading, Through Trees, Renfrewshire
Oil on canvas
18 x 22in (45.5 x 56cm)
£1,450–1,650 / €2,100–2,400
$2,650–3,000 ⊞ WrG

▶ **Margaret Ballantyne**
British (20thC)
St Ives, Cornwall
Oil on canvas
24in (61cm) square
£2,050–2,300 / €3,000–3,350
$3,700–4,200 ⊞ CFAG

◄ **Muriel Barclay**
Scottish (20thC)
Con Carino
Oil on canvas
40in (101.5cm) square
£3,150–3,500
€4,600–5,100
$5,800–6,400
⊞ **CFAG**

► **Thomas Barker of Bath**
British (1767–1847)
Young peasant girl in a woodland clearing
Signed, oil
9 x 6in (23 x 15cm)
£210–250
€310–370
$380–450 ⚒ **GH**

William Henry Barnard
British (1769–1818)
Mountain Pass in Greece, with figures by a cross
Pencil and watercolour on paper,
heightened with bodycolour
14 x 10in (35.5 x 25.5cm)
£230–270 / €340–410
$420–500 ⚒ **DW**

Shona Barr
Scottish (20thC)
Sunset
Watercolour
6 x 8½in (15 x 21.5cm)
£360–400 / €530–590
$660–730 ⊞ **WrG**

Shona Barr studied at Glasgow School of Art and also at Norwegian and English universities. She has received several prestigious Scottish art awards including the Landscape Prize at GSA, the Armour Prize for Still Life at GSA, and the David Cargill Award at the Glasgow Institute. She has exhibited in both solo and mixed shows in Scotland and London, and at the annual RGI and RSW exhibitions. Her work is to be found in the collections of United Distillers, Proctor & Gamble, Robert Fleming Holdings and John Menzies.

Jerry Barrett
British (1824–1906)
A lady with a canary in an interior
Oil on canvas
20 x 15in (51 x 38cm)
£1,800–2,150 / €2,650–3,200
$3,300–3,950 ⚒ **B(Kn)**

◄ **Daniel Barrow**
Canadian (20thC)
In My Head
Watercolour collage
11 x 8½in (28 x 21.5cm)
£330–390 / €480–580
$600–720 ⊞ **OTG**

► **Paul Bassingthwaighte**
British (b1963)
Almond Harvest
Oil on canvas
16 x 20in (40.5 x 51cm)
£240–290 / €350–420
$440–530 ⚒ **B(Kn)**

Henry Mayo Bateman
British (1887–1970)
Diamonds, a Game of Bridge
Signed, pen and wash
9½ x 9¼in (24 x 23.5cm)
£850–1,000 / €1,250–1,500
$1,550–1,850 ⚒ B(Kn)

Gifford Beal
American (1879–1956)
Summer Day, Rockport
Signed, oil on masonite
24 x 30in (61 x 76cm)
£36,000–43,000 / €53,000–63,000
$66,000–79,000 ⚒ S(NY)

◀ **Penelope Beaton, ARSA, RSW**
British (1886–1963)
Storm, Iona
Signed, pen and ink and watercolour
17¼ x 22¾in (44 x 58cm)
£1,800–2,150 / €2,650–3,150
$3,300–3,950 ⚒ B(Ed)

◀ **Roland Becerra**
American (b1973)
Family Portrait
Acrylic
67 x 78in (170 x 198cm)
£4,400–4,850 / €6,400–7,100
$8,000–8,800 ⊞ LaP

Roland Becerra
American (b1973)
On The Roof
Acrylic
24in (61cm) square
£660–730
€950–1,050
$1,200–1,350 ⊞ LaP

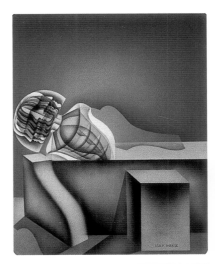

◄ **Arnold Belkin**
Canadian (1930–92)
Marat Asesinato #10
Oil on board
70 x 55¼in (178 x 140.5cm)
£2,500–3,000 / €3,650–4,400
$4,550–5,500 ⚒ **LCM**

Arnold Belkin studied painting in Vancouver but from 1948 until his death he lived in Mexico City. Together with the painter Ernesto Icaza, he founded the group known as the Interioristas (interiorists) of the human inspiration. Owing to a manifesto entitled 'New Presence: Man in Art in our Times', in which Jose Luis Cuevas, Leonora Carrington and Rafael Coronel took part among others, they were known as the group of the New Presence.

Edward Bell
British (19thC)
Gurnard and Flounder
Inscribed, watercolour
7¼ x 10¾in (18.5 x 27.5cm)
£220–260 / €320–380
$400–480 ⚒ **B(Kn)**

► **Richard Bell**
Australian (b1953)
Honest John, 2003
Synthetic polymer paint on canvas
35½in (90cm) square
£1,600–1,900 / €2,300–2,750
$2,900–3,500 ⚒ **SHSY**

George Bellows
American (1882–1925)
Approach of Rain
Signed, inscribed and dated 1913, oil on panel
13¼ x 19½in (33.5 x 49.5cm)
£85,000–102,000 / €124,000–149,000
$155,000–185,000 ⚒ **S(NY)**

Vladimir Belskiy
Russian (b1949)
Golden Beams
Signed, oil on canvas
13 x 21¾in (33 x 55.5cm)
£400–480 / €580–690
$730–870 ⚒ **JNic**

Anthony Benedetto (b1926)

Anthony Benedetto, or Tony Bennett as he is better known to most, was born in 1926 in the Astoria area of Queens, New York. The son of an Italian-born immigrant, he began drawing chalk pictures on the sidewalks around his home when he was five years old, and later attended the High School of Industrial Arts in Manhattan. While he is best known for his musical career that has spanned the last 50 years and won him 12 Grammy Awards, he has also been committed to another passion, his painting and has always made time to paint and draw every day, even when touring. Over the years, he has enjoyed experimenting with a range of styles and now works mainly in oils and watercolours. He often paints views of his hometown, New York City, portraits of musician friends, as well as views from his hotel windows. Bennett sees his paintings as performance art saying 'my canvasses are seen by an audience and communicate my vision'. He feels strongly that an artist can always improve and, in an effort to continue to learn and grow, Bennett takes classes at the Art Students League in New York whenever he has the opportunity. Elsewhere he often arranges private tuition with artists such as Robert Wade and high school friend and artistic mentor Everett Raymond Kinstler. The UN has commissioned his artwork twice and he has work in permanent collections at the Butler Institute of American Art and the National Arts Club, Manhattan. For the last ten years, Tony has donated a winter scene to the American Cancer Society's Holiday Card Program to be reproduced as a card to raise funds for the charity. He has also been involved with such diverse projects as the 2001 Kentucky Derby (as their official artist) to producing original artwork for *The Simpsons* trading cards after appearing on the show himself. He signs his work with his family name of Benedetto.

▶ **Anthony Benedetto (Tony Bennett)**
American (b1926)
Sedona, Arizona
Watercolour
15 x 22in (38 x 56cm)
**£6,200–6,900 / €9,000–10,000
$11,300–12,500** ⊞ BENE

Anthony Benedetto (Tony Bennett)
American (b1926)
A Rainy Day
Watercolour
12 x 16in (30.5 x 40.5cm)
**£5,900–6,600 / €8,600–9,600
$10,700–12,000** ⊞ BENE

For more Anthony Benedetto pictures
see Celebrity Art (pages 50–51)

◀ **Anthony Benedetto (Tony Bennett)**
American (b1926)
Palace of Fine Arts, San Francisco
Watercolour
11 x 15in (28 x 38cm)
**£6,700–7,400 / €9,800–10,800
$12,200–13,500** ⊞ BENE

Frank Moss Bennett (1874–1953)

Frank Moss Bennett was a London painter of portraits, genre and historical subjects in oils and watercolour, as well as being an illustrator. Bennett was born in Liverpool and studied at St John's Wood School of Art, the Slade School of Art and at the Royal Academy School of Art, where he won a gold medal and a travelling scholarship. Bennett exhibited at the Royal Academy between 1898 and 1928, as well as at the Royal Institute of Painters in Watercolour and the Paris Salon. As with other artists from his period, he turned to the 17th and 18th centuries for some of his subjects, which proved a popular move among his patrons. *A Surprise Move* sold for a higher price than *One More for Luck* simply because it is a larger picture.

◄ **Frank Moss Bennett**
British (1874–1953)
A Surprise Move
Signed and dated 1943, oil on board
20½ x 14½in (52 x 37cm)
£17,900–19,900
€26,100–29,000
$32,000–36,000
⊞ **HFA**

Frank Moss Bennett
British (1874–1953)
One More for Luck
Signed and dated 1932, oil on canvas
16 x 12in (40.5 x 30.5cm)
£11,500–12,800 / €16,800–18,700
$20,900–23,300 ⊞ **HFA**

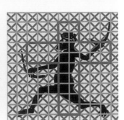

What to buy

Prices for works by well-known artists depend on condition and the period in which they were painted. Work from certain periods of an artist's life is often acknowledged to be better than that from another. Paintings in good condition always achieve higher prices.

Gordon Bennett
Australian (b1955)
Home Décor
Four, signed, inscribed and dated, screenprints on paper
7in (18cm) square
£1,580–1,900 / €2,300–2,750
$2,900–3,450 ➚ **SHSY**

▶ **Margaretann Bennett**
Scottish (20thC)
Fisherman's Gable and Lilac Trawler
Mixed media
17½ x 5½in (44.5 x 14cm)
£430–480 / €630–700
$780–860 ⊞ **WrG**

Alexander Nicholaevich Benois
Russian (1870–1960)
Moored Boats
Signed, inscribed and dated 1934,
watercolour over pencil on paper
10½ x 14¾in (27 x 37.5cm)
£4,800–5,700 / €7,000–8,400
$8,700–10,400 ➚ **S**

Jean Baptiste Emile Beranger
French (1814–83)
The Final Touches
Signed, oil on panel
16¼ x 12½in (41.5 x 32cm)
£12,500–13,900 / €18,200–20,300
$22,800–25,300 ⊞ HFA

▶ **Emile Bernard**
French (1868–1941)
Crouching Boy
Charcoal and watercolour on paper
10 x 15in (25.5 x 38cm)
£4,500–5,000 / €6,600–7,300
$8,200–9,100 ⊞ WoF

Bernard attended the Académie of Fernard Cormon,
where he was a contemporary of Louis Anquetin and
Henri de Toulouse-Lautrec. In 1886, he made his first trip
to Brittany and by 1888 he was working in Pont-Aven,
had been befriended by Claude-Emile Schuffenicker and
had met Paul Gauguin. In 1889, he returned to Paris
where he participated in the 'Synthetist' exhibition
together with Gauguin at the Café Volpini. In 1892, he
arranged the first retrospective exhibition of Vincent van
Gogh's work. Later he developed his career as a writer
and publisher.

Leon Berkowitz
American (b1919)
After the Cloud
Signed, oil on canvas
73½ x 94½in (186.5 x 240cm)
£1,450–1,750 / €2,100–2,500
$2,600–3,100 ↗ LHA

◀ **Mike Bernard, RI**
British (20thC)
Harbour Cottages, Polperro
Mixed media
18in (45.5cm) square
£700–780 / €1,000–1,100
$1,250–1,400 ⊞ BM

Mike Bernard trained at the West Surrey College of Art and Design, Farnham, followed by
postgraduate studies at the Royal Academy Schools. Since then he has exhibited at the Royal
Festival Hall and many other galleries in London and the provinces. He has also gained awards
and prizes for his paintings, was elected a member of the Royal Institute of Painters in
Watercolour in 1997, and in their 1999 exhibition at the Mall Galleries he was presented with
the Kingsmead Gallery Award. Mike Bernard enjoys experimenting with media techniques,
often using mixed media incorporating collage and acrylics. He also uses oil and watercolour.
He strives for exciting textures and light, combining these qualities into original semi-abstract
images of landscapes, seascapes, street scenes, still lifes and figurative compositions. One of
his favourite locations is the Cornish coast.

John Berry (b1920)

John Berry 's work is familiar to those of us who grew up reading Ladybird Books. He worked as an illustrator for Ladybird from 1960 to 1972 on the People at Work series, and as these books are now being sought after at collectors' fairs the value of his original illustrations are increasing. Berry was a war artist during WWII and his work is displayed in the Imperial War Museum. In the mid-1990s he was commissioned to paint a life size portrait of George Bush Snr to hang in the Admiral Nimitz Museum in Fredericksburg, Texas. His large oils always fetch much more than his gouache illustrations as seen here.

◄ **John Berry**
British (b1920)
The Favourites
Oil
20 x 30in
(51 x 76cm)
£4,000–4,500
€5,900–6,500
$7,400–8,200 ⊞ Dr

John Berry
British (b1920)
Speed Trap from *The Policeman*
Ladybird book illustration,
1970s, gouache
11 x 7in (28 x 18cm)
£400–450 / €580–640
$730–810 ⊞ Dr

◄ **André Bicât**
British (1909–96)
Landscape Woman
Signed and dated
1965, oil on canvas
20 x 24in (51 x 61cm)
£500–600
€730–880
$910–1,100
⚒ B(Kn)

Harold Harrington Betts
American (1881–1915)
Untitled landscape
Signed, oil on canvas
25 x 30in (63.5 x 76cm)
£1,700–2,050 / €2,500–3,000
$3,100–3,700 ⚒ LHA

► **Samuel John Lamorna Birch**
British (1869–1955)
Down-falling stream Lamorna
Signed and dated 1954, oil on canvas
20 x 42in (51 x 61cm)
£4,500–5,400 / €6,600–7,900
$8,200–9,800 ⚒ DN

Dorrit Black
Australian (1891–1951)
Untitled landscape
Signed, watercolour on paper
10¾ x 14¼in (27.5 x 36cm)
£3,000–3,600 / €4,400–5,300
$5,400–6,500 🔨 SHSY

Laverne Nelson Black
American (1887–1938)
Cowboy Herding Cattle
Signed, oil on canvas
20¼ x 24¼in (51.5 x 61.5cm)
£20,000–24,000 / €29,000–35,000
$36,000–43,000 🔨 S(NY)

▶ **David Blackburn**
British (b1939)
Wooded Coastline,
Morning Light 2001
Pastel on paper
19¼ x 15in
(49 x 38cm)
£1,050–1,200
€1,500–1,750
$1,900–2,200
⊞ HG

Charles Henry Blair
British (19thC)
Two kittens looking
at a vase of flowers
Signed, oil on canvas
10 x 14in
(25.5 x 35.5cm)
£800–950
€1,150–1,350
$1,450–1,750
🔨 WW

Peter Blake
British (b1932)
Regatta
Signed and numbered 5/50, lithograph
17¼ x 25¾in (44 x 65.5cm)
£340–410 / €500–600
$620–740 🔨 B

▶ **Jacques-Emile Blanche**
French (1861–1942)
Portrait of the Duchess
of Clermont-Tonnerre
with her dog
Oil on canvas
50 x 40in
(127 x 101.5cm)
£4,500–5,400
€6,600–7,900
$8,200–9,800 🔨 S(P)

◄ **Sandra Blow, RA**
British (b1925)
Untitled 2000
Signed and dated
2000, watercolour,
felt-tip, pen and
collage on paper
12 x 14in
(30.5 x 35.5cm)
£880–980
€1,300–1,400
$1,600–1,750
⊞ **JLx**

Robert Henderson Blyth, RSA, RSW
British (1919–70)
Gateway
Signed and inscribed, oil on board
10¾ x 8¾in (27.5 x 22cm)
£880–1,050 / €1,300–1,550
$1,600–1,900 ⚒ **B(Ed)**

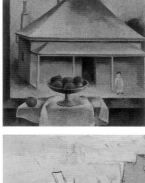

◄ **Nancy Borlase**
New Zealander (b1914)
Suburban Scene
Signed, oil on board
21¾ x 17¾in (55.5 x 45cm)
£500–600 / €730–880
$910–1,100 ⚒ **B(Kn)**

Rosa (Marie-Rosalie) Bonheur
French (1822–99)
Lion in a landscape
Signed, oil on canvas
13 x 15in (33 x 38cm)
£4,200–5,050
€6,100–7,300
$7,600–9,100 ⚒ **LHA**

► **Francis Bott**
German (b1904)
Composition in blue and grey
Signed and dated 1956,
acrylic on board
25½ x 38¼in (65 x 97cm)
£1,200–1,450 / €1,750–2,100
$2,200–2,600 ⚒ **B(Kn)**

Giuseppe Bottani
Italian (1717–84)
Study of a male nude
Inscribed, chalk on brown prepared paper
8 x 10¾in (20.5 x 27.5cm)
£360–430
€530–640
$660–790 ⚒ **B(Kn)**

► **Bob Bourne**
British (b1931)
Cape Cornwall
Signed and dated 1985,
oil on canvas
39¾ x 47¾in (101 x 121.5cm)
£600–720 / €880–1,050
$1,100–1,300 ⚒ **B(Kn)**

Day Bowman (20thC)

Day Bowman grew up in west Somerset and the county's coastline and countryside has strongly influenced her work. Her earlier work was more figurative but after the death of her son, and later that of her husband, she continued to paint landscapes of the west of England but in a more abstract style. She feels the sea has a healing quality and her paintings have swirling strokes like waves. She creates the swirls with a piece of cardboard.

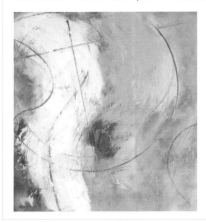

◄ **Day Bowman**
British (20thC)
Compass IV
Oil, charcoal and oil sticks
on canvas
71¾ x 66¼in (182.5 x 168.5cm)
£4,000–4,500 / €5,800–6,500
$7,300–8,200 ⊞ **DB**

Day Bowman
British (20thC)
Polewatch V
Oil, charcoal and oil sticks on canvas
71¾ x 66¼in (182.5 x 168.5cm)
£4,000–4,500 / €5,800–6,500
$7,300–8,200 ⊞ **DB**

◄ **George Price Boyce, RWS**
British (1826–97)
South Precinct of Cleeve Abbey,
West Somerset
Signed, inscribed and dated
1874, watercolour
7½ x 11in (19 x 28cm)
£2,300–2,750 / €3,350–4,000
$4,200–5,000 ➚ **HN**

► **Alexander Stuart Boyd**
Scottish (1854–1930)
Samples of Solicitors
Signed, ink sketches on wove
18 x 14¼in (45.5 x 36cm)
£950–1,100 / €1,400–1,600
$1,750–2,000 ➚ **B**

Hercules Brabazon Brabazon, NEAC
British (1821–1906)
Embarkation of the Queen of Sheba, after Claude Lorrain
Signed, watercolour with scratching out
7 x 14½in (18 x 37cm)
£750–900 / €1,100–1,300
$1,350–1,600 ➚ **B(B)**

Hercules Brabazon Brabazon, NEAC
British (1821–1906)
Figures in an interior
Signed, watercolour
8¼ x 11½in (21 x 29cm)
£700–840 / €1,000–1,200
$1,250–1,500 ➚ **B**

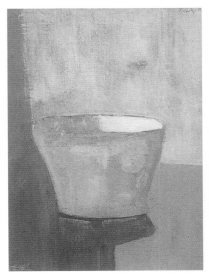

Charles Brady, HRHA
Irish (1929–97)
Bowl
Signed and dated 1974, oil on board
15½ x 12in (39.5 x 30.5cm)
£5,500–6,600 / €8,000–9,600
$10,000–12,000 ↗ WA

Antonietta Brandeis
Bohemian (1849–1920)
On the Grand Canal, Venice
Signed, oil on panel
6 x 9½in (15 x 24cm)
£7,200–8,600 / €10,500–12,500
$13,100–15,600 ↗ B

► **Georges Braque**
French (1882–1963)
L'Atelier
Signed and numbered 74/75, lithograph
16¾ x 20½in (42.5 x 52cm)
£3,150–3,800 / €4,600–5,500
$5,800–6,900 ↗ BUK

After Georges Braque
French (1882–1963)
The Boat
Signed, lithograph
9½ x 13¾in (24.5 x 35cm)
£400–480 / €590–700
$730–870 ↗ BUK

Erich (Arik) Brauer
Austrian (b1929)
Round Well
Signed and dated 1974, oil on board
13½ x 15¾in (34.5 x 40cm)
£5,800–7,000 / €8,500–10,200
$10,500–12,700 ↗ DORO

James Brereton
British (b1954)
Place de la Concorde
Oil
12 x 16in (30.5 x 40.5cm)
£720–800 / €1,050–1,200
$1,300–1,450 ⊞ Dr

◀ **John Brett, ARA**
British (1830–1902)
Oystermouth Castle, Swansea
Signed, titled and dated 1887
7 x 14in (18 x 35.5cm)
£3,500–4,200 / €5,100–6,100
$6,400–7,600 🔨 S(O)

Charles A. Brindley
British (fl1888–98)
A brief respite on a crisp,
autumnal day
Signed and dated 1904,
watercolour
28½ x 21in (72.5 x 53.5cm)
£900–1,050 / €1,300–1,500
$1,650–1,900 🔨 B(Kn)

Nicholas Richard Brewer
American (1857–1949)
Highwood Study
Signed
9 x 12in (23 x 30.5cm)
£880–1,050 / €1,300–1,500
$1,650–1,900 🔨 TREA

Molly Brett
British (fl1934)
The Four Seasons
Set of four, signed, watercolour
8 x 6in (20.5 x 15cm)
£1,150–1,350 / €1,650–1,950
$2,100–2,450 🔨 B(Kn)

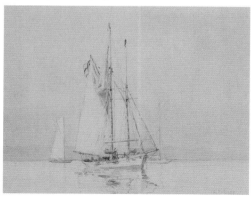

Arthur John Trevor Briscoe
British (1873–1943)
A topsail schooner under reduced sail offshore
Signed, watercolour
9 x 12½in (23 x 32cm)
£1,300–1,550 / €1,900–2,250
$2,350–2,800 🔨 B

Miller Gore Brittian
Canadian (1912–68)
Contemplative Head
Pastel and pencil
17¼ x 11¾in (44 x 30cm)
£360–430 / €530–630
$650–780 🔨 B(Kn)

Gerald Leslie Brockhurst
Australian (1890–1978)
Marquett, 1925
Signed and inscribed, etching
8½ x 6¾in (21.5 x 17cm)
£75–90 / €110–130
$135–160 🔨 DW

Gerald Leslie Brockhurst
Australian (1890–1978)
Two Girls
Signed, etching
4³⁄₄ x 5¾in (12 x 14.5cm)
£650–780 / €950–1,100
$1,200–1,400 ⤢ DN

Deborah Brown
Irish (b1927)
Man Sea and Sky
Signed and inscribed, oil on board
18 x 22in (45.5 x 56cm)
£1,800–2,150 / €2,600–3,100
$3,250–3,900 ⤢ WA

Painted between 1951 and 1953, Man Sea and Sky is an early example of Deborah Brown's work, predating her move into abstract painting and later sculpture. Born in Belfast, she enrolled at the Belfast College of Art in 1946, spending only 12 months there before switching to the National College of Art in Dublin. In 1950, she went to Paris for a year, absorbing the lessons of the Old Masters while being inspired by contemporary trends in art. On her return to Belfast in 1951, the Arts Council of Northern Ireland gave her a solo show in their gallery at Donegal Place. Man Sea and Sky bears comparison with both Basil Blackshaw's similarly titled Men, Sea and Moon of 1952, and with Daniel O'Neill and Colin Middleton's work of the late 1940s and early '50s in which figures are pressed up close to the picture plane and brooding dark colours lend the scenes a poetic romanticism.

► **Horace Brodzky**
Australian
(1885–1969)
Rural scene
Signed and dated
1941, watercolour
9 x 10¾in
(23 x 27.5cm)
£280–330
€410–480
$510–600 ⤢ B(Kn)

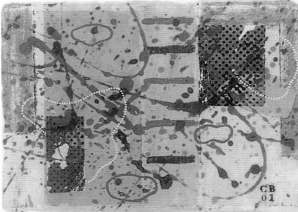

Colin Brown
Scottish (b1962)
Routes
Mixed media
6½ x 9in (16.5 x 23cm)
£340–380 / €500–550
$620–690 ⊞ WrG

Colin Brown was born in Dundee. He studied at Duncan of Jordanstone College of Art, and was awarded the John Kinross Scholarship by the Royal Scottish Academy.

Edwin J. Bruns
American (b1899)
Road to the Cove – Gaspe Penninsular c1955
Signed, inscribed and dated, oil on canvas
9 x 12in (23 x 30.5cm)
£110–130 / €160–190
$200–240 ⤢ JAA

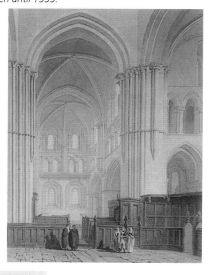

Gordon Bryce, RSA, RSW
Scottish (b1943)
Fruits and Fan
Signed and inscribed, oil on board
8½ x 11½in (21.5 x 29cm)
£1,050–1,250 / €1,500–1,800
$1,900–2,250 ⚒ **B(Ed)**
Gordon Bryce studied at Edinburgh College of Art with Sir Robin
Philipson and Sir William Gillies. He was Head of Fine Art at Gray's
School of Art, Aberdeen until 1955.

Claude Buckle
British (b1905)
The Horseman
Signed, watercolour
14 x 22in (35.5 x 56cm)
£360–400 / €530–590
$650–730 ⊞ **TGG**

▶ **John Chessel**
Buckler
British (1793–1894)
The transept of the
church of Saint Cross,
near Winchester;
The choir of the
church of Saint Cross,
near Winchester
A pair, signed and
dated 1829,
watercolour over
pencil with
scratching out
14½ x 10½in
(37 x 26.5cm)
£800–960
€1,200–1,400
$1,450–1,750
⚒ **B(B)**

Ernest Buckmaster
Australian (1897–1968)
Grey Day, Yarra Glen, 1943
Signed and dated 1943, oil on canvas
21¼ x 30¾in (54 x 78cm)
£3,800–4,550 / €5,500–6,600
$6,900–8,300 ⚒ **LJ**

◀ **Bernard Buffet**
French (1928–99)
Still life with coffee pot
Signed and numbered
192/300, lithograph
19½ x 23¾in (49.5 x 60.5cm)
£520–620 / €760–900
$940–1,100 ⚒ **BUK**

▶ **Anne Bull**
British (b1940)
The Card Players
Oil
29 x 24in (73.5 x 86.5cm)
£950–1,050 / €1,350–1,500
$1,700–1,900 ⊞ **Stl**

Ferdinand Burgdorff
American (1881–1954)
Desert landscape at sunrise
Signed and dated 1911, oil on canvas
9¾ x 13½in (25 x 34.5cm)
£710–850 / €1,050–1,250
$1,300–1,550 ⚒ LHA

Gustav Burghardt
German (b1875)
The ship *Europa*
Signed, oil on canvas
32¼ x 47¼in (82 x 120cm)
£1,500–1,800 / €2,200–2,600
$2,700–3,250 ⚒ DORO

Tim Burns
British (20thC)
Net Huts, Hastings
Signed, acrylic
12 x 20in (30.5 x 51cm)
£300–330 / €430–480
$540–600 ⊞ WrG

John Busby, ARSA, RSW, SWLA
British (b1928)
Crane Dance, Hornborgasjon, Sweden
Watercolour
6 x 8in (15 x 21.5cm)
£340–380 / €500–550
$620–690 ⊞ WrG

*Tim Burns was born in London. He studied at Medway College of Art and Design
in 1974 and then at West Surrey College of Art and Design where he completed
his degree in painting and printmaking. Tim focuses his attention on the beaches,
boats and paraphernalia of the fishing industry. He paints in oils and acrylics on
board or canvas and he also collects driftwood and other materials found on the
beach, which he incorporates in some of his works. He lives and paints in
Hampshire, and has exhibited widely in the South of England. His work is held in
collections in the USA, Australia and Scandinavia.*

▶ **Chris Bushe, RSW, SAAC**
Scottish (b1958)
Faded Glory
Oil on paper
27 x 24in (68.5 x 61cm)
£1,600–1,800 / €2,300–2,600
$2,900–3,250 ⊞ P&H

*Born in Aberfeldy, Perthshire, Chris Bushe studied at the Gray's School of Art,
Aberdeen. He has had many solo exhibitions in Scotland and his recent awards
include the Morton Fraser Milligan Award, Russell Flint Trust, Glasgow Arts Club
Fellowship and Scottish Arts Club Award. His work can be found in the collections
of Murray International Metals, Premier Property Group, Aberdeen Hospitals
Trust, Grampian Regional Council, Edinburgh Hospitals Trust and Scottish Life.*

Botanical & Flower Painting

The tradition of flower painting started in the Netherlands. The original distinct style – coloured flowers against a dark background – was revolutionized by Jan van Huysum (see page 34) who bathed his flowers in sunlight. His compositions were much freer and his flowers curled and twisted which complemented the emerging rococo trends popular in interior design. His work can fetch seven-figure sums. Fortunately paintings by his contemporaries are much more affordable. Other notable flower artists such as Jean-Baptiste Monnoyer of France received his training in Antwerp in the 17th century before returning to Paris where he was employed by the architect Charles Lebrun to decorate the many new chateaux. He also painted for Queen Anne in London.

Flower artists painted mainly for beauty with artifice, but during the 19th century botanical art developed and flowers and plants were now portrayed in greater detail and could be used for educational purposes. This was inspired by the Victorians who were great explorers and brought back specimens of many plant species from their travels, all of which had to be catalogued. Pierre-Joseph Redouté is probably best known for his famous botanical paintings of roses which have been reproduced by the thousand. Contemporary botanical artists include Bryan Poole, Rodella Purves and Rosie Sanders.

There was a strong market for decorative flower paintings in Victorian Britain, but many did not achieve the luminous quality that the Dutch painters did. Among the best known flower painters in this genre are the Clare brothers and Eloise Stannard (see *Miller's Pictures Price Guide 2003*). However, as painting flowers at this time was seen as a suitable pastime for young ladies, many decorative, competent but unsigned watercolours can be found in provincial auction houses for around £50 / €75 / $90.

The techniques of flower painting did not change radically until the advent of the Impressionists. More recently, artists such as Stanley Cursiter and Frederick Gore (see pages 33–34), with their bold brushstokes and colours, were less interested in detail and formal settings. Russian artists were also influenced by the Impressionists and other European art movements, David Davidovich Burliuk (see below) placed his flowers in a surreal setting.

Flowers in art are not always purely decorative. In still lifes they can be symbols representing innocence, long life, betrothal, love and friendship, for example. Sought-after contemporary artist Endellion Lycett Green expresses her feelings through her floral pictures with metaphysical titles.

◄ Edwin Alexander, RSA, RSW, RWS
British (1870–1926)
Hawkweed Seeds Dispersing
Signed and dated 1903,
watercolour on brown paper
9½ x 6in (24 x 15cm)
£800–960 / €1,150–1,350
$1,450–1,750 ➤ L&T

Pat Albeck
British (b1930)
Tulips
Watercolour
8 x 5½in (20.5 x 14cm)
£400–450 / €590–660
$730–820 ⊞ ALBE

► Helen Bradley
British (1900–79)
Flowers from our Hedgerow
Signed, titled and dated 1966,
oil on canvas board
9 x 7¼in (23 x 18.5cm)
£2,800–3,350 / €4,100–4,900
$5,100–6,100 ➤ B

David Davidovich Burliuk
American/Russian (1882–1967)
Sunflowers by the Sea
Signed in Latin, oil on canvas
36 x 26in (91.5 x 66cm)
£57,600–69,000
€84,000–100,000
$105,000–125,000 ➤ S

Alfred Joseph Casson
Canadian (1898–1992)
Irises
Signed and dated 1944, gouache on paper
laid down on board
11 x 28in (28 x 71cm)
£2,000–2,400 / € 2,900–3,500
$3,650–4,350 SCAN

John (Jack) Richard Chambers
Canadian (1931–78)
Mantel Group
Signed, titled and dated 1966
oil on panel
45 x 60in (114.5 x 152.5cm)
£8,500–10,200 / € 12,400–14,900
$15,500–18,600 SCAN

Further information

Artists mentioned in the introduction may have
works appearing elsewhere in this Guide.
Consult the index for page numbers.

Peter Coker
British (b1926)
Sunflowers
Signed, oil on board
48 x 32in (122 x 81.5cm)
£5,000–6,000 / € 7,300–8,700
$9,100–10,900 B

▶ **Thomas Frederick Collier**
British (fl1848–74)
Still life of pansies
Signed, watercolour
7½ x 11in (19 x 28cm)
£500–600 / € 730–870
$910–1,100 G(L)

Antoine Chazal
French (1793–1854)
A Study of Camellias
Signed and dated 1845,
oil on paper laid down on canvas
15 x 10in (38 x 25.5cm)
£3,000–3,600 / € 4,400–5,300
$5,500–6,500 S(NY)

▶ **William Crosbie, RSA**
Scottish (1915–99)
Autumn Flowers
Signed and inscribed,
oil on canvas
36 x 28in (91.5 x 71cm)
£2,300–2,750 / € 3,300–3,950
$4,200–5,000 L&T

Stanley Cursiter, RSA, RSW
Scottish (1887–1976)
A still life of red and yellow roses
Signed and dated 1958, oil on board
16 x 18in (40.5 x 45.5cm)
£1,000–1,200 € 1,500–1,750
$1,850–2,200 L&T

Gustav Feith
Austrian (1875–1951)
Violets
Signed and dated 1929, watercolour on paper
6¼ x 5in (16 x 13cm)
£2,350–2,800 / €3,400–4,100
$4,300–5,100 ↗ **DORO**

Frederick Gore, RA
British (b1913)
Hibiscus on a covered terrace, July
Signed, oil on canvas
32 x 40in (81.5 x 101.5cm)
£2,800–3,350 / €4,100–4,900
$5,100–6,100 ↗ **B**

Duncan Grant
British (1885–1978)
Flowers on a Guéridon
Signed, watercolour, pen and ink
on paper
12¼ x 10½in (31 x 26.5cm)
£3,150–3,500 / €4,600–5,100
$5,700–6,400 ⊞ **JLx**

▶ **Jenny Jowett**
English (b1936)
Peony
Pencil and watercolour
19 x 14in (48.5 x 35.5cm)
£2,150–2,400 / €3,150–3,500
$3,900–4,400 ⊞ **GC**

Jan van Huysum
Dutch (1682–1749)
A still life of flowers in a terracotta vase upon
a marble ledge before a niche
Signed and dated 1734, oil on panel
32 x 34in (81.5 x 86.5cm)
£3,030,000–3,636,000
€4,362,600–5,235,100
$5,515,000–6,618,000 ↗ **S**

*Jan van Huysum was the son of a painter
who ran a workshop in which Jan and his
brothers were employed. By 1734, when this
picture was painted, van Huysum was the
foremost flower painter of his day and
commanded higher prices than Rembrandt.
The demand for his pictures was partly due
to the stunning realism with which van
Huysum painted individual blooms, leaves
and fruit as well as more incidental details.*

*Although outside the dateline for this
book, an exception has been made for this
work because of its importance in the history
of flower painting.*

Cecil Kennedy
British (1905–97)
Summer Flowers
Signed, oil on canvas
29½ x 24½in (75 x 62cm)
£16,000–19,200
€23,000–27,000
$29,000–35,000 ↗ **L**

▶ **Karen Kitchel**
American (b1957)
Parking Lot #5, from the
Weeds Series
Oil on wood panel
18in (45.5cm) square
£3,000–3,350 / €4,400–4,900
$5,500–6,100 ⊞ **CDW**

Zhang Kunyi
Taiwanese (1895–1969)
Orchid
Signed, artist's seals, hanging scroll,
ink and colour on paper
27 x 16½in (68.5 x 42cm)
**£3,000–3,600 / €4,400–5,300
$5,500–6,500** ⚒ S(HK)

Endellion Lycett Green
British (b1969)
A
Oil
24 x 36in (61 x 91.5cm)
**£2,700–3,000 / €3,900–4,400
$4,900–5,500** ⊞ CDBA

Circle of Jean-Baptiste Monnoyer
Belgian (1636–99)
Chrysanthemums, narcissi,
pansies and other flowers in a
glass vase on a ledge
Oil on canvas
19½ x 16¼in (49.5 x 41.5cm)
**£5,000–6,000 / €7,200–8,600
$8,400–10,100** ⚒ B

'Circle of' means, in the
opinion of the auctioneer
or gallery, that the work
was executed by someone
closely associated with
the named artist,
but not necessarily
under his direction.

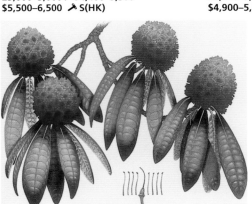

◄ **Bryan Poole**
New Zealander (b1953)
Rhododendron – *Rhododendron Niveum*
Signed, edition of 100, aquatint
and etching
20 x 15in (51 x 38cm)
**£310–350 / €450–500
$560–630** ⊞ BrP

► **Rodella Purves**
Scottish (b1945)
Sweet Chestnut
Pencil and watercolour
22 x 14in (56 x 35.5cm)
**£2,400–2,700 / €3,500–3,950
$4,350–4,900** ⊞ GC

◄ **Rosie Sanders**
English (b1944)
Rosa Iceberg
Pencil and watercolour
14 x 11in (35.5 x 28cm)
**£2,700–3,000 / €3,950–4,400
$4,900–5,400** ⊞ GC

► **Annika Silander-
Hökerberg**
Swedish (b1949)
Double tulips on black ground
Signed and numbered 1/150,
lithograph
18 x 25¼in (45.5 x 64cm)
**£300–330 / €430–480
$540–600** ⊞ IN

Walter Wallor Caffyn
British (d1898)
Country Life
Signed and dated 1898, oil on canvas
16 x 24¼in (40.5 x 61.5cm)
£7,200–8,000 / €10,500–11,700
$13,100–14,600 ⊞ HFA

Alexandre Calame
Swiss (1810–64)
A stone staircase and a doorway in a landscape
Signed, oil on paper, laid down on canvas
15½ x 13in (39.5 x 33cm)
£10,500–12,600 / €15,300–18,400
$19,100–23,000 ⚒ S(NY)

Sir David Young Cameron, RA, RSA, RSW, RE
British (1865–1945)
La Tourettes
Signed, pencil and watercolour
6 x 9in (15 x 23cm)
£1,150–1,400 / €1,700–2,000
$2,100–2,500 ⚒ B(Ed)

◀ Tom Campbell
British (1865–1943)
The Brown Isles,
Lewis
Signed, watercolour
heightened in white
10¼ x 7¼in
(26 x 18.5cm)
£190–220
€280–340
$340–400 ⚒ FHF

Federico del Campo
Peruvian (1837–1927)
Gondolas on a Venetian canal
Signed and dated 1905, oil on canvas
23 x 15¾in (58.5 x 40cm)
£40,000–48,000 / €58,000–70,000
$73,000–87,000 ⚒ B

Jacob Caproens
Belgian (b1680)
Flowers in a gilded vase,
with fruit
Oil on canvas
33 x 26½in (84 x 67.5cm)
£6,200–7,400 / €9,000–10,800
$11,300–13,500 ⚒ DORO

◀ **Ella du Cane**
British (fl1893–1910)
The Kobai plum blossom
Signed, watercolour
15¾ x 9¼in (40 x 23.5cm)
£1,700–2,000 / €2,500–3,000
$3,100–3,700 ⚒ B

Thalia Flora Caravia
Greek (1871–1960)
Woman with a red hat
Oil on cardboard
13¾ x 11in (35 x 28cm)
£6,000–7,200 / €8,800–10,500
$10,900–13,000 ⚒ B

*A dynamic woman and talented artist who
studied with Nicholaos Gysis and Giorgios
Jakobides in Munich, Flora Caravia's artistic
career covered a broad range of subject
matter. In this painting the artist has
captured, with an economy of line and
colour, not only the dry heat of summer but
also a controlled melancholy in the
thoughtful gaze of the woman seated on a
sandy beach. The red sun hat acts as a
powerful foil for the muted tonalities.
Socially and politically involved throughout
her life, Flora Caravia also travelled to the
front as an artist-correspondent, where she
sketched soldiers during the Balkan Wars
(1912–13).*

Jean Albert Carlotti
French (b1909)
Girls on Tour
Signed and dated 1930, watercolour
9¾ x 12½in (25 x 32cm)
£800–900 / €1,150–1,300
$1,150–1,250 ⊞ MI

Emil Carlsen
American (1853–1932)
Trees in full summer
Signed, oil on canvas
25 x 30¼in (63.5 x 77cm)
£52,800–63,000
€77,000–92,000
$96,000–115,000 ⚒ S(NY)

John Wilson Carmichael
French (1799–1868)
Dutch barges riding out a squall off the Low Countries
Signed and dated 1851, oil on canvas
12 x 16in (30.5 x 40.5cm)
£1,250–1,500 / €1,850–2,200
$2,300–2,700 ⚲ B(Kn)

Henry Barlow Carter
British (1803–67)
Alum works, Robin Hood's Bay
Signed and dated 1843, pencil and
watercolour with scratching out
9½ x 13½in (24 x 34.5cm)
£1,600–1,900 / €2,300–2,700
$2,900–3,400 ⚲ TEN

Jean Albert Grand Carteret
French (b1903)
Portrait of a Lady in Fur
Signed and dated 1932, pastel
14¼ x 11in (36 x 28cm)
£500–600 / €730–870
$910–1,050 ⚲ B(Kn)

Reg Cartwright
British (b1938)
Red still life with figs, mandolin and jug
Oil on board
33½in (85cm) square
£2,100–2,300 / €3,050–3,350
$3,800–4,150 ⊞ CAMB

*Born in Leicester in 1938, Reg Cartwright
became a full-time painter and illustrator in
1974. His still life paintings follow the spirit
of Cubism. Through subtle abstraction he
depicts the physical and tonal qualities of his
subject matter. He has received awards and
commissions including the Mother Goose
Award for the most promising new illustrator,
and the MSIA for illustration and graphics.
He has illustrated over 30 books and was
included in the Original Show at the Museum
of 20th Century Illustrators in New York.*

Salvador Castillo
Nicaraguan (20thC)
Garden of Jinotegano
Dated 1997, oil on canvas
35½ x 19¾in (90 x 50cm)
£250–300 / €360–430
$450–540 ⚲ LCM

◀ **Fernando Castro Pacheco**
Mexican (b1918)
Two Women
Oil on canvas
23¾ x 17¾in (60.5 x 45cm)
£3,000–3,600 / €4,400–5,300
$5,500–6,500 ⚲ LCM

*Born in the City of Merida, Yucatan in 1918, Fernando Castro Pacheco is Mayan in spirit. At
14 he entered the Academy of Fine Arts in Merida, under the direction of Alfonso Cardone,
and at 18 he became a master of drawing and history of art, in order to earn a living. From
1932, he began to draw with Cardone. In 1943 he arrived in Mexico, where he soon became
a professor of painting and was prominent in the group following the so-called greats of
Guerrero Galvan, Raul Anguiano and Guillermo Meza. This group was given the title of
Mexican Realist School, and within it Castro Pacheco flourished becoming a consummate
artist, achieving a high sense of the dramatic and a highly-developed artistic technique.*

Patrick Caulfield (b1936)

In the 1960s when the world looked to London for fashion and style, Patrick Caulfield was at the centre of a new type of painting which became known as Pop Art. He is a painter and printmaker and taught at the Chelsea School of Art in the late 1960s; his simple colourful works are often executed in acrylic. During the 1990s there were a number of retrospective exhibitions of his work. The Saatchi Gallery has bought his 1984 painting *Fish and Sandwich*, and many public collections hold his work. Such prominate ownership helps to secure the price of his paintings.

Patrick Caulfield, RA
British (b1936)
Dressed Lobster
Signed and numbered 126/150, screenprint
23 x 28¾in (58.5 x 73cm)
£450–540 / €660–790
$820–980 ⚒ **B(Kn)**

Patrick Caulfield, RA
British (b1936)
Spider Plant
Signed and numbered 69/72, silkscreen
21¾ x 30¾in (55.5 x 78cm)
£300–360 / €440–530
$550–650 ⚒ **B**

▶ **Patrick Caulfield, RA**
British (b1936)
I've only the friendship of hotel rooms
Signed and inscribed, silkscreen
16 x 14in (40.5 x 35.5cm)
£550–660 / €800–960
$1,000–1,200 ⚒ **B(Kn)**

Jules Cavailles
French (1901–77)
Vase of flowers on a table with a chair behind
Signed and dated 1942, gouache over pencil
23¾ x 17¼in (60.5 x 44cm)
£1,300–1,550 / €1,900–2,250
$2,350–2,800 ⚒ **B(B)**

Ann Cawkell
British (b1945)
Anemones
Watercolour
20 x 13in (51 x 33cm)
£400–450 / €590–650
$730–810 ⊞ **LAW**

Abbreviations

Letters after the artist's name denote that the artist has been awarded the membership of an artistic body. See page 233 for the explanation of abbreviated letters.

Charles Ferdinand Ceramano
Belgian (1829–1909)
Prize Merino rams
Signed, oil on canvas
47¼ x 63¾in (120 x 162cm)
£3,300–3,950 / €4,800–5,700
$6,000–7,200 ⚒ **B(Kn)**

Canadian Art

Paintings played an important role in the early years of the 20th century in Canada. With the creation of the Dominion of Canada in 1867 the Canadian people were keen to define their self image. They saw themselves as pioneers and frontiers people and looked towards the untamed lands of the Canadian northwest for inspiration. Artists illustrated wild landscapes both in their strong, free and impassioned oils and in drawings and illustrations for magazines and posters to further the Canadian dream.

Lawren Harris, who was part of a very influential and talented group of artists known as the Group of Seven, opined: 'Art in Canada is an upstart art and its source is not the same as that of the art of Europe. The Canadian artist serves the spirit of his land and people.'

The Group of Seven – Harris, Tom Thomson, M. E. Macdonald, Arthur Lismer, Frederick Varley, Frank Johnson and Franklin Carmichael – all socialized at the Arts and Letters Club in Toronto to debate new directions for Canadian art in the first decade of the 20th century. In 1913, Harris raised enough money to build the Studio Building for Canadian Art in Toronto, where several of the artists worked until the 1920s.

Although Alfred Casson, who joined the Group five years before it disbanded in 1931, was strongly influenced by an exhibition in Canada of French Post-Impressionists and Pointillists including Pissarro and Signac in 1917, most of his colleagues preferred north European and Scandinavian pictures because they identified with the terrain.

Emily Carr was a contemporary of the Group of Seven but because she lived in British Columbia, did not exhibit with them. She studied the conventional Victorian landscapes of artists such as John Bell Smith, father of Frederick Bartlett Bell Smith, but decided she wanted to break free from the rather formal and mannered description of landscape of the previous generation. Technically her work differed because she painted with thinned-down oil on paper but her style, too, was freer and therefore more atmospheric. She depicts wind and movement in the dark forests through her swirling brushstrokes. Other paintings are imbued with a strong light which gives them a surreal quality. She studied Native Indian myths and iconography and often included totem poles in her work. Arthur Lismer was younger than Carr and loved the forest as much as she did, although he painted in a bolder more solid way and had a more restricted colour palette. The feel of the forest is evident in his subtle use of greens and browns.

The next generation of Canadian artists after the Group of Seven felt more confident to experiment with other styles of art. Edward John Hughes and Rene Richard continued in the sharp illustrative tradition. Lloyd Fitzgerald painted figures in landscape, but Jack Bush began to be interested in abstract art and surrealism in the 1940s. He said that he wanted to break away from the idea of landscape art and that it should be the scenery that appeals. 'Paint how you feel,' he declared. Lawren Harris embraced abstract art when in his sixties. John Chambers, who had studied in Madrid, called his work perceptual realism, which he explained was surrealism based on his dreams.

Post-war immigrants such as Ischcowitz studied under Oskar Kokoshka in Munich and brought a new style of painting to the Canadian art scene. Nowadays there is a huge and flourishing community of artists in Canada, all painting in many different styles.

In the 21st century, when an increasing number of us live in urban or suburban environments, the beautiful depictions of the great outdoors by so many Canadian artists have great appeal. The big names of the early 20th century still fetch considerably less than their contemporaries from the United States or Europe. Tom Thomson's work prior to 1911 consists mainly of pen and ink drawings and would be a good starting point for someone interested in collecting Canadian art.

Brian M. Atyeo
Canadian (b1950)
Margaritaville
Signed, acrylic on canvas
36 x 48in (91.5 x 122cm)
£1,850–2,050 / €2,700–3,000
$3,350–3,750 ⊞ HarG

Further information
Artists mentioned in the introduction above may have works appearing elsewhere in this Guide. Consult the index for page numbers.

► **Frederick Bartlett Bell Smith**
Canadian (1846–1923)
Mount Aberdeen
Signed and titled,
watercolour on paper
laid down on cardboard
9¼ x 6¾in (23.5 x 17cm)
£1,650–2,000 / €2,450–2,900
$3,000–3,600 ↗ SCAN

Emily Carr (1879–1945)

Canadians identified themselves with wilderness landscape after the beginning of Independence from the British in 1867. They saw themselves as pioneers and frontiers people opening up the northwest of the country. Emily Carr epitomized this pioneering spirit, by living in the newly opened-up British Columbia and was a very innovative artist. She gave spirit and movement to her pictures by breaking with the formal European style of landscape and often incorporated Native American icons in her work. As a consequence her work fetches high prices today.

◀ **Emily Carr**
Canadian
(1879–1945)
Glade
Titled, oil on
paper laid down
on board
24 x 36in
(61 x 91.5cm)
£40,000–48,000
€59,000–70,000
$73,000–87,000
⚒ SCAN

▶ **Alfred Joseph Casson**
Canadian (1898–1992)
Building the Campfire
Signed and dated 1918, gouache on board
18½ x 22¾in (47 x 58cm)
£4,300–5,150 / €6,300–7,500
$7,800–9,300 ⚒ SCAN

This early work was executed by Casson the year following his first public exhibition at the Canadian National Exhibition in 1917. Works by the French Post-Impressionists including Signac, Pissarro and Denis were shown, and no doubt impressed Casson, who successfully incorporated their technique of pointillism into this picture.

◀ **Ivan Eyre**
Canadian (b1935)
Bye Plain
Acrylic on canvas
44 x 77in (112 x 195.5cm)
£23,600–26,200
€34,000–38,000
$43,000–48,000 ⊞ LOCH

Jacques Deshaies
Canadian (b1947)
Jacques' Cabin
Mixed media on heavy gauge paper
36in (91.5cm) square
£1,800–2,000
€2,600–2,900
$3,300–3,650 ⊞ BRID

Lloyd Fitzgerald
Canadian (b1941)
Apple in Bloom
Signed, titled and dated 1987, acrylic on canvas
30 x 40in (76 x 101.5cm)
£1,550–1,850 / €2,250–2,700
$2,800–3,350 ⚒ SCAN

Patricia Fyfe
Canadian (b1940)
Circles of Life
Acrylic on canvas
36¼ x 60¼in (92 x 153cm)
£1,850–2,200 / €2,700–3,200
$3,350–4,000 ⊞ PFY

Lawren Stewart Harris
Canadian (1885–1970)
Mountain Sketch
Graphite on paper
10½ x 8½in (26.5 x 21.5cm)
£1,900–2,300 / €2,800–3,350
$3,500–4,200 ➚ SCAN

Lawren Stewart Harris
Canadian (1885–1970)
Untitled (Abstract Painting 117)
Signed and titled, oil on canvas
48½ x 38½in (123 x 98cm)
£12,800–15,400
€18,700–22,500
$23,300–28,000 ➚ SCAN

Prudence Heward
Canadian (1896–1947)
Bermuda House
Signed, titled, oil on canvas
22 x 25in (56 x 63.5cm)
£11,800–14,100 / €17,200–20,600
$21,500–25,700 ➚ SCAN

◄ **Douglas Kirton**
Canadian (b1955)
Toxic Pool Group (8)
Signed, titled and dated 1987, oil on panel
35¾ x 80in (91 x 203cm)
£2,500–3,000 / €3,700–4,400
$4,600–5,500 ➚ SCAN

Daniel P. Izzard
Canadian (b1949)
October's Promise
Signed, oil on canvas
36 x 48in (91.5 x 122cm)
£1,900–2,100 / €2,750–3,050
$3,450–3,800 ⊞ HarG

Arthur Lismer
Canadian (1885–1969)
Dark Spruce and Logs
Signed, titled and dated 1955,
oil on panel
16 x 12in (40.5 x 30.5cm)
£5,200–6,200 / €7,600–9,000
$9,500–11,300 ➚ SCAN

► **F. Scott Macleod**
Canadian (b1954)
Storm over
Minas Basin
Signed, oil on canvas
36 x 48in
(91.5 x 122cm)
£1,450–1,600
€2,100–2,350
$2,650–2,950
⊞ HarG

Manly Edward MacDonald, OSA, RCA
Canadian (1889–1971)
A stream in spring sun
Signed, oil on canvas laid to board
10½ x 13¾in (26.5 x 35cm)
£900–1,100 / €1,350–1,600
$1,700–2,000 ⚒ B

Pierre Pivet
Canadian (b1948)
Les Lys
Signed, oil on canvas
40in (101.5cm) square
£2,250–2,500 / €3,300–3,650
$4,100–4,550 ⊞ HarG

Rene Jean Richard
Canadian
(1895–1982)
Far Houses by
Lakeshore
Signed, oil on masonite
16 x 20in
(40.5 x 51cm)
£1,900–2,300
€2,800–3,350
$3,500–4,200
⚒ SCAN

◄ **Jean-Paul
Riopelle**
Canadian
(1923–2002)
Tempo
1958, oil on canvas
9½ x 8in
(24 x 20.5cm)
£8,000–9,600
€11,700–14,000
$14,600–17,500
⚒ B

Thomas (Tom) John Thomson
Canadian (1877–1917)
Summer Landscape
Oil on board
9½ x 12½in (24 x 32cm)
£14,200–17,000 / €20,800–25,000
$25,800–30,900 ⚒ SCAN

◀ **Paul Cézanne**
French (1839–1906)
Bathers
Lithograph
8¾ x 10¾in (22 x 27.5cm)
£7,000–8,400
€10,200–12,200
$12,700–15,300
🔨 **L&T**

▶ **Marc Chagall**
Russian/French
(1887–1985)
Aragon poems
Signed, etching
15½ x 11½in
(39.5 x 29cm)
£3,150–3,750
€4,600–5,500
$5,700–6,800
🔨 **BUK**

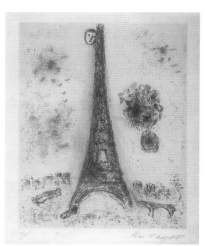

Lithographs

Owning work by a world renowned artist is more affordable in the form of a lithograph. A signed example will retain its value better.

▶ **Lilian Cheviot**
British (fl1894–1930)
Wake Up England
Signed and inscribed, oil on canvas
28 x 34in (71 x 86.5cm)
£12,100–14,500 / €17,600–21,200
$22,000–26,400 🔨 **DNY**

Alexander Innokentovich Chirkov
Russian (1865–1913)
Hayricks
Signed, oil on card
14¾ x 11in (37.5 x 28cm)
£2,150–2,500 / €3,100–3,700
$3,900–4,650 🔨 **S**

H. C. D. Chorlton
British (20thC)
La Fête de Dieu, Concarneau, 1901
Signed and inscribed, watercolour
9½ x 12in (24 x 30.5cm)
£300–360 / €440–530
$550–650 🔨 **LAY**

◄ **N. H. Christiansen**
Danish (19thC)
Evening Glow
Signed, oil on board
8½ x 18¾in (21.5 x 47.5cm)
£3,600–4,000 / €5,300–5,900
$6,600–7,300 ⊞ HFA

◄ **Nguyen Tien Chung**
Vietnamese (1914–76)
Pigeon
Signed and dated 1970, ink and watercolour on paper
6¼ x 9in (16 x 23cm)
£2,250–2,700
€3,300–3,950
$4,100–4,900
⚒ S(SI)

Joseph Clark
British (1834–1926)
Riding a Tiger
Signed, oil on canvas
£4,000–4,500 / €5,900–6,600
$7,300–8,200 ⊞ Man

Granville Daniel Clarke (b1940)

Granville Daniel Clarke was born in Keighley, Yorkshire and attended Barnsley College of Art. Following a period as a songwriter and poet, he returned to watercolour painting, specializing in snow scenes for the fine art publisher Michael Stewart. He works with large canvases in a fluid atmospheric Impressionist style, and favours landscapes, seascapes and townscapes. He is the only artist to paint around the world in 90 days, and has supported many eye camps in India through donations of his paintings. The original watercolour of this print was commissioned by Midlands Expressway in December 2003 to commemorate Britain's first motorway toll.

► **Granville Daniel Clarke**
British (b1940)
Transport Travel & Toll
Signed and numbered 98/100, limited edition print
15 x 22in (38 x 56cm)
£1,800–2,150
€2,600–3,100
$3,300–3,900 ⊞ GDC

◄ **William J. Clayton**
British (20thC)
Etude
Signed and dated 1975, oil on canvas
35 x 23in (89 x 58.5cm)
£5,800–6,500 / €8,500–9,500
$10,500–11,800 ⊞ Bne

► **William Clusmann**
American (1859–1927)
Twilight Landscape
Signed, oil on canvas
15 x 20in (38 x 51cm)
£760–910 / €1,100–1,300
$1,400–1,650 ⚒ JAA

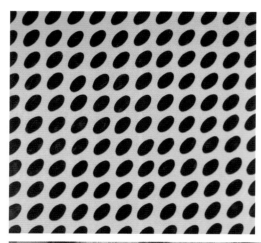

◄ **Jon Coffelt**
American (b1964)
Navy Blue with Citrus
Background
Acrylic-wax on birch
24in (61cm) square
**£1,000–1,100 / €1,450–1,600
$1,800–2,000** ⊞ GALG

► **Cosimo Colella**
Italian (b1966)
Danseur
Acrylic on canvas
48 x 35½in (122 x 90cm)
**£1,550–1,750 / €2,250–2,600
$2,800–3,200** ⊞ GALG

Charles Caryl Coleman
American/Italian (1840–1928)
My Studio Window, Island of Capri
Signed and dated 1897, oil on canvas
21 x 31½in (53.5 x 80cm)
**£39,500–47,000 / €58,000–69,000
$72,000–86,000** ↗ S(NY)

Marcus Collin
Finnish (1882–1966)
Fishmarket, and another
Two, signed, oil on canvas
24 x 28¾in (61 x 73cm)
**£4,600–5,500 / €6,700–8,000
$8,400–10,000** ↗ BUK

Edward Harrison Compton
British (1881–1960)
River valley from the hills
Signed and dated 1914
9½ x 14in (24 x 35.5cm)
**£280–330 / €410–480
$510–600** ↗ GH

Marvin D. Cone
American (1891–1965)
Old Stone Quarry
Signed, oil on board
18 x 15in (45.5 x 38cm)
**£45,000–54,000 / €66,000–79,000
$82,000–98,000** ↗ JAA

Attributed to John Constable
British (1776–1837)
River landscape and trees
Pencil study on off-white paper
7 x 12in (18 x 30.5cm)
£370–440 / €540–650
$670–800 ♪ DW

*This picture fetched only a modest amount at auction
because it is not signed and therefore cannot be verified
as a Constable. Today we require proof, by way of a
signature or other documentary evidence. If it could
proved that this picture was definitely by Constable then
it could be worth around £10,000 / €14,600 / $18,200.*

'Attributed to' means, in the opinion of the
auctioneer or gallery, that the work is assumed
to have been produced by the said artist. The
uncertainty arises because the artist has not
verified that the work does not exist, nor is his
signature on the painting.

Louis Contoit
Canadian (19th/20thC)
English setters working
A pair, signed, oil on canvas
16 x 20in (40.5 x 51cm)
£2,600–3,100 / €3,800–4,500
$4,750–5,750 ♪ DNY

George E. Cook
American
(1867–1930)
Western Landscape
Signed, oil on canvas
16 x 20in
(40.5 x 51cm)
£470–560
€690–820
$850–1,000
♪ TREA

Elizabeth Cope
Irish (b1952)
Interior, Shankill Castle, Paulstown, Co Kilkenny
Signed and inscribed, oil on canvas
40 x 48in (101.5 x 122cm)
£2,750–3,300 / €4,000–4,800
$5,000–6,000 ♪ WA

◄ **Norman Cornish**
British (b1919)
The Gantry
Signed, pastel heightened with white, on buff paper
11¼ x 16in (28.5 x 40.5cm)
£1,500–1,800 / €2,200–2,600
$2,750–3,250 ♪ M

▶ **Malcolm Coward, SEA**
British (b1948)
Spanish Cowboys
Oil on panel
24 x 48in (61 x 122cm)
£3,150–3,500 / €4,600–5,100
$5,700–6,400 ⊞ SMi

◀ **Malcolm Coward, SEA**
British (b1948)
A Wild Boar
Oil on canvas
8 x 10in (20.5 x 25.5cm)
£340–380 / €500–550
$620–690 ⊞ SMi

Sébastien-Melchior Cornu
French (1804–70)
Italian woman with a tambourine
Monogrammed and dated 1853, oil on canvas
39½ x 29¼in (100.5 x 74.5cm)
£7,400–8,900 / €10,800–13,000
$13,500–16,000 ⚒ S(P)

*Cornu studied under Fleury Richard at the
School of Fine Arts, Lyon in 1820, before
becoming a pupil of Ingres in Paris and
Bonnefond in Lyon. In 1828, he was in Italy,
working with Gleyre and living in Rome for
seven years before travelling to the Orient.
He is known today for his religious paintings,
although he regularly exhibited genre, historical,
Oriental and literary works in Lyon and Paris.*

David Crone
Irish (b1937)
Street
Signed, inscribed and dated 1983,
gouache on paper
29 x 20½in (73.5 x 52cm)
£960–1,150 / €1,400–1,650
$1,750–2,100 ⚒ WA

▶ **Fleur Cowles**
American (20thC)
Tryst
Signed and dated 1971, acrylic on board
24 x 18in (61 x 45.5cm)
£150–180 / €220–260
$270–320 ⚒ WW

Ray Austin Crooke
Australian (b1922)
A Farmstead
Signed, oil on canvas
24 x 35¾in (61 x 91cm)
£2,800–3,300 / €4,100–4,800
$5,100–6,000 ⚒ S

James Henry Crossland
British (1852–1939)
Autumn in the Highlands
Signed, oil on canvas
20 x 30in (52 x 76cm)
£5,800–6,500 / €8,500–9,500
$10,500–11,800 ⊞ Bne

◄ **Robert Cruikshank**
British (1789–1856)
Listons Dream
1825, etching with
hand colouring
on wove
10 x 14¼in
(25.5 x 36cm)
£700–840
€1,000–1,250
$1,250–1,500 ⚒ B

Charles Cullen
Irish (b1939)
Emer and Veronica, Berlin
Signed, inscribed and dated 1983,
acrylic and charcoal on paper
20½ x 30in (52 x 76cm)
£1,150–1,350 / €1,700–2,000
$2,100–2,500 ⚒ WA

*Charles Cullen was born in Longford and studied at the
National College of Art, Dublin, later returning there to teach
and, until 2000, serve as head of the painting department.
He is a founder member of the Project Arts Centre and
has been included in a number of major survey shows of
contemporary art in Ireland, including 'The Delighted Eye'
(1980) and the 'Decade Show' at the Guinness Hop Store
(1990). In 1997 the Hugh Lane Gallery held a retrospective
of his work. He is represented in the collections of the
Hugh Lane Gallery, Allied Irish Banks, The Arts Council
and Trinity College Dublin among others.*

Fred Cuming, RA, NEAC
British (b1930)
Dawn Sea
Oil on board
17½ x 29½in (44.5 x 75cm)
£5,800–6,500 / €8,500–9,500
$10,500–11,800 ⊞ BSG

*Born in London and educated at Sidcup School of Art and the Royal College of
Art, Fred Cuming is among Britain's most outstanding and respected painters.
Winner of many art awards, he was elected Royal Academician in 1974 and to
the New English Art Club in 1960. He has exhibited widely, including the Royal
Academy since 1952, and has had numerous one-man shows. His work is in
collections worldwide, including Monte Carlo Museum, Ministry of Works, Royal
Academy, National Museum of Wales, Cardiff, Bradford and Scunthorpe
Museums and the Department of the Environment.*

Charles Courtney Curran
American (1861–1942)
A Seat on the Summit
Titled, signed and dated 1920, oil on canvas
mounted on masonite
25 x 30in (63.5 x 76cm)
£30,000–36,000 / €44,000–53,000
$54,000–65,000 ⚒ S(NY)

*This painting is thought to have been cut down from a
30in (76cm) square canvas and mounted on masonite by
the artist in 1939. Curran changed the title from Cloud
Fancies to A Seat on the Summit at this time.*

◄ **Stanley Cursiter, CBE, RSA, RSW**
Scottish (1887–1976)
A view in Ayrshire
Signed, oil on canvas
9½ x 13½in (24 x 34.5cm)
£2,400–2,800 / €3,500–4,100
$4,350–5,200 ⚒ B(Ed)

Celebrity Art

With our insatiable appetite for the lives and loves of the rich and famous, are the paintings by a prime minister, the sketches by an actress or the watercolours by a popstar of greater value because of the artist? 'Works by royalty and famous statesmen such as Nelson Mandela and Winston Churchill will probably always be of interest even in years to come,' says Anna Hunter of the Belgravia Gallery. 'Mandela may not paint in the style of Rembrandt but his pictures reflect the man and his struggles. He has a fresh, charming and direct style. He worked on his prints in the same way as Matisse, doing all the colour separation himself.' Mandela's prints of the prison on Robin Island are very sought after because there are so few. The Hand of Africa series, in which his hand print represents Africa, although numerous are also desirable.

Buying a picture by a celebrity can make us feel good. Mandela, Prince Charles and many others auction their work in aid of charity. 'Prince Charles is a very accomplished watercolour artist. The signed limited edition lithographs of his watercolour *Hong Kong from HMY Britannia* sold out and would now command high prices,' reckons Anna Hunter. Similar to Queen Victoria's work, his watercolours act as a visual journal. Prince Albert and Queen Victoria set up a print studio at Buckingham Palace and, according to Hunter, 'Prince Albert was very good at cross-hatching.' Queen Victoria did not make many prints after he died but she continued to paint in watercolour. Their work was never sold but given away as gifts.

Fame is fickle and for most celebrities it does not last beyond their death. While celebrities are in the public eye, prices for their paintings could be artificially high, but the next generation is more likely to judge a picture on its merits, rather than on who painted it. When a singer or actor falls from popularity the value of their work could well drop. Some famous people just happen to be reasonably good at painting. It seems a bit unfair that artists in Southern California objected to Jane Seymour showing her pictures at an arts festival – her work is no worse than that of some who merely call themselves artists.

Perhaps it is best to buy a picture by a young actor or singer before they achieve worldwide fame. Fifty years ago, Rolf Harris sold his pictures to fund his trip from Australia to England. The Halcyon Gallery, who sold the picture illustrated below, interestingly say it was bought by an American who had never heard of Rolf Harris the television star.

Bryan Ferry and David Bowie went to art school before they decided to become popstars. David Bowie has always been a collector of modern art and his own very colourful paintings have been exhibited by a Cork Street gallery. The Jacksonville Gallery in Florida also holds examples of his work.

The Beatles, of course, are very collectable. The market for their work is growing all the time, and scribblings and sketches by John Lennon are becoming increasingly valuable. Paul McCartney came to painting long after the Beatles disbanded. A meeting with artist Willem de Kooning inspired him and today, 18 years later, he has produced 500 pictures. There has recently been an exhibition of the Art of Paul McCartney at the Walker Gallery in Liverpool.

So, as with any artist, buy a picture by a celebrity because you like it – most will not cost a fortune and, if in the future their fame increases, their work may increase in value as well.

◄ **Anthony Benedetto (Tony Bennett)**
American (b1926)
Positano, Italy
Watercolour
14 x 10in (35.5 x 25.5cm)
£5,700–6,800 / €8,300–9,900
$10,400–12,400 ↗ BENE

The entertainer Tony Bennett has worked as an artist throughout his life and, while he is best known for his hit songs, he has always made time for his art. He enjoys sketching and painting daily, and his work is now in the collections of Oprah Winfrey, Whoopi Goldberg, Mickey Rooney and Donald Trump. He signs his work with his family name Benedetto.

Rolf Harris
Australian (b1930)
The Boxer
Oil
15½in (39.5cm) square
£54,000–60,000 / €79,000–88,000
$98,000–109,000 ⊞ HnG

► HRH The Prince of Wales
British (b1948)
Balmoral Winter Scene
Signed, limited edition,
lithograph
19¾ x 18¼in (50 x 46.5cm)
£2,000–2,250 / €2,900–3,300
$3,650–4,050 ⊞ Bel

◄ HRH The Prince of Wales
British (b1948)
Ballochbuie, Balmoral, April
Signed, limited edition,
lithograph
22 x 20in (56 x 51cm)
£2,000–2,250 / €2,900–3,300
$3,650–4,050 ⊞ Bel

Paul McCartney
British (b1942)
Ancient Connections
Series of three, signed, limited edition print of 200
25½ x 33in (65 x 84cm)
£900–1,000 / €1,300–1,450
$1,600–1,800 ⊞ TR

Paul McCartney
British (b1942)
Big Mountain Face
Series of three, signed, limited
edition of 200
25½ x 33in (65 x 84cm)
£900–1,000 / €1,300–1,450
$1,600–1,800 ⊞ TR

Nelson Mandela
South African (b1918)
The Guard Tower
Signed, limited edition, lithograph
25½ x 19¾in (65 x 50cm)
£3,600–4,000 / €5,200–5,800
$6,500–7,300 ⊞ Bel

Nelson Mandela
South African (b1918)
The Courtyard
Signed, limited edition, lithograph
25½ x 19¾in (65 x 50cm)
£2,700–3,000 / €3,900–4,400
$4,900–5,500 ⊞ Bel

Jane Seymour
British (b1951)
September on the Beach
Signed, oil on panel
9 x 12in (23 x 30.5cm)
£5,500–6,200 / €8,000–9,000
$10,000–11,300 ⊞ CCP

Leon Dabo
American (1868–1960)
Sunset
Signed, oil on canvas
22 x 30in (56 x 76cm)
£2,750–3,300 / €4,000–4,800
$5,000–6,000 ⚒ TREA

Michael D'Aguilar, RA, RSBA
British (1916–2002)
On the Promenade – A Gust of Wind
Signed, oil on canvas, laid down on board
17¾ x 23¾in (45 x 60.5cm)
£720–860 / €1,050–1,250
$1,300–1,550 ⚒ B(B)

◀ **Peter Dahl**
Swedish/Norwegian (b1934)
Dancing
Signed, watercolour
19¾ x 28¼in (50 x 72cm)
£3,000–3,600 / €4,400–5,300
$5,500–6,500 ⚒ BUK

▶ **Augusto Daini**
Italian (1860–1920)
Good News
Signed, oil on canvas
16½ x 12in (42 x 30.5cm)
£400–480 / €580–700
$730–870 ⚒ WW

Samuel Daniell (1775–1811)

Samuel Daniell was the younger brother of William Daniell and the most talented of the family. He visited Africa and the Cape from 1799 to 1803, and in 1805 left England for Ceylon, where the Governor appointed him Ranger of the Woods and Forests. He remained on the island until his death.

▶ **Samuel Daniell**
British (1775–1811)
Native women bathing in a river, Ceylon
Pencil and watercolour
14¼ x 17¾in (36 x 45cm)
£9,500–11,400
€13,800–16,600
$17,300–20,700
⚒ B

◀ **Samuel Daniell**
British (1775–1811)
Colored (sic) Birds from the East, an album of nineteen bird studies
Watercolour
14¼ x 15¼in (36 x 38.5cm)
£10,000–12,000 / €14,600–17,500
$18,200–22,000 ⚒ B

Charles François Daubigny
French (1817–78)
Banks of the River Oise
Signed and dated 1869, oil on panel
6 x 10in (15 x 25.5cm)
£5,800–7,000 / €8,500–10,200
$10,500–12,700 ➚ L&T

Alan Davie
British (b1920)
Abstract composition
Signed, inscribed and dated 1965, numbered
9/25, lithograph printed on wove
21¼ x 30¾in (54 x 78cm)
£320–380 / €460–550
$580–690 ➚ B

Alan Davie
British (b1920)
Incantation
Signed and numbered 14/100,
lithograph
26¾ x 21¾in (68 x 55.5cm)
£240–290 / €350–420
$440–530 ➚ B(Kn)

Mary Davidson
Scottish (20thC)
Red Poppies
Mixed media
17½in (44.5cm) square
£1,400–1,650 / €2,000–2,400
$2,500–3,000 ⊞ WrG

*Mary Davidson was born in Dundee, and moved to
Glasgow in 1986. She studied part time at Glasgow
School of Art, combining it with work as a secretary/PA,
and turned to full-time painting in 1994. She has taken
part in many exhibitions, both in Britain and abroad. She
is a member of the Glasgow Society of Women Artists
and the Paisley Art Institute, and is a regular exhibitor at
the RSW, RGI and Laing Art Exhibitions. Mary works
mainly in water-based media, in gouache and acrylics.
She likes to paint the shorelines from both the east and
west coasts of Scotland.*

Arthur B. Davies
American (1862–1928)
Figures in a Landscape
Signed, oil on canvas
23¾ x 28¼in (60.5 x 72cm)
£9,300–11,100 / €13,600–16,100
$16,900–20,200 ➚ S(NY)

James Davis
Scottish (b1944)
Waiting to Go On
Acrylic on gesso panel
17 x 19in (43 x 48.5cm)
£1,800–2,150 / €2,600–3,100
$3,300–3,900 ⊞ WrG

◀ **Stuart Davis**
American
(1892–1964)
Lady on the Beach
Signed, inscribed
and dated 1917,
oil on canvas
29½ x 18in
(75 x 45.5cm)
£19,700–23,600
€29,000–35,000
$36,000–43,000
🔨 **S(NY)**
*The subject of this
painting is based on
a postcard sent to
Stuart Davis by Henry
Glintenkamp in 1913,
his close friend and
fellow artist. David
and Glintenkamp
met through the
Henri School and
went on to share a
studio in Hoboken,
New Jersey in 1912
and later in
Manhattan in 1913.*

Edwin Dawes
American (1872–1945)
Autumn Lake
Signed, oil on board
16 x 20in (40.5 x 51cm)
£550–660 / €800–960
$1,000–1,200 🔨 **TREA**

Montague Dawson (1895–1973)

Montague Dawson comes from a family of marine
artists – his grandfather was painter Henry Dawson.
After serving in the Royal Navy Montague began to
paint full time. He is technically very competent and his
eternal popularity plays on our nostalgia for the great
age of shipping. Most of his pictures are the same but
American ships always fetch a lot more than British
ones. His work is held at the National Maritime
Museum in Greenwich, London.

▶ **Montague Dawson**
British (1895–1973)
Fair Weather – *The Charles H. Lunt*
Signed, oil on canvas
20 x 30in (51 x 76cm)
£15,000–18,000 / €22,000–26,000
$28,000–33,000 🔨 **B**

Locate the source

The source of each illustration
can be found by checking the
code letters below each caption
with the Key to Illustrations,
pages 234–236.

◀ **Montague Dawson**
British (1895–1973)
The American full-rigger *Abner Coburn*
running before the wind
Signed, oil on canvas
20 x 30in (51 x 76cm)
£30,000–36,000 / €44,000–53,000
$55,000–66,000 🔨 **B**

◀ **Suzanne Daynes-Grassot**
French (1884–1976)
The Red Hair
Oil on canvas
29 x 21in (73.5 x 53.5cm)
£6,300–7,000 / €9,200–10,200
$11,500–12,700 ⊞ JN

A French School painter of portraits, figurative subjects, nudes, landscapes and still life, Suzanne Daynes-Grassot was born in Paris. She was a regular exhibitor at the Paris Salon and the Société Nationale between 1918 and 1935, and was awarded the Armand Berton Poussielgue Prize at the Salon in 1930 for La Femme Rousse. Most of her work is in oils on canvas, but she also occasionally painted in watercolours.

Rachel Deacon
British (20thC)
Woman Reclining with Pot
Oil on canvas
39½ x 47¼in (100.5 x 120cm)
£1,250–1,400 / €1,800–2,000
$2,300–2,600 ⊞ CAMB

Rachel Deacon studied Illustration at Chelsea School of Art and now lives and works in London. Her dramatic paintings of women in fruit groves and sultry settings are inspired by poetry and literature. She has received commissions for MCA Records, Ikea and Sony among others and has also received awards for her work. She has featured in numerous exhibitions throughout Britain, including the Outstanding Printmakers National Print Exhibition *at the Mall Galleries, London.*

Henry Jacques Delpy
French (1877–1957)
River at Sunset
Oil on canvas
15½ x 24¼in (39.5 x 61.5cm)
£1,950–2,300
€2,850–3,350
$3,550–4,200
⚒ DORO

◀ **Siri Derkert**
Swedish
(1888–1973)
Elsa Thorling
Dated 1911,
oil on panel
9½ x 7¼in
(24 x 18.5cm)
£1,150–1,350
€1,650–1,950
$2,100–2,450
⚒ BUK

Gabriel Deschamps
French (b1919)
A Marina on the Mediterranean
Signed, oil on canvas
13½ x 10¼in (34.5 x 26cm)
£2,100–2,500 / €3,050–3,650
$3,800–7,600 ⚒ B(B)

▶ **Achille Jacques Jean Marie Devéria**
French (1800–57)
A Turkish gentleman and lady seated in an interior
Signed, black and white chalk on buff paper
18½ x 23¼in
(47 x 59cm)
£3,350–4,000
€4,900–5,800
$6,000–7,300 ⚒ S

Arthur Devis (1711–87)

Arthur Devis depicts the life of well-to-do families in Georgian England, particularly excelling at the Conversation Piece – a family grouped in front of their estate. Many were north of England families as Devis came from Preston in Lancashire. His large Conversation Pieces always fetch considerably more than his smaller individual portraits. It is unlikely that Gainsborough saw Devis' Conversation Pieces but Gainsborough's early work shows a resemblance to that of Devis.

▶ **Arthur Devis**
British (1711–87)
Portrait of a Lady of the Lister Family
Oil on panel
19 x 13½in (48.5 x 34.5cm)
£18,000–21,000 / €26,000–31,000
$33,000–38,000 ⚒ S

Arthur Devis
British (1711–87)
Portrait of a gentleman with his wife and child, possibly Captain the Hon The Rev Robert Cholmondeley and his wife Mary
Oil on canvas
39 x 49in (99 x 124.5cm)
£66,000–79,000 / €96,000–115,000
$120,000–144,000 ⚒ S

◀ **Henry Cotterill Deykin**
British (1905–89)
St Leonard's, Bank Holiday
Oil on canvas
25 x 30in (63.5 x 76cm)
£4,500–5,000 / €6,600–7,300
$8,200–9,100 ⊞ JN

Henry Cotterill Deykin studied at the College of Arts and Crafts and the Slade School of Fine Art. He taught at Warwick School from 1936 to 1965, except for a period in camouflage work during WWII.

Herbert Dicksee
British (1862–1942)
Tigers watering
Signed, 1911, etching on wove
17¾ x 27in (45 x 68.5cm)
£300–360 / €430–520
$550–650 ⚒ B

Robert Dighton
British (1752–1814)
A puppy's dress; A choice of fruit; The harmony of courtship; The discord of marriage
Set of four, signed and inscribed, watercolour
5½ x 4½in (14 x 11.5cm)
£2,400–2,900 / €3,500–4,200
$4,400–5,300 ⚒ B

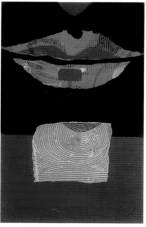

Gerard Dillon
Irish (1916–71)
Lips
Signed, oil and collage on board
21 x 14in (53.5 x 35.5cm)
£4,300–5,000
€6,200–7,300
$7,800–9,100 ⚒ WA

Jim Dine
American (b1953)
Rainbow
Signed, dated 1972 and numbered 8/50, lithograph
14½ x 17¾in (37 x 45cm)
£360–430 / €520–620
$650–780 ⚒ B(Kn)

◄ **Charles Edward Dixon, RI**
British (1872–1934)
Off Billingsgate
Signed and dated 1922, oil on canvas
43 x 75¼in (109 x 191cm)
£6,300–7,000 / €9,200–10,200
$11,400–12,700 ⊞ HFA

*Charles Edward Dixon was a painter of river, coastal and marine subjects
in oil and watercolour. He was the son of the genre and historical
painter, Alfred Dixon. Charles first exhibited at the Royal Academy at
the age of 16, before he became a regular contributor to the Illustrated
London News, the Graphic and the Sphere. He exhibited at many
venues, including the New Watercolour Society, and was elected RI in
1900. He is well known for his port scenes, particularly on the Thames.*

Charles Edward Dixon, RI
British (1872–1934)
The Lower Pool, London
Signed and dated 1912, watercolour
10½ x 30in (26.5 x 76cm)
£7,600–8,500 / €11,100–12,400
$13,800–15,500 ⊞ Bne

► **Frank Dobson**
British (1886–1963)
Portrait of Rollo Peters III
Oil on canvas
18 x 16in (45.5 x 40.5cm)
£3,150–3,500 / €4,600–5,100
$5,700–6,400 ⊞ WoF

*Frank Dobson attended Leyton School of Art
from 1900 to 1902 and was apprenticed as a
sculptor from 1902 to 1904 with Sir William
Reynolds-Stephens. He trained at Hospitalfield
Art Institute, Arbroath and at the City and
Guilds School, Kennington. He had his first
one-man show at the Chenil Galleries in 1914.*

Josef Dobrowsky
German (1889–1964)
Yellow and orange jugs with flowers, bowl
with fruits
Signed and dated 1935, gouache on paper
29¼ x 19¾in (74.5 x 50cm)
£2,650–3,200 / €3,850–4,650
$4,800–5,800 ↗ DORO

Frank Dobson
British (1886–1963)
Sulphur and White Breasted Toucans
Signed, titled and dated 1946, pastel and watercolour
13¾ x 19in (35 x 48.5cm)
£360–430 / €520–620
$650–780 ↗ B(O)

Joseph Josiah Dodd
British (1809–80)
Milan Cathedral
Signed, inscribed and dated 1878, oil on canvas
27½ x 35½in (70 x 90cm)
£1,550–1,850 / €2,250–2,650
$2,800–3,350 ↗ B(B)

◄ **Tom Dodson**
British (1910–91)
Northern street
scene
Signed and dated
1977, oil on canvas
17¼ x 13¼in
(44 x 33.5cm)
£920–1,100
€1,350–1,600
$1,750–2,000
➢ **B(NW)**

William Dommersen
Dutch (1850–1927)
A Flemish market place
Signed, oil on canvas
38¼ x 57¾in (97 x 146.5cm)
£6,000–7,200 / €8,700–10,500
$10,900–13,100 ➢ **B**

Pieter Cornelis Dommersen
Dutch (c1823–1908)
Rough Seas
Oil on panel
11 x 15in (28 x 38cm)
£11,300–12,500 / €16,500–18,200
$21,000–23,000 ⊞ **JN**

Pieter Cornelis Dommersen was a member of the Dommershuizen family of artists who originally came from Utrecht, Holland and settled in England towards the end of the 19th century, changing their name to Dommersen. He travelled extensively in Europe on painting expeditions with his son, William, who painted in a similar style. His work combines a mastery of light, shade and depth with an ability to paint figures, ships and water. He also painted some Dutch street scenes which are quite rare and usually much admired.

◄ **Edmond van Dooren**
Dutch (1895–1965)
Landscape in the Ardennes
Oil on canvas
19¾ x 27½in (50 x 70cm)
£420–500 / €610–730
$760–910 ➢ **BERN**

David Donaldson, RSA, RP
British (1916–96)
Japanese Girl
Signed, 1980, oil on canvas
40 x 37in (101.5 x 94cm)
£4,000–4,800 / €5,800–7,000
$7,300–8,700 ➢ **B(Ed)**

► **Kenneth Draper**
British (b1944)
Many Moons
Mixed media
24½ x 21¾in (62 x 55.5cm)
£2,500–2,800 / €3,650–4,050
$4,550–5,100 ⊞ **HG**

Kenneth Draper was born in Yorkshire, the son of a coal miner. His early years drew on the experience of the extremes of the northern industrial landscape where the effects of mining and steelworks were enclosed by the rugged moorlands of Derbyshire and Yorkshire. Over the years he has travelled widely, visiting India and Pakistan, East Africa, South West America, Egypt and Menorca, where he now lives. Although he was well known as a painter during the 1990s, he has recently returned to his original medium – sculpture.

A good provenance can make a huge difference to the price of a picture. Collectors like something new to the market; a good picture that has been in a family for generations will fetch more than a picture that has been in and out of auction houses.

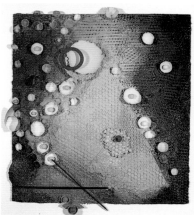

Alexander J. Drysdale
American (1870–1934)
Louisiana Bayou
Signed, watercolour on paper
8 x 11in (20.5 x 28cm)
£880–1,050 / €1,300–1,550
$1,600–1,900 ♪ TREA

William Duffield
British (1816–63)
Still life
Monogrammed, oil on canvas
24 x 20in (61 x 51cm)
£1,100–1,300 / €1,600–1,900
$2,000–2,350 ♪ B(Kn)

Raoul Dufy
French (1877–1953)
The Orchestra
Lithograph
20½ x 17¼in (52 x 44cm)
£200–240
€290–350
$360–430 ♪ BBA

Edward J. Duval
British (fl1880–1916)
Largo, Coast of Fife
Signed, inscribed and dated 1878, watercolour heightened with white
17½ x 27¼in (44.5 x 69cm)
£700–840 / €1,000–1,200
$1,250–1,500 ♪ Bea

*Known as a landscape painter with a fondness for depicting expanses
of water, Edward J. Duval exhibited at numerous venues, including the
Royal Academy, the Walker Art Gallery, Liverpool, and the Ridley Art Club.*

Christopher Dunkley
Canadian (b1956)
Template T, 101
Acrylic on canvas
47 x 36in (119.5 x 91.5cm)
£1,900–2,100
€2,800–3,100
$3,450–3,800 ⊞ GALG

► Marcel Dyf
French (1899–1985)
French Landscape
Signed
23¼ x 28¼in (59 x 72cm)
£4,400–5,300 / €6,400–7,700
$8,000–9,600 ♪ AH

◀ **Joan Eardley, RSA**
British (1921–63)
A Stormy Sea IV
Signed, oil on board
12½ x 22¾in
(32 x 58cm)
£7,800–9,400
€11,400–13,700
$14,200–17,100
🔨 B(Ed)

Tom Early
British (1914–67)
Gypsy Caravan on the Helston Road
Signed, titled and inscribed, oil on canvas board
15½ x 17¾in (39.5 x 45cm)
£1,550–1,750 / €2,250–2,500
$2,800–3,150 ⊞ JLx

Albert Edelfelt
Finnish (1854–1905)
Interior
Oil on canvas
9¾ x 11¾in (25 x 30cm)
£5,600–6,700 / €8,200–9,800
$10,200–12,200 ⊞ BUK

Norman Edgar, RGI
Scottish (b1948)
Soup Tureen
Signed, oil on canvas
28 x 36in (71 x 91.5cm)
£2,300–2,750 / €3,350–4,000
$4,200–5,000 🔨 L&T

Ric Elliot
Australian (1933–95)
Historic Shop, Hunters Hill
Signed, oil on masonite board
15¾ x 27½in (40 x 70cm)
£370–440
€540–640
$670–800 🔨 SHSY

▶ **Tracy Emin**
British (b1963)
Figure study
Oil on board
6 x 9in (17 x 23cm)
£1,800–2,150 / €2,600–3,100
$3,300–3,900 🔨 B

Magnus Enckell
Finnish (1870–1925)
Coastal Landscape
Signed and dated 1915, watercolour
11¾ x 14½in (30 x 37cm)
£420–500 / €610–730
$760–910 ⚘ BUK

Oscar B. Erickson
American (1883–1963)
Winter Stream
Signed, oil on canvas
16 x 13in (40.5 x 33cm)
£470–560 / €690–820
$860–1,050 ⚘ JAA

◀ **David Evans**
British (b1942)
Still life of plate
and cutlery
Oil on canvas
15¾ x 19¾in
(40 x 50cm)
£460–550
€670–800
$740–1,000
⚘ **B(Kn)**

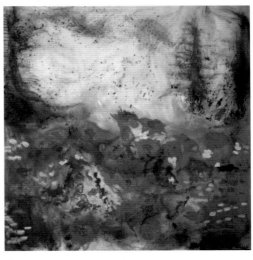

▶ **Kyle Evans**
American (b1958)
Adrift Upon
The Poppies
Encaustic in birch panel
24in (61cm) square
£1,000–1,150
€1,450–1,650
$1,850–1,000
⊞ **GALG**

◀ **William Evans
of Eton, OWS**
British (1798–1877)
On the Brocas, Eton
Signed and dated
1845, watercolour
9¾ x 14in
(25 x 35.5cm)
£500–600
€730–880
$910–1,100
⚘ **B(Kn)**

Ray Evans
British (b1920)
Hillside with cottages
Signed and dated 1963, gouache
15½ x 21½in (39.5 x 54.5cm)
£460–550 / €670–800
$840–1,000 ⚘ GH

Equestrian Art

The way a horse is depicted in a painting tells us so much about the culture of a country. In England, the 18th century was the classical period of horse portraiture; by then horses were not purely instruments of battle or conveyances. The thoroughbred had been refined and racing became a popular and glamorous sport.

Those who could paint the horse were in great demand. One such artist is John Wootton (not to be confused with 20th-century foxhunting artist Frank Wootton). His panoramic views of George I visiting Newmarket project an image of comfortable confidence. The picture says British racing is the best and the sport of kings. A high price was reached for the John Wootton illustrated on page 67 (the estimate was £6,000 / €8,800 / $10,900). Notable sporting art dealers prefer larger Woottons with more background detail. If a Wootton was to be sold from one of England's country houses such as Badminton House in Gloucestershire it could fetch around £250,000 / €365,000 / $455,000. These large pictures are acknowledged to be some of his best.

While Wootton was in his prime one of the greatest English horse painters of all time was perfecting his craft. George Stubbs would take equestrian art to a new level and it is said that a nobleman once offered him £100 / €145 / $180 to paint his horse but only £50 / €75 / $90 to paint his wife. Stubbs, who used to drag corpses from the knacker's yard to study them, gives the horses in his pictures muscle and sinew. His horses always glisten and Stubbs brilliantly illustrates how light reflects off their coats. Prices for his paintings are therefore very high. More affordable contemporaries of Stubbs are Francis and John Nott Sartorius. Francis's work is more primitive and naïve than the work of his son John. Some prefer Francis's small pictures which are available at reasonable prices to John Nott's more expensive work. Original 18th-century horse paintings will always increase in value but check authenticity as there are many reproductions.

The 19th century saw work for English equestrian artists grow enormously as foxhunting became the sport of the gentry. New money meant new large country houses, the walls of which needed covering with fine paintings.

You can pick up small oils of a horse in a stable, often labelled English School, from £100 / €145 / $180, but you can expect to pay around £5,000 / €7,300 / $9,100 for an equestrian subject with a background by a well respected Victorian artist.

In France, horses were depicted differently and did not feature in sporting paintings. They were chargers and war-horses in the age of Napoleon. Eugene Delacroix included horses in his huge mythological paintings. In America, the second half of the 19th century saw an increased interest in horse racing and therefore work for equestrian artists such as Frederick Arthur Bridgman (see page 63).

The end of the 19th century saw the emergence of Sir Alfred Munnings. His early work is extremely desirable and continues to increase in value but his hunting scenes are worth less than his later pictures of famous racehorses which he painted after the loss of one eye. These pictures can fetch seven- or eight-figure sums.

The modern era has seen the horse assume a more abstract role in paintings. The animal no longer needs to be painted to illustrate the social position of its owner or just as an extra in a battle scene. In America horses were used by cowboys and a tradition of cowboy art grew up around it (see *Miller's Picture Price Guide 2004*). Leonora Carrington is a surrealist and not a specific equestrian artist – her picture illustrated on the next page went for twice its estimate. Elisabeth Frink produced prints from her sculptures and some of her horses' heads seem influenced by Chinese porcelain. Her work is much copied, so make sure that you buy a numbered and signed print executed in her lifetime.

Nowadays, there are fewer traditional horse painters working but there is still a demand for equestrian art. The best equestrian artists now interpret horses in a new way, and the static traditional image in oil has been replaced by a more sketchy impression of a horse in motion. Jo Taylor's paintings (see page 66) emphasize the sinews of the horse and her work is collected by aristocratic patrons who in former times would have bought paintings by Wootton or Stubbs.

◄ **Cecil Charles Windsor Aldin, RBA**
British (1870–1935)
Rotund huntsman with horse at the edge of a field
Signed, watercolour
18 x 11in (45.5 x 28cm)
£1,250–1,500 / €1,800–2,150 $2,300–2,750 ↗ **GAK**

► **Vladimir Belskiy**
Russian (b1949)
The Duel
Signed, oil on cardboard
18¼ x 13in (46.5 x 33cm)
£450–540 / €660–790 $820–980 ↗ **JNic**

Frederick Arthur Bridgman
American (1847–1928)
Barbary Horses at Cairo
Signed, oil on canvas
19 x 22½in (48.5 x 57cm)
**£6,000–7,200 / €8,800–10,500
$10,900–13,100** ⚒ S

Leonora Carrington
British (b1917)
Horses
Signed and dated 1960, tempera on ceramic
8½ x 23¾in (21.5 x 60.5cm)
**£3,300–3,950 / €4,800–5,700
$6,000–7,000** ⚒ LCM

Leonora Carrington was born in Lancashire. She met Max Ernst in London before going to Paris where she worked with the Surrealists and took part in exhibitions of this school in Paris and Amsterdam. As a consequence of WWII she went to Mexico in 1941, where she continued her artistic career. Her works have been shown in Museums of Modern Art in Mexico, New York, Paris, London and San Francisco. She is, without doubt, one of the principal exponents of surrealism and her pictures, engravings and sculptures are to be found in the most prestigious private collections and museums in the world.

◄ **Neil Cawthorne**
British (b1936)
Over the Hedge
Signed, oil on panel
24 x 35¾in (61 x 91cm)
**£1,900–2,300 / €2,800–3,350
$3,500–4,200** ⚒ B(Kn)

William Albert Clark
British (20thC)
Grey hunter, standing four square with bridle before a house
Signed and dated 1930, oil on canvas
15¾ x 19¾in (40 x 50cm)
**£450–540 / €660–790
$820–980** ⚒ B(Kn)

Henry Enrico Coleman
Italian (1846–1911)
Lassoing the wild horses
Signed and inscribed, watercolour
18 x 25½in (45.5 x 65cm)
**£11,000–13,200
€16,100–19,300
$20,000–24,000** ⚒ B

► **Malcolm Coward, SEA**
British (20thC)
The Arab
Watercolour
12 x 10in (30.5 x 25.5cm)
**£270–300 / €390–440
$490–540** ⊞ SMi

Joseph Crawhall, RSW
British (1861–1913)
Your Money or Your Life
Watercolour
6¼ x 8¼in (16 x 21cm)
£1,000–1,200 / €1,500–1,750
$1,850–2,200 ⚒ L&T

Isaac J. Cullin
British (fl1881–1920)
Lemberg and Greenback before the race; Lemberg and Greenback leading the parade to the start
A pair, signed, inscribed and dated 1911 and 1910, watercolour
6¼ x 10in (16 x 25.5cm)
£1,800–2,150
€2,650–3,150
$3,300–3,900
⚒ B(Kn)

John Dalby of York
British (fl1826–53)
Floss – a hunter in a loosebox
Signed, inscribed and dated 1939, oil on canvas
12½ x 16½in (32 x 42cm)
£1,050–1,250 / €1,500–1,800
$1,950–2,300 ⚒ B(B)

▶ **Vu Cao Dam**
Vietnamese
(1908–2000)
Man and Horse
Signed, titled and
dated 1967,
oil on canvas
10½ x 14¾in
(26.5 x 37.5cm)
£3,500–4,200
€5,100–6,100
$6,400–7,600
⚒ S(Sl)

Elisabeth Frink, RA
British (1930–93)
Small horse lying down
Signed, edition of 70, lithograph
13½ x 18¾in (34.5 x 47.5cm)
£1,150–1,300 / €1,700–1,900
$2,100–2,350 ⊞ JLx

Harry Hall
British (1814–82)
Untitled
Oil on canvas
33¾ x 46in (85.5 x 117cm)
£14,500–17,400 / €21,200–25,400
$26,400–31,700 ⚒ RTo
This picture depicts the racehorse Fisherman, ridden by jockey 'Brushe' Wells wearing the colours of Fisherman's owner, Mr J. B. Starky.

◄ **Charles Hancock**
British (1796–1868)
A hunter and a dog in a landscape
Oil on canvas
16 x 19in (40.5 x 48.5cm)
£1,400–1,700 / €2,100–2,500
$2,500–3,000 ⚒ WW

John Frederick Herring, Jnr
British (1815–1907)
A farmyard scene with horses, pigs, cattle and poultry
Signed, oil on canvas
24¼ x 36¼in (64 x 92cm)
£20,000–24,000 / €30,000–35,000
$36,000–43,000 ⚒ B

Maqbool Fida Husain
Indian (b1915)
Horse – II
Signed and numbered 26/125, serigraph on paper
31¼ x 41in (79.5 x 104cm)
£550–660 / €800–960
$1,000–1,200 ⚒ B(Kn)

Terry Barron Kirkwood, DA
Scottish (20thC)
Trotting horse
Watercolour
15 x 22in (38 x 56cm)
£100–120 / €150–175
$190–220 ⚒ GH
*Terry Barron Kirkwood graduated from Glasgow School of Art in
1971. Renowned for her paintings of modern landscapes, equestrian
subjects and cats, she works in oils and produces brush drawings on
hand-made rag paper. She has exhibited at RSA, Royal Glasgow
Institute of Fine Arts, and Forbes Gallery, New York.*

◄ **Sir Alfred Munnings, PRA, RWS**
British (1878–1959)
Huntsman
Signed, titled and dated 1914, oil on canvas
20 x 10¼in (51 x 26cm)
£24,000–28,800 / €35,000–42,000
$44,000–52,000 ⚒ B

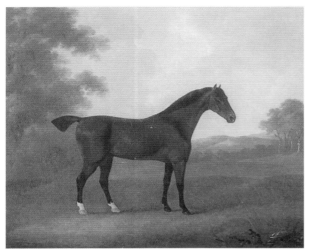

John Nott Sartorius
British (1759–1828)
A chestnut hunter in a landscape
Signed and dated 1799, oil on canvas
13½ x 17in (34.5 x 43cm)
£3,800–4,550 / €5,500–6,600
$6,900–8,300 ⚒ WW

Dennis Syrett, RBA, RSMA
British (b1932)
La Feria, Seville
Signed, oil on canvas
35 x 40in (89 x 101.5cm)
£4,450–4,950 / €6,500–7,200
$8,100–9,000 ⊞ Man

Jo Taylor (b1969)

Jo Taylor studied at Leeds Metropolitan University. She
has since returned to her native Lancashire and works
as a full-time artist. She depicts a variety of animals,
always aiming to capture their energy and spirit and
recreate a sense of their smell, touch and sound.
Jo's work has been inspired by artists such as Marini,
Gericault and Susan Rothenberg. Jo was recently Artist in
Residence at Liverpool University's Faculty of Veterinary
Science, and this has given her a strong anatomical and
physiological understanding of her subject.

Jo Taylor
British (b1969)
Horseman I
Mixed media on paper
27 x 29in (68.5 x 73.5cm)
£1,750–1,950 / €2,550–3,850
$3,200–3,550 ⊞ TTCG

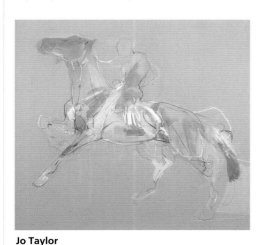

Jo Taylor
British (b1969)
Brave Horse
Mixed media on paper
58 x 30in (147.5 x 76cm)
£2,700–3,000
€3,950–4,400
$4,900–5,500 ⊞ TTCG

Jo Taylor
British (b1969)
Horseman II
Mixed media on paper
27 x 29in (68.5 x 73.5cm)
£1,750–1,950 / €2,550–3,850
$3,200–3,550 ⊞ TTCG

◄ **Jo Taylor**
British (b1969)
Moving Arrow
Mixed media on paper
31 x 26in (78.5 x 66cm)
£1,950–2,200
€2,850–3,200
$3,550–4,000 ⊞ TTCG

Feliks Topolski
Polish (1907–89)
Equestrian study
Signed, pen and watercolour
12½ x 9½in (32 x 24cm)
£540–650 / €790–950
$1,000–1,200 ⚒ B(Kn)

**► John Arnold
Alfred Wheeler**
British (1821–1903)
Sun Star
Signed and inscribed,
oil on board
9½ x 11¾in
(24 x 30cm)
£600–720
€880–1,050
$1,100–1,300
⚒ B(Kn)

Rosemary Sarah Welch, SWA, AAEA
British (b1948)
Into the River at Appleby
Oil
24 x 36in (61 x 91.5cm)
£5,000–5,500 / €7,300–8,000
$9,100–10,000 ⊞ RSW

Rosemary Sarah Welch was born in Ramsbury, Wiltshire, the daughter of the book illustrator Dorothy Welch. After moving to New York at the age of nine, she returned to the UK when she was 15 and attended the St Ives School of Painting in Cornwall, where she studied portraiture. Her love of horses began when she moved to the New Forest and painted the native ponies there. She exhibits widely, including the St Ives Society of Arts and the Society of Women Artists.

Frank Wootton
British (1911–98)
A Bright Morning – Setting Out
Signed, oil on canvas
28 x 38in (71 x 96.5cm)
£13,000–14,500 / €19,000–21,200
$23,500–26,000 ⊞ Bne

John Wootton
British (1683–1764)
A grey hunter with a groom, the owner
standing to the left
Oil on canvas
49 x 39¼in (124.5 x 99.5cm)
£18,000–21,600 / €26,300–31,000
$33,000–39,000 ⚒ S

Thomas Faed
British (1826–1900)
A family group seated in a landscape
Oil on canvas
21 x 27½in (53.5 x 70cm)
£1,300–1,550 / €1,900–2,250
$2,350–2,800 ➚B(Kn)

William J. Fairlie
British (fl1850–60s)
Old Cottage at Aberg Glastyn
Oil
12 x 19in (30.5 x 48.5cm)
£1,500–1,650 / €2,150–2,400
$2,700–3,000 ⊞ Dr

◄ **Alecos Fassianos**
Greek (b1935)
Two Friends
Signed, watercolour
on paper
25½ x 19½in
(65 x 49.5cm)
£3,800–4,550
€5,500–6,600
$6,900–8,300 ➚B

Edmund Fairfax-Lucy
British (b1945)
Lake, early morning
Oil on canvas
18 x 22in (45.5 x 56cm)
£1,800–2,150 / €2,650–3,150
$3,200–3,900 ➚B

Arthur Charles Fare
British (1876–1958)
Beeston Castle and Villages, Cheshire – the Annual Flower Show and Gala
Signed and dated 1936, watercolour
18½ x 12in (47 x 30.5cm)
£230–270 / €330–390
$410–490 ➚FHF

John Faulkner
British (c1830–88)
On the Avon near Stoneleigh, In the Open Country
A pair, signed and inscribed, watercolour
19 x 39in (48.5 x 99cm)
£1,300–1,550 / €1,900–2,250
$2,350–2,800 ➚B(Kn)

Mary Fedden, RA
British (b1915)
Black Cat
Signed and dated 1982, watercolour
6¼ x 8½in (16 x 21.5cm)
£2,200–2,650 / €3,200–3,850
$4,000–4,800 ⚒ B

Neil Faulkner
British (b1952)
The Potting Shed
Signed, watercolour
20½ x 14½in (52 x 37cm)
£1,500–1,650 / €2,150–2,400
$2,700–3,000 ⊞ Bne

► **Mary Fedden, RA**
British (b1915)
Tabby and Pineapple
Signed and dated 1981,
pencil and watercolour
30 x 22in (76 x 56cm)
£2,200–2,600 / €3,200–3,850
$3,700–4,400 ⚒ B

Hans Feibusch
German (1898–1998)
Christ in Glory
Signed and dated 1961, gouache
42½ x 29½in (108 x 75cm)
£500–600 / €730–880
$910–1,100 ⚒ B(L)

Paul Feiler
British (b1918)
Morning Harbour, Mousehole
Signed, inscribed and dated 1954
26½ x 38½in (67.5 x 98cm)
£20,000–24,000 / €29,000–35,000
$37,000–44,000 ⚒ LAY

John Duncan Fergusson (1874–1961)

John Duncan Fergusson was an integral part of the Scottish art scene. He studied in Paris and lived in France from 1911 until the outbreak of WWII and painted nudes and the French landscape in the colourful Fauve style. In 1939 he settled in Scotland and was a founder member of the New Art Club from which emerged the New Scottish Group. He was the author of *Modern Scottish Painting* published in 1943.

John Duncan Fergusson, RBA
British (1874–1961)
Half-length study of an elegant woman in profile
Conte
8 x 4¾in (20.5 x 12cm)
£2,700–3,200
€ 3,900–4,600
$4,900–5,800 ⚒ B(Ed)

John Duncan Fergusson, RBA
British (1874–1961)
The Feather Bonnet
Conte
8½ x 5in (21.5 x 12.5cm)
£1,200–1,450
€ 1,750–2,100
$2,200–2,600 ⚒ B(Ed)

John Duncan Fergusson, RBA
British (1874–1961)
Study for 'Magnolias'
Pencil, watercolour and gouache
8¾ x 6½in (22 x 16.5cm)
£7,800–9,300 / € 11,400–13,600
$14,200–16,900 ⚒ B(Ed)

Moira Ferrier
Scottish (20thC)
Summer Sailing, Isle of Mull
Oil on canvas
16 x 22in (40.5 x 56cm)
£840–930
€ 1,200–1,350
$1,500–1,700 ⊞ WrG

John Fery
Austrian/American (1859–1934)
Lake Josephine and Grinnell Glacier, Glacier National Park
Signed and inscribed, oil on canvas
40 x 60in (101.5 x 152.5cm)
£8,800–10,600 / € 12,900–15,500
$16,000–19,300 ⚒ JAA

John Fery studied art in Vienna, Düsseldorf and Karlsruhe. Fery went to America in 1886 and quickly established himself as a successful painter of American landscape and hunting scenes.

Samuel Luke Fildes
British (1843–1927)
Portrait of a young girl with a pink dress and white veil
Inscribed, oil on canvas
14¼ x 11¾in (36 x 30cm)
£2,000–2,400 / €2,900–3,500
$3,650–4,350 🔨 **B(Kn)**

Paul Fischer
Danish (1860–1934)
Statue of Niels Juels, Gammelholm
Signed, panel
8 x 9½in (20.5 x 24cm)
£4,800–5,800 / €7,000–8,400
$8,700–10,500 🔨 **BUK**

▶ **Horace Fisher**
British (1861–1928)
A young girl carrying a water jug
Signed, oil on canvas
30¼ x 20in (77 x 51cm)
£5,000–6,000 / €7,300–8,700
$9,100–10,900 🔨 **B(Kn)**

Clifford Fishwick
British (1923–97)
Plateau Top
Signed and dated 1966, oil on paper
13¾ x 19¾in (35 x 50cm)
£150–180 / €220–260
$270–320 🔨 **B(Kn)**

◀ **Neville Fleetwood, ROI**
British (b1932)
One Blue Bottle
Oil on board
24 x 28in (61 x 71cm)
£1,500–1,700 / €2,200–2,500
$2,750–3,100 ⊞ **P&H**

Neville Fleetwood graduated from Huddersfield School of Art in the 1950s. He worked as a graphic artist before starting his own successful business, from which he retired early to paint full time. He has exhibited extensively in Yorkshire and London, notably at the New English Art Club, and at the Royal institute of Painters in Oil where he was awarded the President's prize in 1997. Fleetwood's vibrant depiction of his surrounding countryside and vivid abstracted still life paintings have won him a keen following in London.

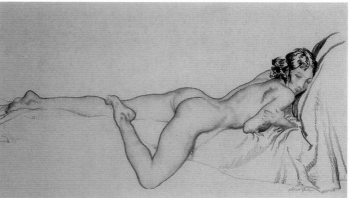

Karl Flieher
Austrian (1881–1958)
Old house with spire, Lötz
Signed, gouache on paper
8 x 10¼in (20.5 x 26cm)
£890–1,050 / €1,300–1,550
$1,600–1,900 ⚒ DORO

Sir William Russell Flint, RA, PRWS
British (1880–1969)
Lavinia
Signed, colour chalks
8 x 13¾in (20.5 x 35cm)
£4,800–5,700 / €7,000–8,300
$8,700–10,400 ⚒ B

Stanhope Alexander Forbes (1857–1947)

Stanhope Alexander Forbes was one of the leading lights in the
British Realist movement of the early 20th century. His rendering
of natural light and colour on the canvas is exceptional and as a
consequence his pictures fetch a lot of money. *The short cut across
the fields* was painted when he was in the later years of his life
and at the peak of his powers. He was a founder member of the
Newlyn School of Art in Cornwall, which nurtured a
generation of British artists. He married Canadian-born artist
Elizabeth Armstrong.

Stanhope Alexander Forbes, RA
British (1857–1947)
The short cut across the fields
Signed and dated 1921, oil on canvas
39½ x 50in (100.5 x 127cm)
£145,000–174,000 / €212,000–254,000
$264,000–317,300 ⚒ B

*Stanhope Forbes's exceptional renderings of natural light and
colour on the canvas are explored in this picture and have
contributed to its success over time and through changes of
fashion. The short cut across the fields was executed in 1921 and
depicts the return of a family from its farming duties in a harmony
of planes, colours and emotions, with the bright and dark colours
distributed sporadically but evenly across the canvas. The artist
reveals the strength of his beliefs in rural domesticity and the
spiritual values of nature.*

◄ **Stanhope Alexander Forbes, RA**
British (1857–1947)
Girls at the quayside, Newlyn
Oil on canvas
20 x 16in (51 x 40.5cm)
£10,000–12,000 / €14,600–17,500
$18,200–22,000 ⚒ B

◀ **Elizabeth Adela Stanhope Forbes, ARWS**
British (1859–1912)
Signed, oil on panel
10½ x 12¼in
(26.5 x 31cm)
£9,500–11,400
€13,800–16,600
$17,300–21,000
⚒ B
Elizabeth Adela married Stanhope Alexander Forbes in 1889. Ten years later, they founded the Newlyn School together.

◀ **Myles Birket Foster**
British (1825–99)
The Thames at Abingdon
Signed, watercolour
10 x 13¾in (25.5 x 35cm)
£10,500–12,600
€15,300–18,400
$19,100–23,000 ⚒ B

John Forrester
New Zealander
(b1922)
Aldila Mark 1962
Oil
39 x 22in (99 x 56cm)
£500–600
€730–870
$910–1,100 ⚒ JNic

Alexis Fournier
American (1865–1948)
Harvest
Signed, oil on canvas
18 x 24in (45.5 x 61cm)
£6,000–7,200
€8,800–10,500
$10,900–13,100 ⚒ TREA

Albert Moulton Foweraker, RBA
British (1873–1942)
The Sloop Inn, St Ives, Cornwall
Signed, watercolour
8½ x 11in (21.5 x 28cm)
£1,700–2,000
€2,500–2,900
$3,100–3,650 ⚒ B

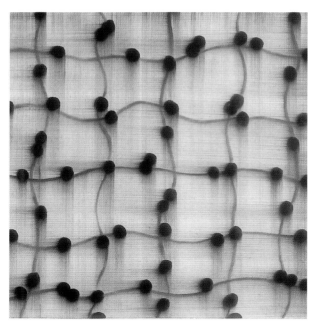

◄ **Mark Francis**
British (b1962)
Untitled (abstract)
Signed, monotype
23in (58.5cm) square
£1,600–1,900 / €2,350–2,750
$2,900–3,450 ⚒ B

► **Donald Hamilton Fraser**
British (b1929)
The Church
Signed, oil on paper
6 x 4¾in (15 x 12cm)
£1,200–1,450 / €1,750–2,100
$2,200–2,650 ⚒ B(Kn)

Colin Fraser
Scottish (20thC)
Sarong
Egg tempera
29½ x 46in (75 x 117cm)
£9,900–11,000 / €14,500–16,100
$18,000–20,000 ⊞ BSG

Colin Fraser was born in Glasgow and studied fine art in Brighton. He now lives and works in Sweden, where the translucent Scandinavian light falling on objects, flooding through windows and casting deep shadow, helps to give his work its extraordinary quality. His favourite medium is egg tempera. He exhibits regularly at the Royal Academy Summer Show, and at galleries in London, New York and Glasgow.

William Miller Frazer, RSA
British (1864–1961)
At Machrihanish
Signed, oil on canvasboard
8 x 13½in (20.5 x 34.5cm)
£1,450–1,700 / €2,100–2,500
$2,650–3,100 ⚒ B(Ed)

Auction or gallery?

All the pictures in our price guide originate from auction houses or galleries. The source of each picture can be found by checking the code letters after each caption with the Key to Illustrations on pages 234–236. When buying at auction prices can be lower than those of a gallery, but a buyer's premium and VAT will be added to the hammer price. Equally when selling at auction, commission, tax and photography charges must be taken into account. Galleries will often restore and authenticate pictures before putting them back on the market. Both galleries and auctioneers will provide professional advice, so it is worth researching both sources before buying or selling your pictures.

Charles Théodore Frère
French (1814–88)
Evening on the Nile
Signed, oil on panel
8¼ x 12½in (21 x 32cm)
£6,600–7,900 / €9,600–11,500
$12,000–14,400 ⚒ S

Elisabeth Frink
British (1930–93)
Small boar
Signed and numbered 21/70, lithograph
19¾ x 25¼in (50 x 64cm)
£380–460 / €550–670
$690–830 ↗ **B**

A. L. Friedrich
American (20thC)
Still Life with Eggs
Oil on canvas
16 x 12in(40.5 x 30.5cm)
£270–320 / €390–470
$490–580 ↗ **TREA**

Donald Friend
British (1915–89)
Friendship
Signed, mixed media on paper
30 x 22in (76 x 56cm)
£3,300–3,950 / €4,800–5,800
$6,000–7,200 ↗ **S(SI)**

Lithographs

Owning work by a world renowned artist is more affordable in the form of a lithograph. A signed example will retain its value better.

Terry Frost (1915–2003)

Painter, printmaker and teacher, Terry Frost was born in Leamington Spa, Warwickshire. After leaving school, Frost served in the army and was held as a prisoner of war, where he met the painter Adrian Heath who encouraged him to paint in oil. After the war, Frost took evening classes at Birmingham College of Art, then studied at St Ives School of Painting and at Camberwell School of Art. He went on to teach at a number of art schools. His abstract painting began in 1949, shortly before returning to St Ives where he worked from 1950 to 1952 as assistant to the sculptor Barbara Hepworth. He exhibited widely both internationally and in England. He was elected RA in 1992 and knighted in 1998. His work is held in the Tate Gallery.

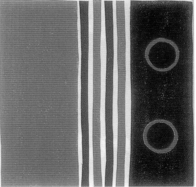

◄ **Terry Frost, RA**
British (1915–2003)
Red, Black and White Rhythm
Signed and dated 1995, collage laid on board
10½in (26.5cm) square
£1,700–2,000
€2,500–2,900
$2,100–3,650
↗ **B(L)**

Terry Frost, RA
British (1915–2003)
Vertical Collage
Signed and dated 2001, acrylic on strips of board
7¼ x 15¾in (18.5 x 40cm)
£3,800–4,200 / €5,500–6,100
$6,900–7,600 ⊞ **JLx**

► **Terry Frost, RA**
British (1915–2003)
Blue, Black & White
Signed, titled and dated 1959, oil on canvas
60 x 36in (152.5 x 91.5cm)
£8,000–9,600
€11,700–14,000
$14,600–17,500 ↗ **B**

Clarence Alphonse Gagnon
Canadian (1881–1942)
Jour de Boucherie
Oil on panel
4½ x 6¾in (11.5 x 17cm)
£4,200–5,000 / € 6,100–7,300
$7,600–9,100 ⚒ **S**
Gagnon was born in Montreal and studied drawing and painting there between 1897 and 1900. With the patronage of the Montreal businessman and collector, James Morgan, he travelled to Europe and studied from 1903 to 1905 at the Académie Julian in Paris, under Jean-Paul Laurens. Gagnon began to grind his own paints, and after 1916 his palette consisted principally of pure whites, reds, blues and yellows, which gave his paintings a brilliancy of colour. Between 1924 and 1936 he lived in Paris and produced illustrations in coloured woodblocks for L. F. Pouquette's Le Grand Silence Blanc. Gagnon became a full member of the Royal Canadian Academy in 1922. This picture comes with a certificate of authentication signed by Lucile Rodien Gagnon.

Yannis Gaitis
Greek (1923–84)
Composition
Signed and dated 1954, tempera on card
19¼ x 25in (49 x 63.5cm)
£4,000–4,800 / € 5,800–7,000
$7,300–8,700 ⚒ **B**

▶ **Eugène Galien-Laloue**
French (1854–1941)
La Place du Chatelet, Paris
Signed, gouache
8 x 12¼in (20.5 x 31cm)
£8,500–10,200
€ 12,400–14,900
$15,500–18,600 ⚒ **B**

◀ **Nicholas Garland**
British (20thC)
Annabel's
Set of 14, signed, titled and numbered 25/50, linocuts
12 x 9in (30.5 x 23cm)
£950–1,100 / € 1,400–1,600
$1,750–2,000 ⚒ **B**

▶ **Attributed to George Garrard**
British (1760–1826)
Mr Bakewell's long-horned cow
Titled and dated 1796, oil on paper
9 x 11in (23 x 28cm)
£160–190
€ 230–270
$290–340 ⚒ **DW**

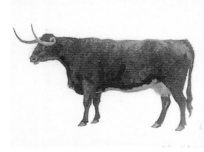

Attributed to Cesare Gennari
Italian (1637–88)
Study of a tree within a landscape with two figures nearby
Pen and brown ink
8¼ x 11½in (21 x 29cm)
£4,400–5,300 / € 6,400–7,700
$8,000–9,600 ⚒ **B(Kn)**

◄ **Herbert Gentry**
African/American
(1922–2003)
Untitled
1987, acrylic on paper
24 x 34in
(61 x 86.5cm)
£5,000–5,600
€7,200–8,100
$8,400–9,400
⊞ **NNA**

Ernest George, RA
British (1839–1922)
Amiens
Signed and titled, watercolour
7 x 10¼in (18 x 26cm)
£105–125 / €155–185
$190–220 ⚒ **DW**

Vassilis Germenis
Greek (1896–1966)
Port entrance
Signed, oil on canvas
26 x 39½in (66 x 100.5cm)
£6,500–7,800 / €9,500–11,400
$11,800–14,200 ⚒ **B**

► **Mark Gertler**
British (1891–1939)
A head. Study for
Nude with Mandolin
Signed and dated
1934, charcoal
8½ x 8¼in
(21.5 x 21cm)
£3,100–3,700
€4,500–5,400
$5,600–6,700
⚒ **LAY**

► **Angelos Giallina**
Greek (1857–1939)
View of Corfu
Signed and dated 1899,
watercolour on paper
15½ x 28¼in (39.5 x 72cm)
£7,000–8,400
€10,200–12,200
$12,700–15,300 ⚒ **B**

◄ **Anthony Gibbs**
British (b1942)
Sunset near Wythall – Warwickshire
Oil
24 x 48in (61 x 122cm)
£3,300–3,750 / €4,800–5,400
$6,000–6,800 ⊞ **Dr**

Oscar H. Gieberich
American (b1886)
Still Life with Game
Signed, oil on canvas
22 x 30cm (56 x 76cm)
£240–290 / € 350–420
$430–520 ⚒ TREA

Gieberich worked in New York and in Boston. He studied with
Charles Hawthorne and at the Art Students League. His work is
in the collection of the Boston Museum.

James Giles, RSA
British (1801–70)
The Averian and Lucerne Lakes, Bay of Baiae, Cape Micenum etc
Signed, inscribed and dated 1826, oil on panel
19½ x 29½in (49.5 x 75cm)
£4,500–5,400 / € 6,600–7,900
$8,200–9,800 ⚒ B(Ed)

▶ **James Gillray**
British (1757–1815)
St George and the
Dragon – a design for
an Equestrian Statue
from the original in
Windsor Castle
Etching with
aquatint finished
with hand-colouring
15¼ in (38.5cm) square
£360–430
€ 520–620
$660–780 ⚒ B

Arthur Gilbert
British (1819–95)
Evening Light
Signed and dated 1862, oil on canvas
8½ x 14in (21.5 x 35.5cm)
£7,200–8,000 / € 10,500–11,700
$13,100–14,500 ⊞ HFA

Edmund Gill
British (1820–94)
Waterfalls
A pair, signed and dated 1862,
oil on panel
9 x 6¾in (23 x 17cm)
£7,200–8,000
€ 10,500–11,700
$13,100–14,600 ⊞ HFA

James Gillray
British (1757–1815)
How to Ride with elegance thro'
the Streets
Etching with contemporary
hand-colouring
13 x 9¾in (33 x 25cm)
£360–430 / € 520–620
$660–780 ⚒ B

Edward Giobbi
American (b1926)
Untitled
Signed and dated 1951, watercolour
21½ x 26in (54.5 x 66cm)
£440–530 / € 640–770
$800–960 ⚒ LHA

Fausto Giusto
Italian (19th/20thC)
Porte Saint-Denis, Paris
Signed, oil on canvas
18 x 30in (45.5 x 76cm)
£9,900–11,900 / € 14,500–17,400
$18,000–21,000 ⊞ HFA

Alfred Augustus Glendening, Snr
British (fl1861–1903)
Tranquil Waters along the Thames
Signed and dated 1888, oil on canvas
8 x 15in (20.5 x 38cm)
£8,100–9,000 / € 11,800–13,100
$14,700–16,400 ⊞ HFA

*Alfred Augustus Glendening was a London landscape painter,
believed to have been born in Greenwich c1840. He worked as a
railway clerk before devoting his life to painting, and soon became
one of the most popular landscape artists of his period, working in
many parts of the British Isles. He particularly enjoyed painting views
of the Thames, Surrey and Sussex, and in the Scottish Highlands he
favoured dramatic landscapes with lochs and cattle. Glendening's
Thames views focus on the quiet and peaceful nature of the river.
Thoroughly British, they give the viewer a tranquil scene of the
laid-back nature of country life. His haymaking scenes contain an
extraordinary level of detail, and are highly sought after among his
collectors. He exhibited at the Royal Academy, British Institution and
Suffolk Street between 1865 and 1903. He was the father of Alfred
Glendening Jnr, who produced similar work.*

Storing your paintings

If you buy a picture with flaking paint store it horizontally
in a damp dark place to stop further deterioration. Never
store a picture in an outbuilding or below freezing point
as damage will occur very quickly. Keep pictures, especially
watercolours, away from direct sunlight. Do not attempt
to clean a good picture yourself but enlist the help of a
specialist – contact a museum or reputable gallery to
recommend a good restorer.

James Gleeson
Australian (b1915)
Genesis No. 2, 1991
Signed and inscribed, oil on canvas
67¾ x 92½in (172 x 235cm)
£12,300–14,800 / € 18,000–21,000
$22,000–26,000 ➚ SHSY

◄ **Ablade Glover**
Ghanean (b1934)
Never again
Oil on canvas
40¼ x 39¾in
(102 x 101cm)
£700–840
€ 1,000–1,200
$1,250–1,550
➚ B(Kn)

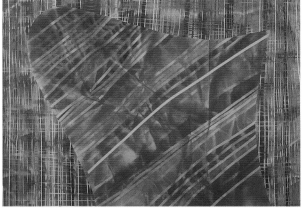

Augustus Goertz
American (b1948)
Untitled
Signed, acrylic on canvas
82 x 95in (208.5 x 241.5cm)
£8,400–10,100 / € 12,500–14,700
$15,300–18,400 ➚ LHA

◄ **Oscar Goodall, RSW**
Scottish (20thC)
Fragments II
Acrylic
24 x 28in (61 x 71cm)
£2,600–2,900 / €3,800–4,200
$4,700–5,300 ⊞ WrG

Oscar Goodall works mainly in pastels, oil and watercolour. He has extensive teaching experience as a lecturer for the Scottish Arts Council, and Dundee, Stirling and St Andrew's extra mural departments. He has exhibited widely in Scotland and abroad, and his work can be found in many public and private collections.

Richard Gorman
Irish (b1946)
Three Nudes
Signed, inscribed and
dated 1981, oil on
canvas
34in (86.5cm) square
£2,100–2,500
€3,100–3,700
$3,800–4,500
↗WA

Alexander Goudie
Scottish (b1933)
The Crystal Lamp
Signed, oil on canvas
36in (91.5cm) square
£1,800–2,150 / €2,650–3,150
$3,250–3,900 ↗L&T

◄ **Duncan Grant**
British (1885–1978)
Untitled: carpet design for
Charleston
Oil pastel on paper
3¾ x 6in (9.5 x 15cm)
£770–850 / €1,100–1,250
$1,400–1,550 ⊞ JLx

Charleston House near Lewes, East Sussex was the home of Duncan Grant and Vanessa and Clive Bell. It was also the meeting place of the writers, artists and intellectuals known as the Bloomsbury Group.

Edmund W. Greacen
American (1877–1949)
Girl with Umbrella in the Garden, Giverny
1908, oil on canvas
28½ x 23½in (72.5 x 59.5cm)
£26,800–32,000 / €39,000–47,000
$49,000–58,000 ↗S(NY)

James Stephen Gresley
British (1829–1908)
Cattle Watering on the Wharfe, Near Barden Tower,
Figures in the Foreground
Signed and dated 1901, watercolour
10¼ x 13½in (26 x 34.5cm)
£900–1,050 / € 1,300–1,500
$1,650–1,900 ⚹ AH

Walter Greaves
British (1846–1930)
The Promenade
Signed, oil on canvas
23¾ x 15¾in (60.5 x 40cm)
£900–1,050 / € 1,300–1,500
$1,650–1,900 ⚹ B(Kn)

Charles Green
British (1840–98)
Dog with pheasant
Signed, oil on panel
15¾in (40cm) square
£35–40 / € 50–60
$65–75 ⚹ BERN

◄ **Katya Gridnev**
Ukranian (b1965)
Friends
Oil on canvas
32 x 40in (81.5 x 101.5cm)
£6,800–7,500 / € 9,900–11,000
$12,400–13,700 ⊞ BSG

*Katya Gridnev studied at the St
Petersburg Academy of Arts and
has exhibited her work in Germany,
Moscow and London. She and
her husband Valery work closely
together, often simultaneously on
portrait commissions, which
results in a similarity in their work.
Since living in England, both
artists have been very successful.*

► **Louis Oscar Griffith**
American (1875–1956)
Summer Sky
Signed, watercolour on paper
11 x 14in (28 x 35.5cm)
£300–360 / € 440–530
$550–660 ⚹ TREA

Valery Gridnev
Russian (b1956)
By the Balcony Door
Oil on canvas
48 x 40in (122 x 101.5cm)
£6,800–7,500 / € 9,900–11,000
$12,400–13,700 ⊞ BSG

*Valery Gridnev was born in the Russian Urals.
He studied at Sverdlovsk Art College, then
spent seven years at the St Petersburg
Academy of Arts, took the advanced course
of studies at the USSR Academy of Arts and,
for his graduation painting, Early Years, he
was awarded the prestigious Gold Medal.
From 1990 to 1994 he worked in the creative
studio at the St Petersburg Academy of Arts.
Since 1991, he has been a member of the
Russian Artists' Federation. He lives in England
with his wife, the artist Katya Gridnev.*

Frederick Landseer Griggs
British (1876–1938)
Lone End, a horse and cart approaching
an abbey
Signed, etching
7 x 10in (18 x 25.5cm)
£380–450 / € 550–650
$690–820 ⚹ B(O)

◄ **Boris Dmitrievich Grigoriev**
Russian (1886–1939)
West Indian street scene
Signed, gouache on paper
14 x 19¼in (35.5 x 49cm)
£4,800–5,700 / € 7,000–8,300
$8,700–10,400 ⚹ S

Pierre Grisot
French (1911–95)
The Ballerinas
Signed, oil on canvas
18 x 14in (45.5 x 35.5cm)
£5,400–6,000 / €7,900–8,700
$9,800–10,900 ⊞ Man

William Gropper
American (1897–1977)
The Senator
Signed, oil on canvas mounted on masonite
28 x 36in (71 x 91.5cm)
£11,400–13,700 / €16,600–20,000
$21,000–25,000 ⚒ S(NY)

Elioth Gruner
New Zealander (1882–1939)
The Blue Hills
Signed, oil on canvas
15½ x 17½in (39.5 x 44.5cm)
£175–210 / €260–310
$320–380 ⚒ LJ

◄ **Isaac Grünewald**
Swedish
(1889–1946)
Figurative composition
Signed, watercolour
13½ x 19¾in
(34.5 x 50cm)
£1,350–1,600
€2,000–2,350
$2,450–2,900
⚒ BUK

Emile Gruppe
American (1896–1978)
Gloucester Harbor
Signed, oil on canvas
20 x 18in (51 x 45.5cm)
£5,700–6,800 / €8,300–9,900
$10,400–12,400 ⚒ TREA

Emile Gruppe was an important New England Impressionist, well-known for his harbour scenes and landscapes. He studied with John Carlson and Richard Miller and exhibited from c1915 to the 1950s at many venues, including the National Academy of Design, the Art Institute of Chicago, and the Connecticut Academy of Fine Arts. Gruppe was one of the central figures in the Cape Ann artists' colony, and his work is an icon of American Impressionism executed in New England in the early 20th century.

James Gunn
British (1893–1964)
Reclining nude
Oil on canvas
17½ x 13½in (44.5 x 34.5cm)
£6,000–7,200 / €8,800–10,500
$10,900–13,100 ⚒ B

Nikolaos Gysis
Greek (1842–1901)
Drunken Maenad
Signed, pastel on paper
20½ x 15in (52 x 38cm)
£17,000–20,000 / €25,000–29,000
$31,000–36,000 ⚒ B

◄ David W. Haddon
British (fl1884–1914)
Head and shoulders portrait of a
young Dutch girl
Signed, oil on board
8½ x 11in (21.5 x 28cm)
£200–240 / € 290–350
$350–430 ↗ FHF

► Brian Hagger
British (b1935)
The Wilton Arms
Signed and dated 1974,
oil on canvas
19¾ x 23¾in (50 x 60.5cm)
£480–570 / € 700–830
$870–1,050 ↗ B(Kn)

Framing your picture

■ A frame should never overpower the picture. Never put a coloured plastic frame on a watercolour. A frame and mount should draw your eye into the picture.

■ Keep mounts and frames in proportion. A heavy frame requires a wider mount, a thin delicate frame a narrower one.

■ Hang watercolours away from direct sunlight. Never hang a glass-fronted picture opposite a door or window. The glass will reflect light and you will not see the picture. Use clear colour glass which eliminates the reflective rays.

Maggi Hambling
British (b1945)
Portrait of an elderly lady in bed with a kitten
Signed and dated 1979, pencil on paper
15 x 11in (38 x 28cm)
£580–690 / € 840–1,000
$1,050–1,250 ↗ BWL

◄ Maggi Hambling
British (b1945)
Sunset
Signed, inscribed and dated 1988, watercolour
23¾ x 19in (60.5 x 48.5cm)
£480–570 / € 700–840
$870–1,050 ↗ B(Kn)

Letitia Marion Hamilton, RHA
Irish (1878–1964)
A Wood in North France
Signed and inscribed,
oil on canvas
20 x 24in (51 x 61cm)
£7,900–9,400
€ 11,500–13,800
$14,400–17,100 ↗ WA

◄ **Richard Hamilton**
British (b1922)
Derek Jarman (Cristea 177)
Signed and titled, edition of 40,
pigment transfer
15¼in (38.5cm) square
£700–840 / €1,000–1,200
$1,250–1,500 ⚒ B

William Lee Hankey
British (1869–1952)
On the Schveldt
Signed, watercolour and pencil
12 x 13½in (30.5 x 34.5cm)
£380–450 / €550–660
$690–820 ⚒ WW

◄ **Father Jack P. Hanlon**
Irish (1913–68)
Canticle to the Sun
Signed and inscribed, oil on canvas
laid on board
24 x 16in (61 x 40.5cm)
£4,900–5,900 / €7,200–8,600
$8,900–10,700 ⚒ WA
This picture relates to the famous 12th-century
poem of the same title by St Francis of Assisi.

Donald Hamilton-Fraser
British (b1929)
Landscape Study, Storm
Oil on paper
4¾ x 7½in (12 x 19cm)
£1,100–1,300 / €1,600–1,900
$2,000–2,400 ⚒ B(Kn)

Father Jack P. Hanlon
Irish (1913–68)
The Sweeper
Watercolour
15 x 11in (38 x 28cm)
£2,050–2,450 / €3,000–3,600
$3,750–4,500 ⚒ WA

Heywood Hardy, ARWS, RPE
British (1842–1933)
Driving a Bargain
Signed, oil on canvas
12 x 19in (30.5 x 48.5cm)
£14,000–16,800 / €20,000–24,000
$25,000–30,000 ⚒ B

Joe R. Hargan
British (b1952)
Room with a View
Signed, oil on canvas
15in (38cm) square
£2,350–2,600 / €3,400–3,800
$4,250–4,750 ⊞ CFAG

Keith Haring
American (1958–90)
New Years 1988
Signed, screenprint in black and
red on japan paper
10¼ x 8in (26 x 20.5cm)
£300–360 / €440–520
$550–650 ➚ B(Kn)

Anne King Harman
Irish (1919–79)
Cottages and Haystacks with Rain Clouds Approaching
Signed, gouache on board
16 x 20in (40.5 x 51cm)
£750–890 / €1,100–1,300
$1,350–1,600 ➚ WA

Joseph Haroutunian
American (b1944)
Deep blue, red
Oil on paper
28 x 20in (71 x 51cm)
£2,000–2,200 / €2,900–3,200
$3,600–4,000 ⊞ GALG

◄ **James Harrigan**
Scottish (b1937)
Red Dredger
Oil on board
20 x 24in (51 x 61cm)
£1,600–1,800 / €2,350–2,600
$2,900–3,250 ⊞ WrG

Born in Ayrshire, James Harrigan studied at Glasgow School of Art. He exhibits in mixed and solo exhibitions in England and Scotland, and participates annually in watercolour shows at the Royal Glasgow Institute of the Fine Arts and Royal Scottish Society of Painters. He won the Laing Landscape Competition in 1980 and The Scotsman's Art Competition in 1985. His work is held in many private and public collections, including the House of Lords and Glasgow University.

Birge (Lovell) Harrison
American (1854–1929)
Shady Valley
Signed and titled, oil on canvas
8 x 10in (20.5 x 25.5cm)
£1,400–1,650 / €2,050–2,400
$2,500–3,000 ➚ TREA

Harrison worked in California and founded the summer school of the Art Students League in Woodstock, New York, in 1897. He was best known for his atmospheric landscapes and moonlit scenes.

John Cyril Harrison
British (1898–1985)
Male and Female Pintails
Signed, watercolour heightened with white
12½ x 18¼in (32 x 46.5cm)
£1,000–1,200 / €1,450–1,750
$1,800–2,150 ➚ B(Kn)

Harrison's work is closely associated with Norfolk, from where he drew much of his inspiration. Guided first by Henry Tonks at the Slade and subsequently by George Lodge, he liked to travel, living in British Columbia, Africa, and even visiting Iceland in order to observe its birds. Favoured subjects were game birds, wildfowl and birds of prey, and Harrison's talent was at its best when capturing the overall character of his subjects, which became the hallmark of his paintings.

Thomas Alexander Harrison
American (1853–1930)
Venice at Dawn with Sailboats
Signed, oil on canvas
20 x 36in (51 x 91.5cm)
£1,550–1,850 / €2,250–2,700
$2,850–3,400 ↗ LHA

Kevin (Pro) Hart
Australian (b1928)
Dragonfly
Signed and titled, oil on board
14 x 18in (35.5 x 45.5cm)
£940–1,100 / €1,350–1,600
$1,700–2,000 ↗ SHSY

Sara S. Hayden
American
(1862–1932)
Meadow Creek
Signed, watercolour
on paper
8½ x 15in
(21.5 x 38cm)
£150–180
€220–260
$280–330 ↗ JAA

Claude Hayes
British (1852–1922)
Harvesting
Signed, watercolour
9 x 13½in (23 x 34.5cm)
£1,200–1,450
€1,750–2,100
$2,200–2,600 ↗ CHTR

Ernest Columba Hayes, RHA
Irish (1914–78)
Light on the Haystacks
Signed and dated 1936, oil on canvas
20 x 24in (51 x 61cm)
£1,300–1,550 / €1,900–2,250
$2,350–2,800 ↗ WA
This very early work of Ernest Hayes was
painted barely two years after his term as a
student at the Dublin Metropolitan School of
Art, where he studied under Seán Keating.
Prior to completing his studies he began
exhibiting at the RHA in 1933 and continued
to do so until his death. He also joined the
Dublin Sketching Club in 1935, and this picture
may have been exhibited there in 1937.

Michael Angelo Hayes
Irish (1820–77)
The London Coach
Signed and dated 1840, oil on board
7 x 10in (18 x 25.5cm)
£420–500 / €610–730
$760–910 ↗ S(O)

Michael Angelo Hayes
Irish (1820–77)
Infantry on the edge of a village
Signed, watercolour
11½ x 16¼in (29 x 41.5cm)
£320–380 / €460–550
$580–690 ↗ WW

Patrick Hayman
British (1915–88)
Mother and Child – Valley and Hills
Signed, oil on board
15½ x 11½in (39.5 x 29cm)
£550–660 / €800–960
$1,000–1,200 ↗ B(Kn)

► **Arthur Hayward**
British (1889–1971)
November Day, St Ives
Signed and inscribed, oil on canvas
10¾ x 14½in (27.5 x 37cm)
£1,400–1,650 / €2,050–2,450
$2,550–3,050 ↗ Bea

Alfred Hayworth, RWS
British (1926–76)
Towards Southwold from Walberswick;
East Wind Walberswick
A pair, signed, watercolour
18¾ x 19¼in (47.5 x 49cm)
£540–640 / €790–930
$980–1,150 ↗ B(L)

◄ **William Heath**
British (fl1899)
State of the Giraffe
Etching with hand colouring on wove
15 x 10¾in (38 x 27.5cm)
£480–580 / €700–840
$870–1,050 ↗ B

Josef Heicke
Austrian (1811–61)
On the Alm
Signed, oil on canvas
20¾ x 27in (52.5 x 68.5cm)
£2,200–2,600 / €3,200–3,800
$4,000–4,800 ↗ DORO

► **Adrian Heath**
British (1920–92)
Untitled
Signed and dated
1962, gouache
and ink
29½ x 21¾in
(75 x 55.5cm)
£400–480
€580–690
$720–870 ↗ B(Kn)

Francisco Eppens Helguera
Mexican (1913–90)
Caravelas
Signed, oil on canvas
27¾ x 19¾in (70.5 x 50cm)
£790–950 / €1,150–1,350
$1,450–1,750 ↗ LCM

The painter, muralist and sculptor Francisco Eppens Helguera was born in San Luis Potosí, Mexico. He attended the Fine Arts Academy of San Carlos, and his work was influenced by the Nationalist ideas of the first painters from the artistic movement called the Mexican School of Painting, or Mexican Renaissance. His works are figurative, and interpret reality in a symbolic way. His smaller paintings are oil on canvas and oil on masonite and his monumental outdoor murals use coloured glass tiles. Helguera has received a number of awards, and his works have been included in many exhibitions, such as the Museum of Modern Art, New York in 1930 and in 1987 the Museum of the Fine Arts Palace (INBA) in Mexico City, and the Cultural Institute Cabañas, Mexico.

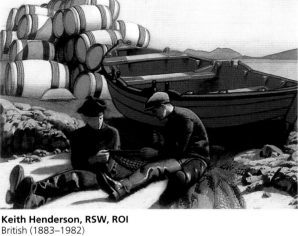

Charles Napier Hemy
British (1841–1917)
Entrance to Falmouth Harbour from Pendennis
(Crab quay; Black Rock; St Anthony's Light; St Mawes)
Signed, watercolour heightened with white
9 x 12½in (23 x 32cm)
£1,000–1,200 / €1,450–1,750
$1,800–2,150 ⚒ B

Keith Henderson, RSW, ROI
British (1883–1982)
Alasdair and Angus
Signed, watercolour and gouache
13¾ x 19in (35 x 48.5cm)
£2,200–2,650 / €3,200–3,850
$4,000–4,800 ⚒ B(Ed)

▶ **James Watterston Herald**
British (1859–1914)
By the River
Oil on panel
12 x 11in
(30.5 x 28cm)
£4,200–5,000
€6,100–7,300
$7,600–9,100
⚒ B(Ed)

George Hepper
British (fl1866–68)
Fashionable Shoppers
Signed and dated 1804,
oil on panel
11¼ x 16in (28.5 x 40.5cm)
£14,400–16,000
€21,000–24,000
$26,000–29,000 ⊞ HFA

▶ **Alfred Herbert**
British (c1820–61)
Low Tide at Scheveningen,
Holland
Signed, watercolour
16¼ x 26¼in (41.5 x 66.5cm)
£5,200–5,800 / €7,600–8,500
$9,500–10,500 ⊞ Bne

Josef Herman (1911–2000)

Josef Herman was born in Warsaw, Poland, the son of a Jewish cobbler. He moved to London in 1940 but a few years later settled for around ten years in the Welsh mining village of Ystradgynlais where he perfected his form of powerful and gritty pictures of the working classes. Herman was interested in the dignity of labour and the depth of the human spirit. He expressed himself in simplified shapes and vivid colours.

Josef Herman, RA
British (1911–2000)
Standing Miners
Signed, oil on board
17½ x 25½in (44.5 x 65cm)
£10,000–12,000
€ **14,600–17,500**
$18,200–21,800 ⚒ B

Josef Herman, RA
British (1911–2000)
Bearded Man
Signed, pen, ink and wash
6½ x 8in (16.5 x 20.5cm)
£500–600 / €730–870
$910–1,100 ⚒ B

▶ **Josef Herman, RA**
British (1911–2000)
Sleeping Figures
Pen and Ink
6¾ x 8¾in (17 x 22cm)
£400–480 / €580–690
$720–870 ⚒ B(Kn)

Josef Herman, RA
British (1911–2000)
Lone Figure
Signed, titled and dated 1978, pencil, watercolour and gouache
9½ x 7½in (24 x 19cm)
£900–1,050 / €1,300–1,550
$1,650–1,950 ⚒ B

Ludwig Hermann
German (1812–81)
Views along the Rhine
A pair, oil on canvas
12½ x 17½in (32 x 44.5cm)
£17,400–19,300 / €25,000–28,000
$31,000–35,000 ⊞ HFA

Rowland Hilder
British (1905–93)
The Valley
Signed, watercolour
7 x 9½in (18 x 24cm)
£720–860 / €1,050–1,250
$1,300–1,550 ⚒ LAY

Bartram Hiles
British (1872–1927)
Country landscape with lone figure beside a stream
Signed, watercolour heightened in white
7 x 20½in (18 x 52cm)
£280–330 / €410–480
$510–600 ⚘ FHF

Roger Hilton
British (1911–75)
Untitled
Signed, edition of 100,
lithograph on wove
13¾ x 11½in (35 x 29cm)
£1,450–1,600 / €2,100–2,350
$2,600–2,900 ⊞ JLx

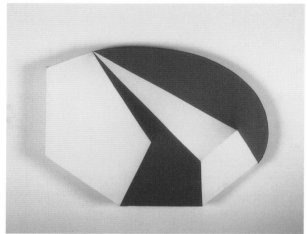

Harry Hine, RI
British (1845–1941)
Gloucester Cathedral
Signed, watercolour
19½ x 15½in (49.5 x 39.5cm)
£1,350–1,500 / €1,950–2,150
$2,450–2,750 ⊞ HN

▶ **Charles Hinman**
American (b1932)
Crystal, 1964
Acrylic emulsion on
shaped canvas
26 x 34 x 7in
(66 x 86.5 x 18cm)
£630–740
€920–1,050
$1,150–1,350
⚘ LHA

Morris Hirshfield
American (1872–1946)
Garden Stand and Birds
Signed and dated 1945, oil on canvas
21 x 25in (53.5 x 63.5cm)
£31,000–37,000 / €45,000–54,000
$57,000–68,000 ⚘ S(NY)

Harold Hitchcock
British (b1914)
A Mediterranean Village, 1968
Acrylic on canvas
20 x 24in (51 x 61cm)
£1,550–1,850 / €2,250–2,700
$2,800–3,350 ⚘ SHSY

◄ **Attributed to Mary Adams Hoagland**
American
(early 20thC)
River Landscape
Signed, oil on canvas
17 x 21in
(43 x 53.5cm)
£360–430
€530–630
$650–780 ⚒ TREA
Hoagland studied at the Art Institute of Chicago and exhibited there from 1900 to 1907.

David Hockney
British (b1937)
Inside the Castle
Signed and numbered 49/100, etching and aquatint
10 x 10¼in (25.5 x 26cm)
£700–840 / €1,000–1,200
$1,250–1,500 ⚒ B

David Hockney
British (b1937)
Painted Environment 2
Signed and dated 1993, numbered 13/25, 16 laser-printed photographs mounted on board
27¾ x 35½in (70.5 x 90cm)
£3,400–4,000 / €4,950–5,900
$6,200–7,300 ⚒ B(Kn)

Felice Hodges
British (b1954)
Untitled
Mixed media and collage
27 x 19in (68.5 x 48.5cm)
£1,700–1,900 / €2,500–2,800
$3,100–3,450 ⊞ FH

Felice Hodges
British (b1954)
Blue Series 6
Mixed media on canvas
23 x 27in (58.5 x 68.5cm)
£720–800 / €1,050–1,200
$1,300–1,450 ⊞ FH

What to buy

Prices for works by well-known artists depend on condition and the period in which they were painted. Work from certain periods of an artist's life is often acknowledged to be better than that from another. Paintings in good condition always achieve higher prices.

► **Edward Henry Holder**
British (fl1864–1917)
A Quiet Backwater – Shiplake-on-Thames
Oil
27 x 20in (68.5 x 51cm)
£4,000–4,450 / €5,800–6,500
$7,300–8,100 ⊞ Dr

George Augustus Holmes, RBA
British (1861–1911)
The Doctor
Signed, oil on board
14 x 16½in (35.5 x 42cm)
£17,500–19,400 / €25,000–28,000
$32,000–36,000 ⊞ HFA

George Augustus Holmes was a painter of genre scenes who exhibited at the Royal Academy between 1852 and 1909. He also exhibited at the British Institution, Suffolk Street, the Grosvenor Gallery and the Paris Salon between 1906 and 1911.

► George Houston, RSA, RSW, RI
Scottish (1869–1947)
Loch Fyne
Signed, oil on canvas
18 x 24in (45.5 x 61cm)
£2,300–2,750 / €3,350–4,000
$4,200–5,000 ⚒ L&T

John Houston, RSA, RSW
Scottish (b1930)
Early Morning Rain
Signed, oil on canvas
40 x 60in (101.5 x 152.5cm)
£2,200–2,600 / €3,200–3,800
$4,000–4,700 ⚒ L&T

► John Hoyland
British (b1957)
Collioure
Oil
45 x 63¾in (114.5 x 162cm)
£2,700–3,000 / €3,900–4,350
$4,900–5,500 ⊞ AHG

John Hoyland was born in Bristol. He studied at Camberwell School of Arts and Crafts, where he won first prize in the Magnolia Landscape Competition, and showed at the National Portrait Gallery, London. He moved to southwest France in 1985 and regularly shows in France and Britain.

Winslow Homer
American (1836–1910)
Boy with Blue Dory
Signed and dated 1880, watercolour and pencil on paper
9 x 17in (23 x 43cm)
£472,000–566,000 / €689,000–826,000
$859,000–1,031,000 ⚒ S(NY)

Winslow Homer is a prominent American artist whose work has challenged other painters' tendencies to sentimentalize landscape. The picture here is unusually idyllic, recalling a happy summer that he would sometimes draw on in his later watercolours. It commanded an exceptionally high price.

Chen Wen Hsi
Singaporean (1906–91)
Singapore Street
Signed, oil on board
24 x 30in (61 x 76cm)
£20,000–24,000 / €29,000–35,000
$36,000–43,000 ↗ S(SI)

▶ **Frederick William Hulme**
British (1816–84)
Near the Common, Woking, Surrey
Oil on canvas
20 x 25in (51 x 66cm)
£14,200–15,800 / €20,000–23,000
$26,000–29,000 ⊞ HFA

William Holman Hunt, ARSA, RSW
British (1827–1910)
The Cornish Coast
Signed and dated 1860, watercolour
7¼ x 9½in (18.5 x 24cm)
£2,000–2,400 / €2,900–3,500
$3,600–4,350 ↗ B

*In September 1860, Holman Hunt went on a walking tour of the West
Country with Alfred Lord Tennyson, the artist Val Prinsep, the sculptor
Thomas Woolner and the writer Francis Palgrave. During this holiday,
Hunt produced a number of sketches of the Cornish coast. The
delightful aspect of the watercolours produced on his trip to Devon and
Cornwall was the fact that, rather than producing the works with their
sale in mind, they were executed purely for the artist's own enjoyment.*

Arthur Foord Hughes
British (fl1878–1927)
Farmyard Doves
Signed and dated 1873, oil on canvas
24½ x 18½in (62 x 47cm)
£2,000–2,400 / €2,900–3,500
$3,600–4,350 ↗ FHF

Daniel Huntington
American (1816–1906)
George Washington and Christopher Gist on the Allegheny River
Oil on canvas
20 x 24in (51 x 61cm)
£87,000–104,000 / €127,000–151,000
$159,000–190,000 ↗ S(NY)

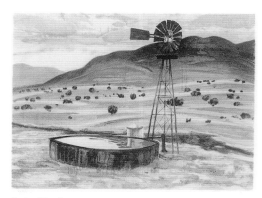

Peter Hurd
American (1904–84)
The Water Tank
Signed, numbered 47/200, lithograph
9 x 12in (23 x 30.5cm)
£180–210 / €260–310
$340–410 ↗ **JAA**

Maqbool Fida Husain
Indian (b1915)
Kerala-I
Signed, numbered 20/325, serigraph on paper
41in (104cm) square
£550–660 / €800–960
$1,000–1,200 ↗ **B(Kn)**

Jean Baptiste Hu't
French (1745–1811)
A court couple in a garden;
A companion
A pair, oil on panel
14 x 10¾in (35.5 x 27.5cm)
£1,900–2,250 / €2,750–3,300
$3,450–4,100 ↗ **B(Kn)**

◄ **Robert Gemmell Hutchison**
RBA, RI, RSA, RSW
British (1865–1945)
Carnoustie
Signed, oil on board
8½ x 10in (21.5 x 25.5cm)
£2,200–2,600 / €3,200–3,800
$4,000–4,800 ↗ **B(Ed)**

► **Nicholas Hely Hutchinson**
Irish (b1955)
Approaching Storm, Easky
Signed and inscribed, gouache and oil pastel
17½ x 20½in (44.5 x 52cm)
£1,300–1,550 / €1,900–2,250
$2,350–2,800 ↗ **WA**

Sarah Hutton (b1962)

Sarah Hutton exhibits widely in the north of England. Born in Haworth, Yorkshire, she set up Haworth Artists' Field Study Centre in 1984. She had previously studied in Leeds and Syracuse University in New York state. She works in various different mediums and is best known for her striking and colourful landscapes that are inspired by the Yorkshire countryside. Sarah has exhibited at Art 91 and Art 97 in London, as well as at the Mall Gallery and the Peach Tree Centre, Atlanta.

◄ **Sarah Hutton**
British (b1962)
Houses by the Sea
Mixed media on paper
22½ x 30¼in (57 x 77cm)
£1,350–1,500 / €1,950–2,200
$2,450–2,750 ⊞ **HUT**

◄ **Sarah Hutton**
British (b1962)
Farm on Moors
Mixed media
on paper
6 x 15in (15 x 38cm)
£590–650
€850–950
$1,050–1,200
⊞ **HUT**

Sarah Hutton
British (b1962)
Jumping Lamb
Mixed media on paper
9½ x 7in (24 x 18cm)
£310–350 / €450–510
$570–640 ⊞ **HUT**

Louis Icart
French (1888–1950)
Don Juan
Signed, numbered 9.335,
etching and aquatint
21 x 14in (53.5 x 35.5cm)
£360–430 / €520–630
$660–780 Bea

► **Filippo Indoni**
Italian (fl1880–84)
A young man lighting his pipe,
a pretty young girl carrying an
umbrella and leaning on a
stone post
Signed, watercolour
20½ x 14in (52 x 35.5cm)
£800–960 / €1,200–1,400
$1,500–1,800 JNic

Rudolph Ihlee
British (1883–1968)
Rachel
Signed and dated 1962, oil on board
24¾ x 21¼in (65.5 x 54cm)
£320–380 / €460–550
$580–690 B(Kn)

► **Robert Clark
Indiana**
American (b1928)
Red and Blue Love
Signed and dated
1996, numbered
110 /200, silkscreen
17¾in (45cm) square
£600–720
€880–1,050
$1,100–1,300
B(Kn)

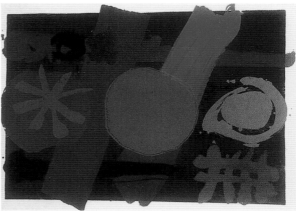

Albert Irvin, RA
British (b1922)
Star III
Signed, dated 1993 and numbered 97/125, silkscreen and
woodblock on wove
23¼ x 33in (59 x 84cm)
£240–290 / €350–420
$440–530 B(Kn)

**Lawrence
Isherwood**
British (1917–88)
Beach and Sky
Signed, oil on board
23¼ x 15¼in
(59 x 38.5cm)
£420–500
€610–730
$760–910 FHF

◄ **Lawrence Isherwood**
British (1917–88)
Bolton
Signed, oil on board
16¼ x 22in (41.5 x 56cm)
£260–310 / €380–450
$470–560 B(Kn)

Nicholas Issaiev
Russian (fl1930s–40s)
Still Life: Tulips in a Blue Vase
Signed, oil on canvas
23¾ x 31½in (60.5 x 80cm)
£3,600–4,300
€5,300–6,300
$6,600–7,800 S

Kurt Jackson
British (b1961)
Lazy Wave
Signed and dated 1989, watercolour
10 x 12in (25.5 x 30.5cm)
£1,200–1,400 / € 1,700–2,000
$2,000–2,350 ⚒ LAY

Rosa Jameson
British (fl1880–1900)
Nutting Strictly Forbidden
Signed, watercolour
20 x 16½in (51 x 42cm)
£3,400–3,800 / € 5,000–5,500
$6,200–6,900 ⊞ Bne

Andrzej Jackowski
British (b1947)
Holding the Tree
Signed, titled and dated 1988,
oil on canvas
119 x 50in (302.5 x 127cm)
£1,400–1,650 / € 2,000–2,400
$2,550–3,000 ⚒ B(Kn)

▶ **Valerie Jaudon**
American (b1945)
Kosciusko, 1975
Oil on canvas
72in (183cm) square
£7,700–9,300
€ **11,200–13,600**
$14,100–16,900 ⚒ LHA

Holger Jensen
American (b1880)
The Blue Barn
Signed, oil on board
19½ x 23½in (49.5 x 59.5cm)
£175–210 / € 250–300
$320–380 ⚒ TREA

◀ **Viggo Johansen**
British (1851–1935)
A young girl knitting
Signed, oil on canvas
22¾ x 17¼in
(58 x 44cm)
£2,500–3,000
€ **3,650–4,400**
$4,550–5,500
⚒ B(Kn)

▶ **Helge
Johansson**
Swedish (1886–1926)
From the banks at
Port D'Orleans
Signed and dated
1924, oil
23¾ x 28⅜in
(60.5 x 73cm)
£1,100–1,300
€ **1,600–1,900**
$2,000–2,400
⚒ BUK

Augustus Edwin John (1878–1961)

Augustus John was primarily a portrait painter although he did paint still lifes and figures in landscapes. The most sought after are pictures of his family. A record £45,000 / €66,000 / $82,000 was reached at Bonhams for *Girl Leaning on Stick*, an impressionistic study of his wife Dorelia, painted in 1910. Work from this period rarely comes up for sale. An undistinguished oil portrait by John can be bought for £10,000 / €14,600 / $18,200 and an attractive small still life in oil between £5,000 / €7,300 / $9,100 and £7,000 / €10,200 / $12,700. Sketchy drawings can be picked up for a few thousand pounds and more intricate pencil portraits around £10,000 / €14,600 / $18,200. To buy one of his pencil drawings is a good way to break into the picture market and own a work by a prominent artist.

Augustus Edwin John, RA
British (1878–1961)
William Butler Yeats
Signed, etching on wove
7 x 4¾in (18 x 12cm)
£1,200–1,450 / €1,750–2,100
$2,200–2,600 ⚒ B

Augustus Edwin John, RA
British (1878–1961)
A Fishergirl of Equihen,
Signed, pencil
12¼ x 7¼in (31 x 18.5cm)
£1,450–1,750 / €2,100–2,500
$2,650–3,200 ⚒ SHSY

◄ **Augustus Edwin John, RA**
British (1878–1961)
Fishergirls at Equihen, Normandy
Signed, pen, ink and wash
13½ x 19in (34.5 x 48.5cm)
£22,000–25,000 / €32,000–36,000
$40,000–45,000 ⊞ Bne

In the summer of 1907, Augustus John came across a group of fishergirls working on the Normandy coast of Equihen near Boulogne. He was struck by their distinctive costumes and made many studies of the girls in different group compositions.

► **Einar Jolin**
Swedish (1890–1976)
San Giorgio Maggiore, Venice
Signed and dated 1962
21¼ x 25½in (54 x 65cm)
£1,700–2,000 / €2,500–2,900
$3,100–3,600 ⚒ BUK

Charles Jones
British (1836–92)
Cattle and Sheep Grazing
Oil on panel
10 x 16in (25.5 x 40.5cm)
£8,900–9,900 / €13,000–14,400
$16,200–18,000 ⊞ HFA

◄ **David Jones**
British (1895–1974)
Town scene
Watercolour
22 x 15in (56 x 38cm)
£4,800–5,700 / €7,000–8,300
$8,700–10,400 ⚒ B

► **Herbert Jones**
British (fl1855–85)
A Four-in-Hand Race at the Five Bells Tavern, New Cross, South London
Signed, oil on canvas
12 x 24in (30.5 x 61cm)
£4,300–4,800 / €6,300–7,000
$7,800–8,700 ⊞ Bne

Hugh Bolton Jones
American (1848–1927)
Adams County, Pennsylvania
Signed and dated 1870, oil on canvas
30 x 53¾in (76 x 136.5cm)
£31,000–37,000 / €45,000–54,000
$57,000–68,000 ⚒ S(NY)

▶ **Raphael Jones**
British (19th/20thC)
A young lady in a landscape
Signed, pen, ink and grey wash
7½ x 5¾in (19 x 14.5cm)
£100–120 / €145–175 / $180–210 ⚒ WW

Wolfgang Joop (b1944)

Wolfgang Joop lives in New York and was a freelance artist and professor of life drawing before becoming a fashion designer. His artwork is held in the permanent collections of several contemporary art museums in Europe, notably the Hamburg Museum of Art and Industry.

▶ **Wolfgang Joop**
German (b1944)
Drawing, Jeans
Signed, crayon, watercolour and gouache on paper
19 x 11in (48.5 x 28cm)
£1,500–1,800 / €2,200–2,600
$2,750–3,250 ⚒ S(NY)

▶ **Wolfgang Joop**
German (b1944)
Drawing, Evening Dress
Signed, crayon, watercolour and gouache on paper
15¾ x 11in (40 x 28cm)
£2,650–3,100
€3,900–4,500
$4,800–5,700
⚒ S(NY)

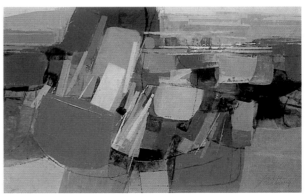

Paul Jouve
French (1880–1973)
Leopard with a Snake
Etching
19¼ x 27½in (49 x 70cm)
£2,850–3,400 / €4,150–4,950
$5,200–6,200 ⚒ S

Jose Joya
Filipino (b1931)
Blue Lake
Signed and dated 1974, oil on paper laid on board
14½ x 22½in (37 x 57cm)
£1,650–1,950 / €2,400–3,000
$2,800–3,550 ⚒ S(SI)

Béla Kádár
Hungarian (1877–1955)
Seated woman
Signed, pen and ink
on paper
7½ x 6½in (19 x 16.5cm)
£200–240 / €290–350
$360–430 ⚒ B

Yakov Yakovlevich Kalinichenko-Babak
Russian (1869–1938)
The Lesson
Signed and dated 1984,
oil on canvas
33¼ x 20⅝in (84.5 x 52.5cm)
£24,000–29,000
€35,000–42,000
$44,000–53,000 ⚒ S
*Kalinichenko studied at the Moscow College
of Painting, Sculpture and Architecture
during the 1890s, later enrolling in the
Imperial Academy of Arts in St Petersburg.*

► **Tony Karpinski**
British (b1965)
Elephant Feeding
Signed and inscribed,
oil on board
12¼ x 17¼in
(31 x 44cm)
£8,100–9,000
€11,800–13,100
$15,000–17,000
⊞ HFA

◄ **Otis Kaye**
American
(1885–1974)
Two to Win
Signed, oil on panel
10½ x 12½in
(26.5 x 32cm)
£30,000–36,000
€44,000–53,000
$54,000–65,000
⚒ S(NY)

Seán Keating, PRHA
Irish (1889–1977)
Portrait of a Young Girl
Signed, pastel on tinted paper
13½ x 10in (34.5 x 25.5cm)
£2,400–2,900 / €3,500–4,200
$4,400–5,300 ⚒ WA

William Keeling
British (fl1891–1904)
A Derbyshire Lane
Signed, oil on canvas
19¼ x 13in (49 x 33cm)
£200–240 / €290–350
$360–430 ➚ FHF

Nicholas Joseph Kellin
French (1788–1858)
The head of the caravan
Signed and dated 1847, watercolour and bodycolour
6¼ x 12½in (16 x 32cm)
£750–900 / €1,000–1,300
$1,350–1,600 ➚ B

Sir Gerald Festus Kelly, PRA
British (1879–1972)
Loretta
Oil on canvas
24¼ x 19in (61.5 x 48.5cm)
£2,600–3,100 / €3,800–4,500
$4,700–5,600 ➚ B

Richard Barrett Talbot Kelly
British (1896–1971)
Lapwings in flight
Signed and dated 1960, watercolour
10½ x 14¼in (26.5 x 36cm)
£300–360 / €440–520
$550–660 ➚ (BKn)

Roger Kemp
Australian (1908–87)
Untitled
Signed, oil on composition board
27½ x 21in (70 x 53.5cm)
£1,600–1,900 / €2,350–2,750
$2,900–3,450 ➚ SHSY

◄ **Thomas Benjamin Kennington**
British (1856–1916)
Sisters
Signed and dated 1912, oil on panel
14 x 10in (35.5 x 25.5cm)
£11,200–12,500
€16,400–18,300
$20,400–22,800 ⊞ Man

► **Janette Kerr**
British (b1957)
Sun Ring II (Marshwood Vale)
Oil on paper
9 x 10in (23 x 25.5cm)
£490–550 / €710–800
$890–1,000 ⊞ BYA

George Keyt
Sri Lankan (1901–93)
Nayika
Signed, oil on canvas
24 x 19in (61 x 48.5cm)
£9,600–11,500 / € 14,000–16,800
$17,500–20,900 ⚒ S

Born in Ceylon (now Sri Lanka), Keyt was educated at Trinity College, Kandy. He started work as a professional painter in 1927, encouraged by Lionel Wendt (1900–44), a celebrated Ceylonese photographer and musician, and his subjects were the Kandyan landscape, people and their culture. In the 1930s, he was influenced by Hindu mythology and art and Buddhism, and his depiction of episodes from the Jatakas culminated in the representation of the life of the Buddha on the walls of the circumambulatory shrine room of the Gotami Vihara, Columbo. He was an original member of the 43 Group of artists which earned an identity for Ceylon in the international art world. At the the same time, Keyt was exposed to the influence of early Cubist landscapes, as well as the work of Picasso. He fused these Western influences with his Eastern subject matter. In 1954, his work was exhibited at the ICA in London by Sir Herbert Read and afterwards the exhibition travelled to the Art Institute, Rotterdam. Keyt's paintings are in the permanent collections of the Victoria and Albert Museum, and British Museum, London.

Cecil King
British (1881–1942)
View of Oporto, Portugal
Signed, watercolour
6¾ x 10¼in (17 x 26cm)
£320–380 / € 470–550 / $580–690 ⚒ B(Kn)

◄ **Joseph Bartholomew Kidd after John James Audubon**
British (c1801–89)
The Baltimore Oriole
Oil on canvas
26 x 20½in (66 x 52cm)
£17,000–20,000
€ 25,000–29,000
$30,000–36,000 ⚒ S(NY)

► **George Goodwin Kilburne**
British (1839–1924)
Sunday
Signed, watercolour
10½ x 14in (26.5 x 35.5cm)
£1,200–1,400 / € 1,750–2,050
$2,200–2,550 ⚒ B(B)

Sarah Louisa Kilpack
British (1839–1909)
Figures and Sheep on Cliffs at Sunset
Signed, oil on card
5½ x 4in (14 x 10cm)
£950–1,100 / € 1,350–1,550
$1,600–1,850 ⚒ B&L

► **Ernst Ludwig Kirchner**
German (1880–1938)
Dancing in a pleated skirt
Graphite on wove paper
8¼ x 6¾in (21 x 17cm)
£1,100–1,300 / € 1,600–1,900
$2,000–2,350 ⚒ B

'After' means, in the opinion of the auctioneer or gallery, that the work was produced by someone in the style of the named artist and at roughly the same date, but not necessarily by his pupil.

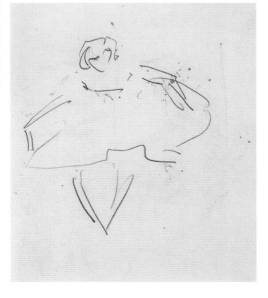

Norman Kirkham, RGI
Scottish (b1936)
Rhum from Eigg
Signed, oil on linen
22in (56cm) square
£2,700–3,000 / € 3,950–4,400
$4,900–5,500 ⊞ **WrG**

Norman Kirkham trained at Glasgow School of Art,
where he later held various teaching posts. He is a past
President of the Glasgow Art Club and a past Honorary
Secretary of the Royal Glasgow Institute of the Fine Arts.
He has exhibited at the Royal Academy, Royal Society of
Portrait Painters and the Royal Scottish Academy, among
others. His work is held in many public and private
collections in Europe, America, South Africa and Hong Kong.

Nadia Kisseleva
Anglo/Russian (b1956)
African Sunset
Oil
32 x 40in (81.5 x 101.5cm)
£1,050–1,200 / € 1,550–1,750
$1,900–2,200 ⊞ **Dr**

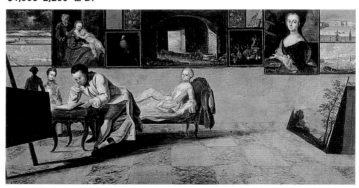

Johann Jakob Kleemann
German (1739–90)
Interior of a Gallery
Gouache on paper
4¾ x 9in (12 x 23cm)
£5,600–6,700 / € 8,200–9,800
$10,200–12,200 ➚ **S(NY)**

◀ **Gustav Klimt**
Austrian (1862–1918)
Bending nude with raised
leg to the right
Pencil on paper
21¾ x 14½in (55.5 x 37cm)
£18,000–21,000 / € 26,000–31,000
$33,000–38,000 ➚ **DORO**

▶ **Clara Klinghoffer**
British (1900–72)
Portrait of a girl
Signed and dated 1960,
watercolour and pastel
21½ x 16½in (54.5 x 42cm)
£190–230 / € 280–330
$340–410 ➚ **WW**

Dame Laura Knight, RA
British (1877–1970)
Carmo's Circus, Southsea
Signed, inscribed and dated
1929, watercolour and pastel
7 x 5in (18 x 12.5cm)
£2,500–3,000 / €3,650–4,400
$4,550–5,500 ➚ GAK

Anthony Robert Klitz
British (1917–2000)
Yachts on the Water
Signed and dated 1978, oil on canvas
20 x 40in (51 x 101.5cm)
£1,500–1,800 / €2,200–2,600
$2,700–3,250 ➚ WA

◀ **Dame Laura Knight, RA**
British (1877–1970)
Seated Clown
Signed, charcoal and crayon
14 x 10¼in (35.5 x 26cm)
£4,000–4,800 / €5,800–7,000
$7,300–8,700 ➚ LAY

Louis Aston Knight
American (1873–1948)
Above the Mill
Signed, oil on canvas
25½ x 32in (65 x 81.5cm)
£20,000–24,000 / €29,000–35,000
$36,000–43,000 ➚ S(NY)

George Sheridan Knowles
British (1863–1931)
Summer's Day on the River
Signed and dated 1903, oil on canvas
29 x 40in (73.5 x 101.5cm)
£21,000–24,000 / €31,000–35,000
$38,000–44,000 ⊞ HFA

Jack Knox
Scottish (b1936)
Beach
Signed, watercolour
6 x 8½in (15 x 21.5cm)
£580–650 / €850–950
$1,050–1,200 ⊞ WrG

Danish (1868–1944)
Spring Thaw
Signed, oil on canvas :
34 x 28in (86.5 x 71cm)
£7,600–8,500 / € 11,100–12,400
$13,800–15,500 ⊞ **Bne**

Martin Knox
American (b1923)
Woman
Oil on canvas
21 x 42¼in (53.5 x 107.5cm)
£175–210 / € 260–310
$320–380 ⚒ **LCM**

► **Unto Koistinen**
Finnish (1917–94)
Reclining model
Signed and dated
1960, oil on board
11 x 15¾in
(28 x 40cm)
£1,850–2,200
€ 2,700–3,200
$3,350–4,000
⚒ **BUK**

Paul Koester
German (1855–1946)
Alpine Cabin in the Mountains
Signed, oil on canvas
37 x 43¾in (94 x 111cm)
£2,800–3,300 / € 4,000–4,800
$5,100–6,000 ⚒ **DORO**

► **Erkki Koponen**
Finnish (1899–1996)
Vertical Element
Signed, oil on canvas
46in (117cm) square
£820–960 / € 1,200–1,400
$1,500–1,750 ⚒ **BUK**

Ang Kiu Kok
Filipino (b1931)
Rooster
Signed and dated 1966,
mixed media on paper
29 x 19in (73.5 x 48.5cm)
£5,500–6,600 / € 8,000–9,600
$10,000–12,000 ⚒ **S(SI)**

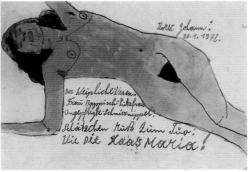

◄ **Johann Korec**
Austrian (b1937)
The Essence of Woman
Signed and dated 1972, pen,
ink and watercolour on paper
4 x 11½in (10 x 29cm)
£310–370 / € 450–540
$560–670 ⚒ **DORO**

Insuring your picture

No one likes to pay high insurance premiums. To get coverage at the best price here are some points to consider:

■ Have your picture valued at an auction house or specialist gallery and update the valuation every three years.

■ If your works of art have a combined value over £50,000 / €73,000 / $72,500 it is worth insuring them with a company specializing in fine art. It may be cheaper than using a general insurance company.

■ Many insurance companies allow a discount off the premium if a burglar alarm is fitted to the premises.

■ In case of theft keep a photographic record of your pictures. If you are the victim of theft, post photographs on the Internet website of Art Loss Register www.artloss.com

Konstantin Alexeevich Korovin
Russian (1861–1939)
Songs around the Campfire
Signed and inscribed, oil on board
13¼ x 16in (33.5 x 40.5cm)
£30,000–36,000 / €44,000–52,000
$55,000–65,000 ⚒ S

▶ **Jerzy Kossack**
Polish (1886–1955)
The round-up
Signed and dated 1907, oil on board
21 x 30¾in (53.5 x 78cm)
£1,100–1,300 / €1,600–1,900
$2,000–2,350 ⚒ B(Kn)

▶ **For more Cowboy Art**
see Frederic Remington (page 156)

Leon Kossoff
British (b1926)
Composition
Lithograph
12¼ x 16¼in (31 x 41.5cm)
£150–180 / €220–260
$270–320 ⚒ B

Oleg Kudryashov
Russian (b1932)
Untitled
Signed and dated 1993, numbered 1/1,
hand-coloured drypoint
41 x 28in (104 x 71cm)
£700–840 / €1,000–1,200
$1,300–1,550 ⚒ B(Kn)

Johannes Gerardus Kuelemans
Dutch (1842–1912)
Wren Chirruping
Signed, watercolour
8¾ x 6¼in (22 x 16cm)
£400–480 / €580–700
$730–870 ⚒ B(Kn)

Georges LaChance
American
(1888–1964)
Peace and Content
Signed, oil on canvas
20 x 24in (51 x 61cm)
£1,200–1,450
€ **1,750–2,100**
$2,200–2,650
⚒ **TREA**

Edward Ladell
British (1821–86)
Still Life
Signed and dated 1860, oil on panel
10 x 12in (25.5 x 30.5cm)
£16,600–18,500 / € 24,200–27,000
$30,000–34,000 ⊞ HFA

Edward Ladell was a self-taught artist, having originally followed the profession of his father, a coachbuilder. He specialized in still lifes composed of fruit, flowers and a variety of objects including glass, tankards, china vases and birds' nests, and his technique achieved an astonishing degree of realism. He exhibited at the Royal Academy between 1856 and 1886 and at the British Institution, the Royal Society of British Artists, Suffolk Street and local West Country venues.

Annie Rose Laing
British (1869–1946)
Afternoon
Signed, oil on canvas
24 x 20in (61 x 51cm)
£25,000–30,000
€ **36,000–43,000**
$45,000–54,000 ⚒ **B(Ed)**

▶ **Eugène Galien Laloue**
French (1854–1941)
Chartres
Signed, gouache
9½ x 11½in
(24 x 29cm)
£17,400–19,300
€ **25,000–28,000**
$31,000–35,000
⊞ **HFA**

William Bradley Lamond, RBA
British (1858–1924)
Fisherfolk, Angus
Signed, oil on canvas
14 x 21in (35.5 x 53.5cm)
£900–1,100 / € 1,350–1,600
$1,700–2,000 ⚒ **B(Ed)**

◀ **Augustus Osbourne Lamplough, ARA**
British (1877–1930)
Dhows by the banks of the Nile
Signed, watercolour
13½ x 19¾in
(34.5 x 50cm)
£850–1,000
€ **1,250–1,450**
$1,550–1,800 ⚒ **B**

Zygmunt Landau
Polish (1898–1962)
Portrait of a girl
Signed and dated 1951,
mixed media
29½ x 21½in (75 x 54.5cm)
£240–290 / €350–420
$440–530 ⚒ WW

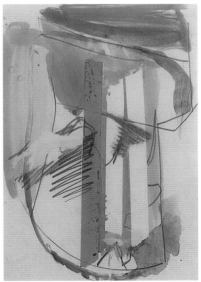

◄ **Peter Lanyon**
British (1918–64)
Untitled (San Gimignano)
Signed and dated 1964, pencil, watercolour, collage and
scratching out on paper
13¾ x 10in (35 x 25.5cm)
£2,600–3,100 / €3,800–4,500
$4,750–5,600 ⚒ B

Georgina Lara
British (fl1862–71)
Village Scenes
A pair, oil on canvas
14 x 24in (35.5 x 61cm)
£12,100–13,500 / €17,600–19,700
$22,000–24,600 ⊞ HFA

*A painter of farmyard and village scenes, Georgina Lara
exhibited at the British Institution as well as exhibiting 16
works at Suffolk Street. Very little is known about her life.
Her work is sometimes attributed to Edward Masters,
whose style is very similar to her own. She is noted for
putting large numbers of doll-like figures into her
paintings and setting them in country and village scenes
where they are going about their daily chores and duties.*

Georgina Lara
British (fl1862–71)
The Meeting Place
Oil on canvas
9 x 13in (23 x 33cm)
£6,300–7,000 / €9,200–10,200
$11,500–12,800 ⊞ HFA

► **Karolina Larusdottir**
Icelandic (b1944)
Time To Leave
Oil on canvas
24 x 30in (61 x 76cm)
£2,300–2,500 / €3,300–3,650
$4,200–4,600 ⊞ CAMB

*Karolina Larusdottir was born in Reykjavik, Iceland. She
studied at the Sir John Cass College, London, the Ruskin
School of Art, Oxford and Barking College of Art. Her
watercolour and oil paintings and handmade etchings
are often inspired by her childhood in Iceland – her
grandfather's hotel in Reykjavik providing a wealth of
imagery. Her work contains a wry humour that enhances
the surreal and timeless qualities she creates when
dealing with her favourite topic – people. She is a
member of the New English Art Club, the Royal Society of
Painter Printmakers and the Royal Watercolour Society.
She lives and works in East Anglia.*

Josef Lauer
Austrian (1818–81)
Still life
Signed and dated 1843,
watercolour on paper
23¾ x 19in (60.5 x 48.5cm)
£4,100–4,900 / € 6,000–7,200
$7,500–8,900 ➚ DORO

June Launder
British (20thC)
Huts and Boats
Acrylic on board
15 x 23in (38 x 58.5cm)
£630–700
€ 900–1,000
$1,150–1,300 ⊞ WrG

► **Simon Laurie**
Scottish (b1964)
The Blue Twins
Acrylic on board
9 x 10in (23 x 25.5cm)
£500–550 / € 730–800
$910–1,000 ⊞ P&H

Sir Thomas Lawrence, RA
British (1769–1830)
Portrait of Lady Georgiana Agar-Ellis,
with her son Henry
Oil on canvas
51 x 41in (129.5 x 104cm)
£180,000–216,000
€ 263,000–315,000
$328,000–393,000 ➚ WW

Sir Thomas Lawrence was probably the most successful portrait painter of the early 19th century, and his subjects included most of the notable people of the day. In 1792 he was appointed Painter in Ordinary to King George III, and President of the Royal Academy in 1820. Lawrence's portraits always command high prices, which reflects the importance of his work.

Ahti Lavonen
Finnish (1928–70)
Sensation Black and Yellow
Signed, oil on canvas
19 x 39½in (48.5 x 100.5cm)
£3,400–4,100 / € 5,000–6,000
$6,200–7,400 ➚ BUK

Ahti Lavonen studied painting at the Workers' Institute and at the Free School of Art, Helsinki. His early work, produced in the 1950s, used striking colours to create abstract pictures, but once he discovered French and Italian art in Paris and Rome in the 1960s, and in particular art connected with Roman Catholicism, he adopted a more informal means of expression and a colour symbolism that pivoted on the ascetic use of black and white.

Frederick 'Fred' Lawson
British (1888–1968)
The market place at Leyburn with a fairground and
figures, motor vehicles nearby
Signed, pencil and watercolour
12¼ x 14¼in (31 x 36cm)
**£2,400–2,900 / € 3,500–4,200
$4,350–5,250** ➤ TEN

Ernest Lawson
British (1873–1939)
View of Segovia
Signed, oil on canvas
12 x 16in (30.5 x 40.5cm)
**£16,500–19,800
€ 24,100–28,900
$30,000–36,000**
➤ S(NY)

Sonia Lawson, RA, RWS
British (b1934)
The Rubbish Dump
Initialled, oil on canvas laid down on board
24¼ x 23¾in (61.5 x 60.5cm)
**£1,350–1,600 / € 1,950–2,300
$2,450–2,900** ➤ B(L)
*Sonia Lawson, daughter of Fred Lawson,
studied at Worthing, Doncaster and the
Royal Academy, where she won a travelling
Scholarship to France. In 1991 she was
elected a full member of the RA, and has
lectured at the Royal College of Art and the
Royal Academy Schools.*

▶ **Edward Lear**
British (1812–88)
Honister from near
Buttermere
Inscribed and dated
1836, pencil and
black chalk on
blue paper
7 x 10¼in (18 x 26cm)
**£1,500–1,800
€ 2,200–2,600
$2,800–3,300** ➤ B

Noel Harry Leaver
British (1889–1951)
Trading on the Street
Signed, bodycolour
7 x 10¼in (18 x 26cm)
**£950–1,100 / € 1,400–1,600
$1,700–2,000** ➤ B(Kn)

Noel Harry Leaver
British (1889–1951)
Almost Home
Signed, watercolour
7 x 10in (18 x 25.5cm)
**£2,700–3,000 / € 3,900–4,400
$4,900–5,500** ⊞ HFA

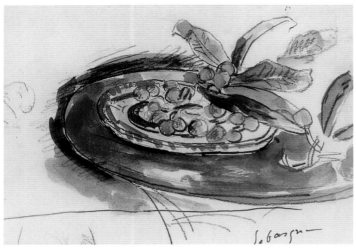

Henri Lebasque
French (1865–1937)
Still Life
Watercolour and gouache over pencil
6 x 9¼in (15 x 23.5cm)
£2,400–2,650 / €3,500–3,850
$4,350–4,800 ⊞ WoF

*Lebasque studied at the Ecole des Beaux Arts at Angers. He is
regarded as a Post-Impressionist artist in the spirit of Matisse. He used
a strong palette over controlled drawing, and much of his responsive
work was done in watercolour or a mixture of watercolour and
gouache, as in this particular piece.*

Rene Legrand
British (b1953)
Girls on the shore
Oil
20 x 24in (51 x 61cm)
£2,900–3,250 / €4,250–4,750
$5,300–5,900 ⊞ Dr

Martin Leman
British (20thC)
Sandbank
Oil on board
10in (25.5cm) square
£810–900 / €1,150–1,300
$1,500–1,650 ⊞ WrG

*Martin Leman studied typographic design at the Central School of
Arts and Crafts and became a part-time lecturer in graphic design at
Hornsey College of Art. He began to paint pictures in 1968 and in the
early '70s he had a one-man show at the Portal Gallery. In 1979, his
work was so successful he became a full-time artist, painting and
illustrating cat books. He spends the summer months in St Ives,
where the strong light of the West Penwith area has had a marked
effect on his paintings.*

Robert Lenkiewicz (1941–2002)

Robert Lenkiewicz loved women, as can be seen in his highly sexualized nudes. Equally he painted pictures of the poor and underprivileged as well as undertaking murals for stately homes in Devon and Cornwall where he lived. Lenkiewicz is revered in the southwest of England but was not part of the London art scene. His death forced the sale of pictures which had been owned by him, including those shown here. At the moment his work is quite unfashionable so it may be a good time to buy his work if it appeals to you.

◄ **Robert Lenkiewicz**
British (1941–2002)
Self Portrait
Oil on board
8½ x 6¼in (21.5 x 16cm)
£4,550–5,500
€6,700–8,000
$8,300–10,000 ⚒ S(O)

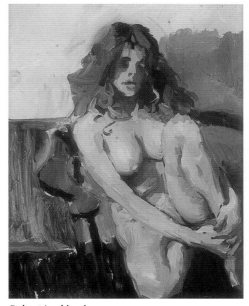

Robert Lenkiewicz
British (1941–2002)
Study of Belle Pecorini in the Kitchen, Priory Road
Signed, titled and inscribed, oil on board
10¾ x 8¾in (27.5 x 22cm)
£3,100–3,700 / €4,550–5,400
$5,600–6,700 ⚒ S(O)

Robert Lenkiewicz
British (1941–2002)
Foot of the Stairs
Signed and inscribed,
oil on canvas
59½ x 36in (151 x 91.5cm)
£3,350–4,000
€4,900–5,800
$6,100–7,300 ⚒ S(O)

◄ **Robert Lenkiewicz**
British (1941–2002)
Punk Family
Oil on hessian
67 x 47½in (170 x 120.5cm)
£7,200–8,600
€10,500–12,600
$13,100–15,700 ⚒ S(O)

◄ **Stanislas Victor Edouard Lepine**
French (1835–92)
Fontainebleau Forest
Signed, partially inscribed, oil on paper laid down on panel
9¼ x 12in
(23.5 x 30.5cm)
£3,500–4,200
€5,100–6,100
$6,300–7,500 ⚒ TEN

▶ **Charles Leslie**
British (19thC)
Highland Waters
A pair, oil on canvas
12 x 10in
(30.5 x 25.5cm)
£5,200–5,800
€7,600–8,500
$9,500–10,600 ⊞ HFA

Thérèse Lessore (1884–1945)

Thérèse Lessore was the third wife of painter Walter Sickert (1860–1942). She was from an artistic family; her father was painter Jules Lessore and she was the sister of the sculptor Frederick Lessore. While at the Slade School of Art she won the Melville Nettleship Prize for Figure Composition. Her charming pictures – many of which depict life in the circus and music hall for which she and her husband shared a passion – are becoming increasingly collectable.

◄ **Thérèse Lessore**
French (1884–1945)
Lady at the Theatre
Signed and dated
1918, oil on canvas
24 x 20in
(61 x 51cm)
£900–1,100
€ **1,350–1,600**
$1,700–2,000 ⚒ B

Thérèse Lessore
French (1884–1945)
The Upper Circle
Signed and dated 1918, oil on canvas
18 x 24in (45.5 x 61cm)
£2,800–3,350 / €4,100–4,900
$5,100–6,100 ⚒ B

► **Thérèse Lessore**
French (1884–1945)
Street Scene
Signed and dated
1940, oil on canvas
25 x 26in
(63.5 x 66cm)
£950–1,150
€ **1,450–1,700**
$1,750–2,100 ⚒ B

Hayley Lever
American (1876–1958)
Gloucester Harbor
Signed, oil on canvas
24 x 30in (61 x 76cm)
£40,000–48,000 / €59,000–70,000
$73,000–87,000 ⚒ S(NY)

Maurice Levis
French (1860–1940)
Saint Dye sur Loire
Signed, oil on paper laid on panel
8½ x 12¼in (21.5 x 31cm)
£5,200–5,800 / €7,600–8,500
$9,500–10,500 ⊞ Bne

If possible, it is advisable to sell a landscape in a gallery or auction house that is near to the place depicted in the picture – it will have a greater chance of achieving a good price. However, this does not apply to works by famous artists: you will get better results in a larger city as there will be a considerably higher number of potential buyers.

Roy Lichtenstein
American (1923–97)
The Living Room (Interior Series)
Signed and dated 1990, numbered 37/60, woodcut and screenprint
on four-ply board
52 x 66in (132 x 167.5cm)
£5,500–6,600 / € 8,000–9,600
$10,000–12,000 ⚒ B

▶ **G. Lieneman**
American (20thC)
Winter Stream
Signed, oil on board
10 x 12in (25.5 x 30.5cm)
£360–430 / € 530–630
$660–780 ⚒ TREA

Thomas Hodgson Liddell
British (1860–1925)
Peking: The Lama Temple
Signed, watercolour over pencil heightened with bodycolour
20½ x 29in (52 x 73.5cm)
£2,900–3,500 / € 4,250–5,100
$5,300–6,300 ⚒ S

*This painting depicts the Lama group of temples in the northeast corner
of the Tartar City, built as an Imperial palace by the son of Kanghi.
Liddell visited China in 1908 and his Chinese watercolours were used to
illustrate his book* China – Its Marvel & Mystery, *published the following
year. The painting shows students being taught by their teachers in
the open air. Their yellow robes denote Imperial patronage.*

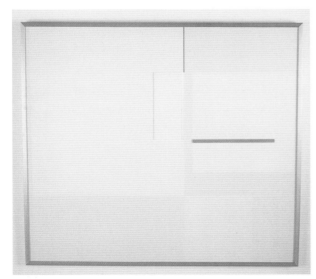

Richard Lin
American (b1933)
Painting Relief
Aluminium, perspex and oil
on canvas
36 x 40in (91.5 x 101.5cm)
£3,550–4,250
€ 5,200–6,200
$6,400–7,700 ⚒ LHA

▶ **Juhani Linnovaara**
Finnish (b1934)
Nainen Ja Väreilevä Maisema
Signed, oil on canvas
16½ x 20½in (42 x 52cm)
£9,600–11,500
€ 14,000–16,800
$17,500–20,900 ⚒ BUK

Edward Barnard Lintott
American (1875–1951)
Orchid Spray
Oil on canvas mounted on board
8½ x 10½in (21.5 x 26.5cm)
£180–210 / €260–300
$330–380 ⚹LHA

Ana Livingston
Argentinian (b1941)
Two Mangoes
Oil on canvas
31 x 51in (78.5 x 129.5cm)
£3,400–3,800 / €4,900–5,500
$6,200–6,900 ⊞ BSG

Ana Livingston was born in Argentina. In 1968, she married a British diplomat, whose postings included Paris in the mid-1970s, where she began to take life classes at the Ecole des Beaux Arts. She subsequently attended classes at the Heatherly School of Arts, London before returning to Paris in 1981 and joining the studio of Sophia Vari, a painter and sculptress. It was during this period that she developed her fascination for space and volume, which is reflected, in particular, in her paintings of fruit.

Thomas Ivester Lloyd
British (1873–1942)
Gone to Ground
Signed, oil on board
15 x 21in (38 x 53.5cm)
£950–1,150
€1,450–1,700
$1,700–2,000 ⚹CGC

► **Tom Lloyd, RWS**
British (1849–1910)
Winter Ploughing
near Bosham, Sussex
Signed, watercolour
11½ x 27½in
(29 x 70cm)
£2,900–3,500
€4,250–5,100
$5,300–6,350
⊞ Bne

Claire Loder
British (20thC)
Hat Trick
Mixed media
15½in (39.5cm) square
£430–480 / €630–700
$780–870 ⊞ WrG

William Logsdail
British (1859–1944)
Wadham College Chapel, Oxford
Signed, oil on canvasboard
15¾ x 11¾in (40 x 30cm)
£400–480 / €590–700
$730–870 ⚹B(B)

Marten van der Loo
Belgian (1880–1920)
The Farm
Signed and dated 1909, oil on canvas
31½ x 39½in (80 x 100.5cm)
£510–610 / €740–890
$920–1,100 ⚹BERN

◄ **Ross Loveday**
Welsh (b1946)
Untitled
Acrylic on board
24in (61cm) square
£750–830 / € 1,050–1,200
$1,350–1,500 ⊞ CAMB

Ross Loveday was born in Bargoed, Wales. He studied optometry at the University of Wales, Cardiff, and has practised as an ophthalmic optician for many years. Since the early 1990s, he has pursued his interest in painting and is now a professional artist, living and working in East Anglia. Inspired by the landscape, Loveday captures the subtle and dramatic changes created by a brewing storm or a spring morning. His work has featured in numerous public and private collections including Addenbrookes Hospital, Cambridge, HRH Prince of Wales and Warner Bros Music.

Jason Lowes
British (20thC)
Portrait of a lady
Signed and dated 1999, watercolour
30 x 21in (76 x 53.5cm)
£550–660 / € 800–960
$1,000–1,200 ➚ B(Kn)

Laurence Stephen Lowry (1887–1976)

According to the experts the market for Lowry peaked around four years ago. However, his works still fetch good prices because few of his pictures are in private hands. What sells best are large canvases of figures in an industrial landscape, although his considerably cheaper smaller pictures of dogs are selling well. A pencil drawing from 1931 sold at Bonhams recently for £40,000 / € 58,400 / $72,800 because it had never been seen before. Although Lowry appears to be a self-taught artist he spent many years studying art, attending painting and drawing classes in Manchester while working as a tax and rent collector.

◄ **Laurence Stephen Lowry, RA**
British (1887–1976)
Landscape with Farm Buildings
Signed, limited edition reproduction
17 x 20½in (43 x 52cm)
£840–1,000
€ 1,250–1,450
$1,550–1,850 ➚ AH

Laurence Stephen Lowry, RA
British (1887–1976)
Head of Old Man
Signed, oil on board
15½ x 11½in (39.5 x 29cm)
£22,000–26,400
€ 32,000–38,500
$40,000–48,000 ➚ B

Laurence Stephen Lowry, RA
British (1887–1976)
Girl
Signed, oil on panel
7¼ x 4½in (18.5 x 11.5cm)
£15,000–18,000
€ 21,900–26,300
$26,400–33,000 ➚ B

◄ **Maximillien Luce**
French (1858–1941)
Study for Pissarro's orchard at Eragny
Signed, charcoal on irregular shaped paper
8½ x 16½in (21.5 x 42cm)
£2,400–2,650 / € 3,500–3,850
$4,350–4,800 ⊞ WoF

Luce started his artistic career as a printmaker and later attended the Académie Suisse and the Atelier of Carolus-Duran. From 1888, he exhibited at the Salon des Indépendants.

Jean Macalpine (b1953)

Jean Macalpine was born in Lancashire and is a successful and well regarded printmaker and photographer. She uses chemical tinting in the developing process, enabling her to change colour, shift spaces and depth, and redevelop tonal areas. She has shown as part of mixed shows round Britain, and chemicals giant ICI have bought her work.

◄ **Jean Macalpine**
British (b1953)
Prairie
Hand-toned
photograph
18¼ x 22½in
(46.5 x 57cm)
£1,050–1,200
€1,550–1,750
$1,900–2,200
⊞ **HG**

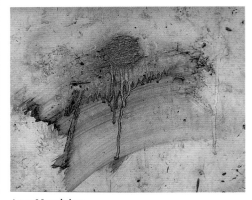

Jean Macalpine
British (b1953)
Meltdown '03
Hand-toned photograph
18¼ x 22½in (46.5 x 57cm)
£1,150–1,300 / €1,650–1,900
$2,100–2,400 ⊞ **HG**

► **Jean Macalpine**
British (b1953)
Intrusion 2003
Hand-toned
photograph
10¾ x 13½in
(27.5 x 34.5cm)
£580–650
€850–950
$1,050–1,200
⊞ **HG**

Horatio MacCulloch, RSA
Scottish (1805–67)
On a drove road
Signed, oil on canvas
13½ x 17¼in (34.5 x 44cm)
£4,200–5,000 / €6,100–7,300
$7,600–9,100 ⋌ **B(Ed)**

William Alister MacDonald
British (fl1893–1910)
Gateway in Vatican Wall, Rome
Signed, inscribed and dated
1908, watercolour
10¾ x 6¾in (27.5 x 17cm)
£380–450 / €550–650
$690–820 ⋌ **B(Kn)**

◄ **James MacIntyre, RUA**
Irish (b1926)
The Fisherman's Dogs,
Roundstone, Connemara
Signed, inscribed and dated
1998, watercolour
17½ x 22in (44.5 x 56cm)
£1,400–1,650 / €2,000–2,400
$2,550–3,000 ⋌ **WA**

Miguel Mackinlay
Spanish (1895–1958)
Laurie and Theresa, the artist's daughters
Signed, oil on canvas
20 x 24in (51 x 61cm)
£400–480 / €580–700
$730–870 ⋌ **B(Kn)**

Brian Mackinnon
Canadian (b1953)
Nude in a Suburban Landscape
Mixed media
24in (61cm) square
£1,900–2,100 / € 2,800–3,100
$3,450–3,800 ⊞ GALG

Mícheál MacLiammóir
Irish (1899–1978)
An Old Woman Beholds a Faery Parade at Night
Signed, watercolour, pen and ink on paper
12½ x 9½in (32 x 24cm)
£1,700–2,050 / € 2,500–3,000
$3,100–3,700 ⚒ WA

◄ **William MacTaggart, PPRSA, RA, FRSE, HonRSW**
British (1903–81)
Norwegian harbour
Pencil and watercolour
on buff paper
8¾ x 10in (22 x 25.5cm)
£1,250–1,500
€ 1,850–2,200
$2,300–2,700 ⚒ B(Ed)

Anna MacMiadhachain
British (20thC)
Purbeck Quarry
Oil on canvas
12 x 14in (30.5 x 35.5cm)
£860–950 / € 1,250–1,400
$1,550–1,750 ⊞ WrG

Although Anna MacMiadhachain was born in London, she comes from west-country seafaring stock and this is reflected very much in her paintings. She attended Watford School of Art before moving to Dorset where she met Padraig MacMiadhachain. They both spent many years travelling and painting. Her distinctive naïve style has become increasingly sought after. Each painting is carefully planned and meticulously executed in a muted palette of blue-grey and earthy greens.

Arthur K. Maderson
Irish (b1942)
Point of Sunset
Signed and inscribed, oil on board
24½ x 22½in (62 x 57cm)
£2,600–3,100 / € 3,800–4,500
$4,700–5,600 ⚒ WA

John Charles Maggs
British (1819–96)
The Bath to London Coach Passing a Hunt on the Road;
The Bath to London Coach at Full Speed Through a Town
A pair, signed, inscribed and dated 1883, oil on canvas
13¾ x 25½in (35 x 65cm)
£1,850–2,200 / € 2,700–3,200
$3,350–4,000 ⚒ B(B)

John Charles Maggs
British (1819–96)
Coaching Scenes
A pair, signed and dated 1884, oil on canvas
14 x 26in (35.5 x 66cm)
£6,100–6,800 / € 8,900–9,900
$11,100–12,400 ⊞ HFA

Cecil Maguire, RHA, RUA
Irish (b1930)
Cutting Rye, Inishmaan
Signed, inscribed and dated 1985, oil on board
18 x 14in (45.5 x 35.5cm)
£5,200–6,200 / € 7,500–9,000
$9,500–11,300 ⚒ WA

Anton Mahringer
Austrian (1902–74)
Winter in St Georgen, Gailtal
Signed and dated 1952, oil on hardboard
33¼ x 33½in (84.5 x 85cm)
£23,000–27,000 / € 34,000–41,000
$42,000–49,000 ⚒ DORO

▶ **Henry Maidment**
British (1889–1914)
Herding the Sheep along the Country Lane
Signed and dated 1899, oil on panel
20 x 30in (51 x 76cm)
£6,200–6,900
€9,000–10,100
$11,300–12,600
⊞ HFA

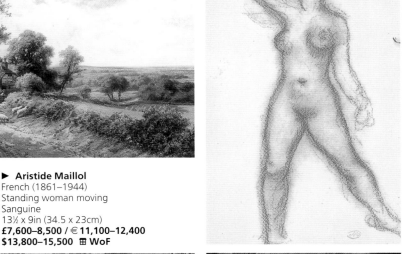

▶ **Aristide Maillol**
French (1861–1944)
Standing woman moving
Sanguine
13½ x 9in (34.5 x 23cm)
£7,600–8,500 / €11,100–12,400
$13,800–15,500 ⊞ WoF

Gustave Maincent
French (1850–87)
Reading in the Park
Signed, oil on canvas
23½ x 19½in (59.5 x 49.5cm)
£7,600–8,500 / €11,100–12,400
$13,800–15,500 ⊞ Bne

Andre Maire
French (1899–1984)
Still Life and Women in the Vietnamese Countryside
Signed, inscribed and dated 1960, oil on panel
19 x 25in (48.5 x 63.5cm)
£2,500–3,000 / €3,650–4,400
$4,550–5,500 🔨 S(SI)

Konstantin Egorovich Makovsky
Russian (1839–1915)
Treasures in the Granovitaya Palata
Signed, oil on canvas
31½ x 23¾in (80 x 60.5cm)
£66,000–79,000 / €96,000–115,000
$120,000–144,000 🔨 S

Konstantin Egorovich Makovsky depicted scenes of simple Russian country life before the appalling upheavals of the 20th century. These works are now being collected, especially by former Soviet citizens who now have money to spend. Makovksy studied in Moscow but was a bit of a rebel. He left the Russian Academy in 1893 to form the Secession group Artel.

◀ **Constantinos Maleas**
Greek (1879–1928)
Pine trees in Halki
Signed, oil on hardboard
11½ x 15¼in (29 x 38.5cm)
£15,000–18,000 / €21,900–26,300
$27,300–32,800 🔨 B

◀ Jean-Baptiste Mallet
French (1759–1835)
A young woman standing in an archway
Oil on panel
17¼ x 13¾in (44 x 35cm)
£5,300–6,300
€7,700–9,200
$9,600–11,500
⚘ S(NY)

Harrington Mann
British (1864–1937)
From the Palatine
Signed, oil on board
6¼ x 10in (16 x 25.5cm)
£980–1,150 / €1,400–1,650
$1,800–2,100 ⚘ B(B)

Peter Marcus
American (1889–1934)
Landscape
Signed, oil on canvas
12 x 16in (30.5 x 40.5cm)
£750–890 / €1,100–1,300
$1,350–1,600 ⚘ TREA
Peter Marcus studied with Charles Davis and Henry Ward Ranger, and in France. He was a member of the Connecticut Association of Fine Artists and the Lotos Club. He exhibited between 1910 and the 1920s at the Art Institute of Chicago and the Pennsylvania Academy of Fine Art.

John Marin
American (1870–1953)
New Mexico Landscape
Signed and dated 1929, watercolour on paper
15 x 20½in (38 x 52cm)
£26,000–31,000 / €38,000–45,000
$48,000–58,000 ⚘ S(NY)

◀ Yoshio Markino
Japanese (1869–1956)
The First Church of Christian Science, Boston
Signed, watercolour
11¼ x 9½in (28.5 x 24cm)
£2,700–3,200 / €3,950–4,700
$4,900–5,800 ⚘ B

▶ Yoshio Markino
Japanese (1869–1956)
Miss John Bull
Signed, watercolour
10¾ x 6¾in (27.5 x 17cm)
£3,000–3,600 / €4,400–5,200
$5,500–6,500 ⚘ B

Reginald Marsh
American (1898–1954)
Street Walker: a double-sided watercolour
Signed, front: ink, wash and watercolour on
paper; back: pencil, ink and wash on paper
en grisaille
21¾ x 15in (55.5 x 38cm)
£8,600–10,300 / €12,500–15,000
$15,600–18,700 ➤ S(NY)

► **Frank Henry
Mason**
British (1876–1965)
Figures in St Mark's
Square
Signed, watercolour
20 x 30in (21 x 76cm)
£1,600–1,900
€2,350–2,750
$2,900–3,450
➤ L&T

John Fitz Marshall
British (1859–1932)
A Trusty Companion
Signed, oil on canvas
21 x 14in (53.5 x 35.5cm)
£11,700–13,000
€17,100–19,000
$21,000–24,000 ⊞ HFA

*John Fitz Marshall was a painter
of animals, landscapes and
flowers and spent most of his
life living in Croydon. The Royal
Academy exhibited twenty of his
paintings from 1883 to 1903
and he was elected to the Royal
Society of British Artists in 1896.*

◄ **Ethel King Martyn, RE**
British (fl1886–c1923)
A collection of etchings and
related artwork
Etchings, trial proofs,
watercolours
Largest 13¾in (30cm) square
£1,050–1,250 / €1,550–1,850
$1,900–2,250 ➤ DW

*Ethel King Martyn worked
principally as an etcher, and
exhibited at the Royal Academy,
the Royal Society of Painter-
Etchers and Engravers, and the
Royal Society of British Artists.
Her work is suffused with the
spirit of the Pre-Raphaelites, and is
largely devoted to the illustration
of literary subjects, including
myths, legends, fables and
related subject matter.*

David Martin, RGI, RSW
Scottish (b1922)
The Red Field
Watercolour
11 x 18½in (28 x 47cm)
£850–950 / €1,250–1,400
$1,550–1,750 ⊞ WrG

*David Martin studied at the Glasgow School of Art from
1940 to 1942 and 1946 to 1948, interrupted by war
service in the Royal Air Force. He was principal teacher of
art at Hamilton Grammar School for ten years and retired
early in 1983 to paint full time. He was elected member
of the Royal Glasgow Institute of the Fine Arts in 1981, the
Royal Scottish Society of Painters in Watercolours in 1984
and honorary member of the Society of Scottish Artists in
1993. Over the years, he has had many major one-man
shows and mixed exhibitions in Scotland and England.*

André Masson
French (1896–1987)
Penthesilée
Signed, inscribed and dated 1960, pastel on canvas
15 x 18in (38 x 45.5cm)
£8,500–9,500 / €12,400–13,900
$15,500–17,300 ➤ WoF

*André Masson studied at the Académie des Beaux-Arts,
Brussels, and then at the Académie des Beaux-Arts, Paris.
He served in WWI and was severely injured. His wartime
experiences left him with a profound and troubled curiosity
about the nature and destiny of man. He had his first
exhibition at the Galerie Simon in Paris in 1922. His early
work is influenced by Cubism, but he later joined the
Surrealists, with whom he exhibited. He was particularly
taken with the Surrealist practice of Automatic painting.
Masson lived in Germany, the Netherlands and Spain during
the 1930s, designing stage scenes and the décor for ballets
and plays. In 1937, he returned to Paris, but left for America
in 1940 where he worked among the New York group of
émigré Surrealists. After his return to France in 1946 he
continued to design stage sets and produced a series of
lithographs and drawings for his portfolios Bestaire and
Mythologies. This painting refers to a mythological story.*

Edwin Masters (Thomas Masters)
British (fl1896)
Village Life
Signed, oil on canvas
18¾ x 29in (47.5 x 73.5cm)
£7,100–7,900 / €10,300–11,500
$12,900–14,400 ⊞ HFA

William Matthison
British (1854–1926)
A nanny and baby standing in the rose garden of a Cotswold stone house
Signed, watercolour
10¾ x 17¼in (27.5 x 44cm)
£800–960 / €1,150–1,400
$1,450–1,750 ⚒ B(O)

Auction or gallery?

All the pictures in our price guide originate from auction houses or galleries. The source of each picture can be found by checking the code letters after each caption with the Key to Illustrations on pages 234–236. When buying at auction prices can be lower than those of a gallery, but a buyer's premium and VAT will be added to the hammer price. Equally when selling at auction, commission, tax and photography charges must be taken into account. Galleries will often restore and authenticate pictures before putting them back on the market. Both galleries and auctioneers will provide professional advice, so it is worth researching both sources before buying or selling your pictures.

◀ **Richard Mayhew**
American (fl1957)
Memories
Watercolour on paper
38 x 30in (96.5 x 76cm)
£4,400–4,850 / €6,400–7,100
$8,000–8,800 ⊞ NNA

Arthur Daniel McCormick
British (1860–1943)
The Song
Signed, oil on canvas
24 x 36in (61 x 91.5cm)
£16,000–17,800 / €23,000–26,000
$29,000–32,000 ⊞ Man

Donald Fraser Gould McGill
British (1875–1962)
So These are Your Dear Twins!; another similar
A pair, signed and inscribed, watercolour and bodycolour
5 x 10¼in (12.5 x 26cm)
£750–900 / €1,100–1,300
$1,350–1,600 ⚒ B

◄ Christine McGinnis
American (b1937)
Blue Idol
Acrylic
36 x 48in (91.5 x 122cm)
£1,700–1,900 / €2,500–2,750
$3,150–3,500 ⊞ LaP

Robert McGregor, RSA
British (1847–1922)
Study for The Knife Grinder
Signed, oil on canvas
8 x 5½in (20.5 x 14cm)
£1,600–1,900 / €2,350–2,800
$2,900–3,450 ⚒ B(Ed)
The Knife Grinder, *one of McGregor's best known works, was painted in 1878 in Largo, Fife.*

Nancy McHarg
Scottish (b1938)
Back Gardens, Pittenweem, Fife
Signed, oil on board
10 x 20in (25.5 x 30.5cm)
£520–580 / €760–850
$950–1,050 ⊞ WrG
Nancy McHarg is a member of the Glasgow Society of Women Artists and the Paisley Art Institute. She exhibits regularly with them and with local galleries in Perth and Edinburgh. Nancy paints mainly around Glasgow and Fife, but tries to go abroad whenever possible to benefit from the warmer weather and rich colours. She enjoys painting still life and tends to do most in the winter as a member of the Glasgow Southern Arts Club.

◄ Donald McIntyre
British (b1923)
White fishing boat
Signed and inscribed, oil on board
7 x 9in (18 x 23cm)
£1,500–1,800
€2,200–2,600
$2,700–3,250
⚒ LAY

► John McLean
British (b1939)
Talisker 1
Acrylic on canvas
7 x 42½in
(18 x 108cm)
£220–260
€320–380
$400–470 ⚒ B(Kn)

Seán McSweeney, HRHA
Irish (b1935)
White Bogland Pool
Signed, inscribed and dated 1998, oil on board
10 x 14in (25.5 x 35.5cm)
£2,850–3,400
€4,200–5,000
$5,200–6,200 ⚒ WA

Insuring your picture

No one likes to pay high insurance premiums. To get coverage at the best price here are some points to consider:

■ Have your picture valued at an auction house or specialist gallery and update the valuation every three years.

■ If your works of art have a combined value over £50,000 / €73,000 / $91,000 it is worth insuring them with a company specializing in fine art. It may be cheaper than using a general insurance company.

■ Many insurance companies allow a discount off the premium if a burglar alarm is fitted to the premises.

■ In case of theft keep a photographic record of your pictures. If you are the victim of theft, post photographs on the Internet website of Art Loss Register www.artloss.com

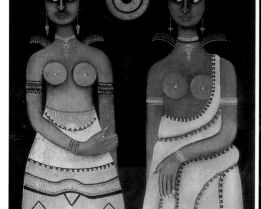

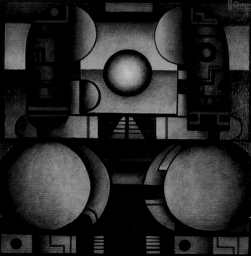

▶ **Santos Medina**
Mexican (20thC)
Oxomoco and Xopaltomalt;
Las Nustas
Two, dated 1994 and 1978,
oil on material
22½ x 16¼in
(57 x 41.5cm);
36¼ x 39¾in
(92 x 101cm)
£60–70 / €85–100
$110–130 ⚒ LCM

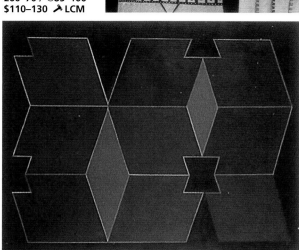

◀ **Robert Medley**
British (b1905)
Thebes
Signed, inscribed and dated 1971,
acrylic on canvas
40¾ x 49¾in
(103.5 x 126.5cm)
£400–480
€580–700
$730–870 ⚒ B(Kn)

▶ **Theo Meier**
Swiss (1908–82)
Balinese maiden
Signed and dated 1936, oil on canvas
21¼ x 17¼in (54 x 44cm)
£2,900–3,500
€4,250–5,100
$5,300–6,400 ⚒ S(SI)

William Mellor (1851–1931)

William Mellor was born in Barnsley, Yorkshire, and worked in Ilkley, Scarborough and Harrogate. He travelled widely and was inspired by the landscape of North Wales and the North East, particularly Yorkshire. His landscapes are easily recognized and are generally scenes in summer or early autumn. The most distinctive feature of Mellor's paintings is the meticulously delicate rendering of trees and foliage heightened by the rich English sunlight that bathes the scene.

He never exhibited in London. The value of his work is rising slowly but steadily. Thirty years ago his pictures would have fetched £100–180 / €150–260 / $180–330.

William Mellor
British (1851–1931)
On the Glaslyn
Signed and inscribed,
oil on canvas
24 x 36in
(61 x 91.5cm)
£14,800–16,500
€21,600–23,800
$27,000–30,000
⊞ **HFA**

William Mellor
British (1851–1931)
On the Wharfe, Yorkshire
Signed and inscribed, oil on canvas
8¼ x 12¼in (21 x 31cm)
£6,200–6,900
€9,000–10,000
$11,300–12,500 ⊞ **HFA**

▶ **William Mellor**
British (1851–1931)
The Fairy Glen
Signed, oil
30 x 20in (76 x 51cm)
£4,250–4,750 / €6,200–6,900
$7,700–8,600 ⊞ **Dr**

Paul Meltsner
American (1905–66)
Workers
Signed, oil on canvas
36 x 28in (91.5 x 71cm)
£13,700–15,200 / €20,000–22,000
$25,000–28,000 ⊞ **FBH**

Emma Mendenhall
American (1873–1963)
Hillside Tree
Signed, oil on board
10 x 8in (25.5 x 20.5cm)
£270–320 / €390–460
$500–600 ⤴ **TREA**

Landscape views of beautiful and famous places are always more valuable. Portraits of well-known figures fetch more than portraits of unknowns.

Mortimer L. Menpes, RI, RBA, RE
British (1860–1938)
A Sunny Garden
Signed, mixed media on board
12½ x 16in (32 x 40.5cm)
£3,000–3,600 / €4,400–5,300
$5,500–6,600 ⤴ **S**

Jean Metzinger
French (1883–1956)
Cubist woman
Signed, pencil on paper
12½ x 9½in (32 x 24cm)
£2,700–3,200 / €3,900–4,700
$4,900–5,800 ➶ B

Colin Middleton, RHA
Irish (1910–83)
Nude Study
Signed and dated 1959, watercolour and crayon
15 x 10in (38 x 25.5cm)
£1,750–2,100 / €2,600–3,100
$3,200–3,800 ➶ WA

John Everett Millais
British (1829–96)
Winter borderlands castle in a snow landscape
Monogrammed and dated 1887, etching
and lithograph highlighted with charcoal
20½ x 17in (52 x 43cm)
£420–500 / €610–730
$760–910 ➶ BR

◀ **Joan Miró**
Spanish (1893–1983)
The Rebel
Signed and numbered 12/50, etching with
aquatint and carborundum on Mandeure paper
36¾ x 25¼in (93.5 x 64cm)
£5,700–6,800 / €8,300–9,900
$10,400–12,400 ➶ BUK

▶ **Joan Miró**
Spanish (1893–1983)
Enrajolats
Signed and numbered, etching in colours
22 x 30in (56 x 76cm)
£2,750–3,300 / €4,000–4,800
$5,000–6,000 ➶ DORO

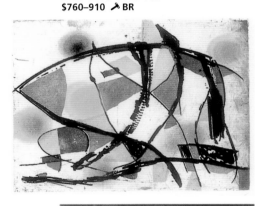

Denis Mitchell
British (1912–93)
Standing Stones
Signed and dated 1947, oil on board
26 x 37¾in (66 x 96cm)
£950–1,100 / €1,400–1,600
$1,750–2,000 ➶ B(Kn)

▶ **Amadeo Modigliani**
Italian (1884–1920)
Portrait of a
young woman
Signed, numbered
217/250, lithograph
on wove
20¾ x 14in
(52.5 x 35.5cm)
£850–1,000
€1,250–1,450
$1,550–1,800 ➶ B

John Mogford
British (1821–85)
Salvaging the Wreck
Signed and dated 1861, watercolour heightened with white
12 x 19½in (30.5 x 49.5cm)
£1,250–1,500 / €2,000–2,400
$2,300–2,750 ⚒ B

Fannie Moody
British (fl1885–97)
Left Behind
Signed and inscribed, coloured chalks on brown paper
18 x 24in (45.5 x 61cm)
£1,500–1,800 / €2,200–2,600
$2,750–3,300 ⚒ DNY

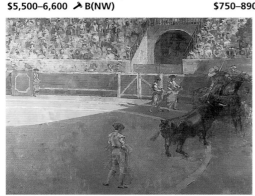

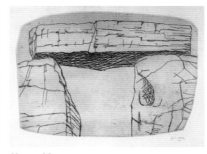

Henry Moore
British (1898–1986)
Reclining Figure: Cave
Signed and numbered, edition of 50 lithograph
11¾ x 16¼in (30 x 41.5cm)
£1,550–1,750 / €2,250–2,550
$2,800–3,200 ⊞ JLx

Edward Hartley Mooney
British (c1878–1938)
The Vale of Clwyd
Signed and dated 1920, oil on canvas
24½ x 29½in (62.5 x 75cm)
£3,000–3,600 / €4,400–5,200
$5,500–6,600 ⚒ B(NW)

Henry Moore
British (1898–1986)
Stonehenge
Signed and numbered
25/60, etching
12¼ x 8¾in (31 x 22cm)
£410–490
€600–720
$750–890 ⚒ BUK

▶ **Rodolfo Morales**
Mexican (1925–2001)
Child embroidering
Signed and
numbered 92/100,
lithograph
25½ x 19¾in
(65 x 50cm)
£500–600
€730–880
$910–1,100
⚒ LCM

Armando Morales
Mexican (b1927)
Bullfighter
Signed and dated 1997, oil on material
25½ x 31½in (65 x 80cm)
£1,950–2,350 / €2,850–3,400
$3,550–4,250 ⚒ LCM

Mary Deneale Morgan
American (1868–1948)
Mountain Landscape
Signed, oil on board
12 x 16in (30.5 x 40.5cm)
£1,600–1,900 / €2,350–2,800
$2,900–3,500 🔨 TREA

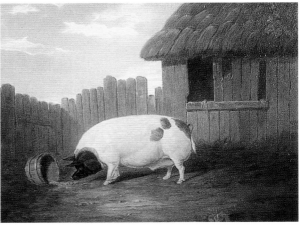

George Morland
British (1763–1804)
The Cottagers' Wealth
Signed and dated 1779, oil on panel
14½ x 18½in (37 x 47cm)
£4,800–5,700 / €7,000–8,300
$8,700–10,400 🔨 WW

Anna Mary Robertson (Grandma) Moses
American (1860–1961)
Springtime Landscape
Signed, oil on masonite
9¾ x 12in (25 x 30.5cm)
£20,000–23,000 / €29,000–34,000
$36,000–43,000 🔨 S(NY)

Marcel Mouly
French (b1918)
Evening Light
Signed
21 x 28¼in (53.5 x 72cm)
£1,100–1,300 / €1,600–1,900
$2,000–2,350 🔨 BUK

▶ **Alice Mumford**
British (b1965)
Two Paper Cups and Rose Hips
Signed and dated 2003, oil on canvas
laid on board
16¼ x 18½in (41.5 x 47cm)
£680–750 / €990–1,100
$1,200–1,350 ⊞ JLx

Alice Mumford
British (b1965)
The Delft Cup and Green Beads
Signed and dated 2003, oil on
canvas laid on board
8¾ x 7¼in (22 x 18.5cm)
£310–350 / €450–510
$560–630 ⊞ JLx

Sir Alfred Munnings, PRA, RWS
British (1878–1959)
The Return from the Fields
Signed and dated 1906,
watercolour over pencil
11½ x 6in (29 x 15cm)
£3,000–3,600 / €4,400–5,200
$5,500–6,600 ✗ B

▲ **For further information**
see Equestrian Art
(pages 62–67)

Frederick Sidney Muschamp
British (1851–1929)
The Letter
Oil on canvas
32 x 15in (81.5 x 38cm)
£8,900–9,900 / €13,000–14,500
$16,200–18,000 ⊞ HFA

Sir Alfred Munnings, PRA, RWS
British (1878–1959)
A portrait of Colonel Harry Egerton Norton,
standing full length, wearing a mixture of
various military uniforms, and portrayed
as a Home Guard
Signed, oil on canvas
30 x 21in (76 x 53.5cm)
£6,200–7,400 / €9,100–10,800
$11,300–13,500 • TEN

*Harry Egerton Norton lived at Wynford,
Somerset, and was a close friend of Alfred
Munnings. Norton was interested in military
uniforms and Munnings appears to have
painted him partially wearing the uniform of
the 15th Hussars as well as the uniform of
the Home Guard.*

August Henri Musin
Belgian (b1852)
Fishing Basin, Ostend
Signed and inscribed, oil on panel
12 x 9½in (30.5 x 24cm)
£2,000–2,400 / €2,900–3,500
$3,600–4,350 ✗ B

Hugh Munro, RGI
Scottish (1873–1928)
Sketching by the River
Signed, oil on canvas
11½ x 15½in (29 x 39.5cm)
£2,200–2,600 / €3,200–3,800
$4,000–4,800 ✗ B(Ed)

▶ **Michael Murfin**
British (b1954)
Crowd Assembly
Signed and
dated 1983,
oil on canvas
54in (137cm) square
£520–620
€760–910
$950–1,150
✗ B(Kn)

Carl Friedrich Mylius
German (1827–1916)
View through an archway
Signed and dated 1891, pen, ink and
wash heightened with bodycolour
11¼ x 8¼in (28.5 x 21cm)
£75–90 / €110–130
$130–160 ✗ DW

Vladislav Nagornov
Russian (b1974)
Nadya
Signed, oil on canvas
16¼ x 13in (41.5 x 33cm)
£450–540 / €660–790
$820–980 ⚒ **JNic**

Makinti Napanangka
Australian (b1930)
Untitled
Inscribed, synthetic polymer
paint on linen
35¾ x 24in (91 x 61cm)
£1,200–1,450 / €1,750–2,050
$2,200–2,500 ⚒ **SHSY**
*These designs are associated
with the Rockhole site of
Lupulnga, South of Kintore.*

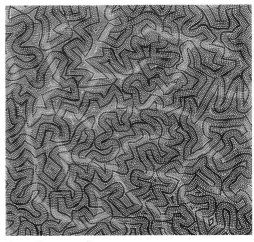

Pansy Napangardi
Australian (b1949)
Untitled (hailstone dreaming at the site of Ilpilli)
Inscribed, synthetic polymer paint on linen
48in (122cm) square
£2,000–2,400
€2,900–3,500
$3,650–4,350
⚒ **SHSY**

▶ **Joseph Nash**
British (1808–78)
Watching the
Cloisters
Signed and dated
1865, watercolour
and bodycolour
20¾ x 15¾in
(52.5 x 40cm)
£550–660
€800–960
$1,000–1,200
⚒ **B(Kn)**

John Nash, RA, NEAC
British (1893–1977)
The Avenue
Signed and dated 1934,
watercolour with pencil
15 x 21¼in (38 x 54cm)
£1,500–1,800 / €2,200–2,600
$2,750–3,250 ⚒ **B**

▶ **Paul Nash**
British (1889–1946)
Shiprail
Signed, pencil and watercolour
9 x 6in (23 x 15cm)
£16,200–18,000
€23,600–26,300
$29,500–33,000 ⊞ **AGN**

Nashar
Indonesian (1928–94)
Abstract
Signed and dated 1978, oil on canvas
55in (139.5cm) square
£2,350–2,800 / €3,450–4,100
$4,250–5,100 ⚒ **S(SI)**

◄ **Patrick Nasmyth**
British (1787–1831)
Wooded Landscape
Oil on panel
12 x 16in (30.5 x 40.5cm)
£5,800–6,500 / €8,500–9,500
$10,600–12,800 ⊞ **HFA**

◄ **Walter Navratil**
Austrian (1950–2003)
Black Cat
tempera on board
27¼ x 39½in
(69 x 100.5cm)
£960–1,150
€1,450–1,700
$1,750–2,100
🔨 **DORO**

Philip Naviasky
British (1894–1983)
The Green Dress
Signed, inscribed and dated 1922, oil
45½ x 35in (115.5 x 89cm)
£700–840 / €1,000–1,200
$1,300–1,550 🔨 **AH**

► **Leroy Neiman**
American (b1921)
Olympic Games
Signed and
inscribed, silkscreen
33 x 48in
(84 x 122cm)
£1,050–1,250
€1,550–1,850
$1,950–2,300
🔨 **JAA**

◄ **Leroy Neiman**
American (b1921)
Innsbruck
Signed, serigraph
15¾ x 11¾in (40 x 30cm)
£310–370 / €450–540
$560–670 🔨 **LHA**

◄ **Ernst Iosipovich Neizvestny**
Russian (b1926)
Torso
Signed and dated
1965, charcoal and
brush on paper
29 x 24½in
(73.5 x 62cm)
£2,150–2,600
€3,100–3,750
$3,600–4,350 ⚒ S

▶ **Nicola Nemec**
British (20thC)
Harbours Series 2
Oil on canvas
15¾ x 19¾in
(40 x 50cm)
£450–500 / €660–730
$820–910 ⊞ HG

Anna Mary Newman
American (d1930)
Pensive
Signed, watercolour on paperboard
36 x 26in (91.5 x 66cm)
£2,500–3,000 / €3,700–4,400
$4,550–5,400 ⚒ TREA

*Anna Mary Newman studied at the Art
Institute of Chicago with Ralph Clarkson,
John Vanderpoel and C. F. Browne. She
also worked with the Overback sisters in
Cambridge City, Indiana, designing ceramics.
Newman's most successful works were
figurative, although she also painted
landscapes and still lifes.*

Laszlo Neogrady
Hungarian (1896–1962)
A Sparkling Winter's Day
Signed, oil on canvas
23½ x 31½in (59.5 x 80cm)
£6,700–7,500 / €9,000–11,000
$12,200–13,600 ⊞ BuP

◄ **Andrew Nicholl, RHA**
Irish (1804–86)
River Landscape
Signed, watercolour
15¼ x 11¼in (38.5 x 28.5cm)
£410–490 / €600–720
$750–890 ⚒ JAd

▶ **Francis Nicholson**
British (1753–1844)
Landscape view of Tintern Abbey and the
River Wye
Watercolour on paper
7½ x 12¼in (19 x 31cm)
£170–200 / €250–290
$310–360 ⚒ DW

◀ **Kate Nicholson**
British (b1929)
Tuscan Landscape
with Campanile
Oil on canvas
27½ x 35½in
(70 x 90cm)
£1,950–2,350
€2,850–3,400
$3,600–4,300 🔨 Bea

▶ **Winifred
Nicholson**
British (1893–1981)
Rustle of Dried Grass
Signed, inscribed
and dated 1967,
oil on canvas
30 x 11¾in (76 x 30cm)
£4,300–5,100
€6,300–7,500
$7,800–9,300 🔨 Bea

◀ **Axel Nilsson**
Swedish (1889–1981)
View of Stadshuskajen,
Stockholm
Signed
25½ x 19¾in (65 x 50cm)
£1,950–2,350 / €2,900–3,450
$3,600–4,300 🔨 BUK

Edmund John Niemann
British (1813–76)
An Afternoon Stroll
Signed and dated 1867,
oil on board
15 x 24in (38 x 61cm)
£4,500–5,000 / €6,600–7,300
$8,200–9,100 ⊞ HFA

▶ **Petr Alexandrovich Nilus**
Russian (1869–1943)
Still life with the artist's paintings
in the background; the reverse
with ladies promenading in the park
Signed and inscribed, oil on canvas
19¾ x 24in (50 x 61cm)
£17,300–20,800
€25,300–30,000
$32,000–38,000 🔨 S

*Petr Alexandrovich Nilus studied
at the Odessa School of Arts
and the Academy of Arts in St
Petersburg, and then set up as
a professional artist in Odessa.
Until the Revolution in 1917,
he took part regularly in the
Wanderers' exhibitions,
specializing in genre scenes and
native landscapes. In 1920 he
emigrated to Paris where he
continued to enjoy considerable
success, showing his works at
major exhibitions and galleries.*

◄ **Norman Clayton Hadlow Nisbett**
British (early 20thC)
Fairfield, Droxford, Hants
Pen, ink and watercolour
12 x 20in (30.5 x 51cm)
£60–70 / €85–100
$110–130 ⚒ DW

Locate the source

The source of each illustration can be found by checking the code letters below each caption with the Key to Illustrations, pages 234–236.

Luis Nishizawa (b1920)

Luis Nishizawa is a painter, draughtsman and sculptor who is usually identified with the Mexican school of painting. He is, however, greatly influenced by Oriental art – his father was Japanese and his mother Mexican – and his landscapes and ink drawings are executed in the traditional manner of Japanese artists. He experiments with various techniques of painting and has notable success working with high temperature ceramics – for example, his mural 'A Song to Life'.

► **Luis Nishizawa**
Mexican (b1920)
Snowcovered mountains from Zacaualpan
Signed, ink on paper
23¾ x 35½in (60.5 x 90cm)
£2,500–3,000
€3,700–4,400
$4,500–5,400
⚒ LCM

Richard Nitsch
German (b1866)
A Well Deserved Pint; A Plucky Companion
A pair, signed, oil on board
7 x 5½in (18 x 14cm)
£10,700–11,900 / €15,600–17,400
$19,500–22,000 ⊞ HFA

Robert Noble, RSA, PSSA
British (1857–1917)
East Linton
Signed, oil on panel
4½ x 8¾in (11.5 x 22cm)
£700–840 / €1,000–1,200
$1,250–1,500 ⚒ B(Ed)

► **Hubert Noi**
Icelandic (b1961)
64°09"54"N 21°56"78"W 311° True North
Oil on canvas
23¾ x 35½in (60.5 x 90cm)
£2,750–3,100 / €4,000–4,500
$5,000–5,600 ⊞ Waa

Hubert Noi was born in Reykjavik. This painting is from a series of works started in 1996: they are locations pinpointed by a GPS instrument and show what meets the eye from that point and given compass direction. Noi is melting together state-of-the-art technology and spirit. The paintings are made from simple sketches and the location and compass direction are written on the frame.

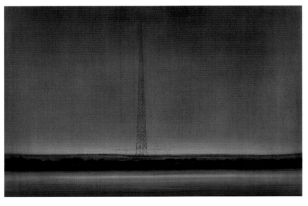

Sidney Nolan (1917–92)

Sidney Nolan is possibly Australia's most important 20th-century artist. He is equally respected in Europe where his work has been shown extensively. In the mid-1950s he moved to Europe, but visited Australia for special projects as well as travelling to Africa, Asia, Europe and Antarctica. He often painted a series of pictures on a theme, among the best known of which are the drawings and paintings of Ned Kelly, the soldiers at Gallipoli and the explorers Burke and Wills. Others are based on ancient myths such as Leda and the Swan. An impassioned artist, Nolan was also a painter of literary themes, a book illustrator, theatre designer and sculptor. He was knighted in 1981.

◄ **Sidney Nolan, RA**
Australian (1917–92)
Kelly at Night
Signed, ripolin on paper
11½ x 9½in (29 x 24cm)
**£7,000–8,400 / €10,200–12,200
$12,700–15,300** ⚒ B

Sidney Nolan, RA
Australian (1917–92)
Prehistoric Animals
Signed, ripolin on card
25 x 20¼in (63.5 x 51.5cm)
**£1,800–2,150 / €2,600–3,100
$3,300–3,900** ⚒ B

◄ **Sidney Nolan, RA**
Australian (1917–92)
Landscape
Signed and dated 1968,
oil and ripolin on paper
20 x 29½in (51 x 75cm)
**£7,200–8,000 / €10,500–11,700
$13,100–14,500** ⊞ WoF

Anna Nordgren
Swedish (1847–1916)
Ducks on the Farm
Signed and dated 1892, oil on canvas
24 x 35¾in (61 x 91cm)
**£960–1,150
€1,400–1,650
$1,750–2,100** ⚒ BUK

► **Pietro Antonio Novelli**
Italian (1729–1804)
The Immaculate Madonna
Pen and black ink with brush and brown wash over traces of black chalk within black ink framing lines
15¾ x 11¾in (40 x 30cm)
**£900–1,050
€1,300–1,500
$1,650–1,900**
⚒ B(Kn)

Hernando Ruiz Ocampo
Filipino (1911–78)
Untitled
Signed and dated 1977, oil on canvas laid on board
33 x 25in (84 x 63.5cm)
£4,700–5,600 / €6,900–8,200
$8,500–10,200 ⚒ S(SI)

Michael O'Dea, RHA
Irish (b1958)
Robbie, Bewley's Café, Dublin
Signed and dated 1988, oil on canvas
20in (51cm) square
£1,650–1,950 / €2,400–2,850
$3,000–3,600 ⚒ WA

Michael O'Dea was born in Ennis, Co Clare, and studied at the National College of Art, Dublin and the University of Massachusetts. Known primarily as a portrait painter, he has exhibited with the Rubicon Gallery and Taylor Galleries, Dublin, Oireachtas and Independent Artists exhibitions. In recent years he has worked extensively to encourage art-making in prisons.

Breon O'Casey
British (b1928)
St Ives 1967
Oil
36 x 24in
(91.5 x 61cm)
£300–360
€440–520
$550–650 ⚒ GH

► **John O'Connor**
British (b1913)
The Sisters and the Crab
Signed, titled and dated 1953, wood engraving on Japanese vellum
13½ x 11in
(34.5 x 28cm)
£290–350
€420–500
$530–630 ⚒ DW

Dorothy Ochtman
American (1892–1971)
Persian Vases
Signed, oil on canvas
30 x 25in (76 x 63.5cm)
£5,100–6,100 / €7,400–8,900
$9,300–11,100 ⚒ LHA

◄ **James O'Halloran**
Irish (b1955)
Brass Bed, Morning Light
Signed, oil on board
20 x 24in
(51 x 61cm)
£1,250–1,500
€1,800–2,150
$2,250–2,700
⚒ WA

Pablo O'Higgins
American (1904–83)
Don Matías
Signed and numbered 57/100, lithograph
13½ x 17in (34.5 x 43cm)
£175–210 / €250–300
$320–380 ✗ LCM

◄ **Lucien Frits Ohl**
Dutch (1904–76)
Under a Flamboyan
Signed, oil on canvas
24 x 35¾in
(61 x 91cm)
£1,750–2,100
€2,500–3,000
$3,200–3,800
✗ S(SI)

► **Aloysius O'Kelly**
Irish (1850–1929)
The Ladies' Land League
Signed, gouache on board, *en grisaille*
11 x 9¼in (28 x 23.5cm)
£3,400–4,100 / €5,100–6,000
$6,200–7,500 ✗ WA
This piece depicts a meeting of the Central Ladies' Land League in their office in Sackville Street, Dublin.

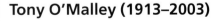

◄ **Erik Olson**
Swedish (1901–86)
Summer's day on the beach, Halland
Signed and dated 1926, canvas laid on board
10½ x 19½in (26.5 x 49.5cm)
£14,200–17,000 / €20,700–25,000
$26,000–31,000 ✗ BUK

Tony O'Malley (1913–2003)

Tony O'Malley was born in Kilkenny, Ireland. In the late 1950s he moved to St Ives – he had fallen in love with the place while on holiday there and felt drawn to the artistic community. Shortly afterwards his paintings became increasingly abstract. He returned to Ireland in the 1980s and, due to the recent economic boom in Ireland, good prices are being paid for his work.

Often a larger canvas by the same artist will command a higher price.

► **Tony O'Malley, HRHA**
Irish (1913–2003)
Entrance to the Orchard, Ashgrove, Fethard-on-Sea
Signed, inscribed and dated 1959, oil on board
31½ x 21¼in (80 x 54cm)
£6,800–8,200
€10,000–12,000
$12,400–14,900 ✗ JAd

► **Tony O'Malley, HRHA**
Irish (1913–2003)
October 1988 After Lanzarote
Signed, inscribed and dated 1989, oil on board
6 x 12in (15 x 30.5cm)
£4,500–5,400 / €6,600–7,900
$8,200–9,800 ✗ WA

Daniel O'Neill
Irish (1920–74)
Scalligstown, Co Donegal
Titled and dated 1953, oil on board
14 x 21in (35.5 x 53.5cm)
£9,600–11,500 / €14,000–16,800
$17,500–21,000 ➚ JAd

Daniel O'Neill
Irish (1920–74)
The Lake
Oil on board
18¼ x 24in (46.5 x 61cm)
£14,400–17,000 / €21,000–25,000
$26,000–31,000 ➚ JAd

George Bernard O'Neill
British (1828–1917)
The Little Gardener
Signed, oil on canvas
14 x 18in (35.5 x 45.5cm)
£12,000–14,400 / €17,500–21,000
$21,800–26,100 ➚ B

Hugh O'Neill
British (1784–1829)
Monnow Bridge, Monmouthshire
Signed, pencil
7 x 11in (18 x 28cm)
£140–165 / €200–240
$250–300 ➚ DW

▶ **Mark O'Neill**
Irish (b1963)
Tartan Chair
Signed and dated 2001,
oil on board
37 x 19in (94 x 48.5cm)
£6,200–7,400 / €9,000–10,800
$11,300–13,500 ➚ WA

◀ **Mark O'Neill**
Irish (b1963)
Peonie (Interior of a country
house in County Laois)
Signed and dated 1995,
oil on canvas laid on board
20 x 30in (51 x 76cm)
£5,900–7,100 / €8,600–10,300
$10,700–12,800 ➚ WA

Vladimir Orlovski
Russian (1842–1914)
Boats During Low Tide
Signed, oil on board
9¾ x 14¼in (25 x 36cm)
£3,000–3,600 / €4,400–5,300
$5,500–6,600 ↗ BUK

James Orr
British (b1931)
House by the Sea, Morar
Acrylic
12 x 14in (30.5 x 35.5cm)
£760–850 / €1,100–1,250
$1,400–1,550 ⊞ WrG

Fergus O'Ryan, RHA, ANCA
Irish (1911–89)
Smith and Pearson Steelworkers on the Liffey Quays, Dublin
Signed, oil on board
22½ x 28½in (57 x 72.5cm)
£2,900–3,500 / €4,200–5,000
$5,300–6,400 ↗ WA

Industrial subjects are rare, and this view of the Liffeyside area of Guinness's brewery in Dublin is particularly interesting because it shows a range of sheds probably for racking or cooperage, under construction. Through the haze of steam or smoke we see the steel structures of a large range of sheds, with the name of the fabricator and contractor, Smith & Pearson, proudly displayed. This quayside was used by Guinness from 1870 until 1960 to ferry barrels of Guinness from the brewery down to the larger ships at Custom House quay, from where they were exported. A Guinness barge may be seen in the foreground, with a lorry which suggests a date between 1945 and 1960. Various malt houses with their steep roofs and a chimney can be seen in the background. O'Ryan's somewhat naïve style of painting captures the busy industrial scene, in the decades just before road transport completely took over from slower means of moving goods.

Fergus O'Ryan, RHA, ANCA
Irish (1911–89)
Millicent,
County Kildare
Signed, oil on board
20 x 24in (51 x 61cm)
£2,350–2,800
€3,400–4,100
$4,250–5,100
↗ WA

► **Frederick Osborne, RHA**
British (1859–1903)
Portrait of Lydia May Montgomery, half length
Signed, pastel
13 x 9½in (33 x 24cm)
£3,750–4,500
€5,500–6,600
$6,800–8,200
↗ JAd

Seán O'Sullivan, RHA
Irish (1906–64)
Gardens with View of a Neoclassical Temple
Signed, oil on board
20 x 24in (51 x 61cm)
£2,600–3,100 / €3,800–4,550
$4,750–5,700 ⚒ **WA**

Nikolaos Othoneos
Greek (1877–1949)
Goats
Signed, oil on
cardboard
8¼ x 12in
(21 x 30.5cm)
£2,800–3,350
€4,100–4,900
$5,100–6,100 ⚒ **B**

Abbreviations

Letters after the artist's name denote that the
artist has been awarded the membership of an
artistic body. See page 233 for the explanation
of abbreviated letters.

▶ **Therese Oulton**
British (b1953)
Song of Deceit
Signed, titled and dated 1988,
oil on canvas
92¼ x 84in (234.5 x 213.5cm)
£2,300–2,750 / €3,350–4,000
$4,200–5,000 ⚒ **B(Kn)**

Ida Rentoul Outhwaite (1880–1960)

Ida Rentoul Outhwaite was a self-taught artist. Her first
published illustrations appeared when she was 15, and
her first illustrated book in 1904, written by her sister
Annie. Her reputatation was firmly established with the
publication of *Elves and Fairies* in1916. Her husband,
Arthur, was a barrister who also wrote stories for her to
illustrate and handled her business affairs. After WWI,
Ida's work was successfully shown in Paris and London
and from 1933 to 1939 she illustrated a regular comic
strip. In her lifetime her black and white art was more
popular as critics felt that her work in colour was
over sentimental.

▶ **Ida Rentoul Outhwaite**
Australian (1880–1960)
The Winter Fairy came in the Snow
Titled and inscribed, watercolour,
ink and bodycolour
10 x 8¼in (25.5 x 21cm)
£7,800–9,400
€11,400–13,700
$14,100–16,900 ⚒ **LJ**

◀ **Ida Rentoul
Outhwaite**
Australian
(1880–1960)
'I would learn to
talk' said the parrot
Titled, watercolour,
bodycolour and ink
10 x 8in
(25.5 x 20.5cm)
£4,550–5,400
€6,600–7,900
$8,300–9,800 ⚒ **LJ**

◀ **Ida Rentoul Outhwaite**
Australian (1880–1960)
One day her special little playmate came
into the forest to look for her
Titled, watercolour and ink
9¾ x 8in (25 x 20.5cm)
£5,700–6,800 / €8,300–9,900
$10,400–12,400 ⚒ **LJ**

Stephen Pace
American (b1918)
Down View of the Artist's House
Signed, watercolour on paper
27½ x 32½in (70 x 82.5cm)
£650–780 / €950–1,100
$1,200–1,400 ↗ LHA

Stephen Pace
American (b1918)
Maine Dining Room ≠1
Signed, watercolour on paper
27½ x 32½in (70 x 82.5cm)
£710–850 / €1,050–1,250
$1,300–1,550 ↗ LHA

Alfred Palmer
British (1877–1951)
Figures by a lake
Signed, oil on panel
20 x 24in (51 x 61cm)
£1,700–2,000 / €2,500–3,000
$3,100–3,700 ↗ WW

Charles Murray Padday
British (1868–1954)
The Arrival
Signed and dated
1893, watercolour
10 x 13¾in
(25.5 x 35cm)
£600–720
€880–1,050
$1,100–1,300
↗ B(Kn)

Samuel Palmer
British (1805–81)
The Sleeping Shepherd
Inscribed, etching
5 x 4in (12.5 x 10cm)
£800–960 / €1,150–1,300
$1,450–1,750 ↗ B

▶ **Epaminondas
Pantazopoulos**
Greek (1874–1961)
Sea view
Signed, oil on panel
12 x 17in
(30.5 x 43cm)
£500–600
€730–880
$910–1,100 ↗ B

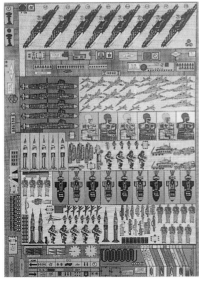

Sir Eduardo Paolozzi
Scottish (b1924)
Zero Energy Experimental Pile
Set of six, signed, dated 1970 and numbered
13/100, offset lithographs
**£1,400–1,650 / €2,050–2,450
$2,550–3,050 ⚡ B**

*Sir Eduardo Paolozzi was born in Edinburgh,
Scotland. He studied at Edinburgh College of
Art and the Slade School of Art, London,
before moving to Paris, where he met
Giacometti and was influenced by Dadaism
and Surrealism. In 1951, while he was
professor at the Central School of Art, he
won his first important sculptural commission
– a fountain for the Festival of Britain.*

Max Papart
French (1911–94)
Married couple by the sea
Signed, inscribed and dated 1966, oil on canvas
31¾ x 31½in (80.5 x 80cm)
**£2,400–2,800 / €3,500–4,100
$4,400–5,100 ⚡ DN**

▶ **John Anthony Park**
British (1880–1962)
Back Road West, St Ives
Signed, oil on canvas
11¼ x 15½in (28.5 x 39.5cm)
**£1,700–2,050 / €2,500–3,000
$3,100–3,700 ⚡ B**

Rene Herbert Renato Paresce
Italian (1886–1937)
Two figures within an interior,
the sea beyond
Signed and dated 1931,
gouache on card
12¼ x 9½in (31 x 24cm)
**£9,000–10,800
€13,100–15,700
$16,400–19,600 ⚡ B**

◀ **Ian Parker**
British (b1955)
Still Life with Six Quinces
Signed, oil on panel
6 x 18in (15 x 45.5cm)
**£1,000–1,100 / €1,450–1,600
$1,800–2,000 ⊞ Bne**

◀ **Alfred William
Parsons, PRWS**
British (1847–1920)
Mi Komori jinja near Yoshino
Signed and inscribed,
watercolour and bodycolour
19½ x 13in (49.5 x 33cm)
**£4,000–4,800 / €5,800–7,000
$7,300–8,700 ⚡ B**

▶ **Victor Pasmore**
British (1908–98)
Anxious Moments
Signed, dated 1985 and
numbered 34/90,
etching and aquatint
39¼ x 27¾in (99.5 x 70.5cm)
**£600–720 / €880–1,050
$1,100–1,300 ⚡ B**

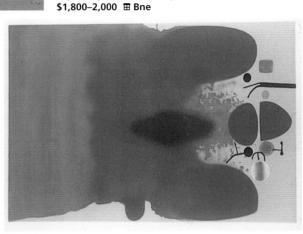

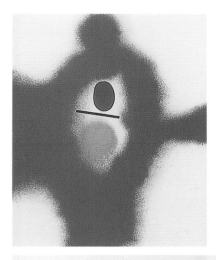

◀ **Victor Pasmore**
British (1908–98)
Abstract in Blue
Signed, silkscreen
22½ x 33in
(57 x 84cm)
£600–720
€880–1,050
$1,100–1,300
🔨 **JNic**

Donald Pass
British (b1930)
Archangel Gabriel
Watercolour
20 x 30in (51 x 76cm)
£1,600–1,800 / €2,350–2,600
$2,900–3,200 ⊞ **BOX**

Watercolours

When framing your watercolours insist on mounting the picture on acid free boards. Poor mounting and the wrong adhesives can cause works on paper to deteriorate.

Gerard Passet
French (b1936)
The Road
Signed and dated
1963, oil on canvas
20in (51cm) square
£220–260
€320–380
$400–480 🔨 **JAA**

◀ **Kevin Pearsh**
Australian (b1951)
Red on Pink
Oil on canvas
39½ x 27½in
(100.5 x 70cm)
£3,400–3,800
€5,000–5,600
$6,200–6,900
⊞ **No9**

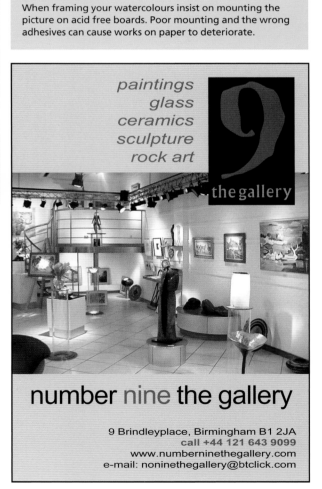

Harry John Pearson
British (1872–1933)
Portrait of a girl with a teddy bear leaning
against a wall
Signed, oil on panel
15½ x 12¾in (39.5 x 32.5cm)
£440–530 / €640–760
$800–960 ⚲ WW

James Peel
British (1811–1906)
Witley Common, Near Mousehill, Surrey
Signed, oil on canvas
16 x 26in (40.5 x 66cm)
£4,500–5,000 / €6,600–7,300
$8,200–9,100 ⊞ HFA

Karl Axel Pehrson
Swedish (b1921)
Lirpa
Signed, oil on canvas
18¼ x 21¾in (46 x 55.5cm)
£1,850–2,200 / €2,700–3,200
$3,400–4,000 ⚲ BUK

George Mnyalaza Milwa Pemba
South African (1912–2001)
Women and Children
Signed, oil on board
19½ x 15¼in (49.5 x 38.5cm)
£4,550–5,400 / €6,600–7,900
$8,300–9,900 ⚲ S

Jack Pender
British (1918–98)
Swinging Boats No. 2
Signed, titled and inscribed,
oil on board
30¾ x 21in (78 x 53.5cm)
£2,050–2,250 / €3,000–3,600
$3,700–4,400 ⊞ JLx

◄ **Arthur Percy**
British (1886–1976)
Still life
Signed and dated 1958, oil
28¾ x 32¼in (73 x 82cm)
£2,250–2,700 / €3,300–3,900
$4,100–4,900 ⚲ BUK

Sidney Richard Percy
British (1821–86)
Cader Idris from the Mawddach
Signed, oil on canvas
9½ x 17in (24 x 43cm)
£4,500–5,400 / €6,500–7,800
$8,200–9,800 ⚲ B

◄ **Vincente de Peredes**
Spanish (20thC)
Parisian Life
Signed, oil on canvas
18 x 15in
(45.5 x 38cm)
£30,000–34,000
€44,000–50,000
$55,000–62,000
⊞ HFA

► **Iosif Yankelevich Perelmann**
Russian (b1876)
After the Easter Vigil
Signed, inscribed
and dated 1907,
oil on canvas
36¼ x 25½in
(92 x 65cm)
£6,600–7,900
€9,600–11,500
$12,000–14,400 ⚒ S

Bui Xuan Phai
Vietnamese (1920–88)
Street, Hanoi
Signed and dated 1978,
oil on panel
9¾ x 13¾in (25 x 35cm)
£4,700–5,600 / €6,900–8,200
$8,500–10,200 ⚒ S(SI)

Jackie Philip
Scottish (b1961)
Red Tulips
Oil on canvas
18 x 22in (45.5 x 56cm)
£1,800–2,000 / €2,600–2,900
$3,250–3,650 ⊞ CFAG

Werner Philipp
German/American (1897–1982)
Santa Clara Hills
Signed and dated 1960, oil on canvas
24½ x 31½in (62 x 80cm)
£450–540 / €650–780
$800–950 ⚒ JAA

► **Robin Philipson, RA, PRSA, FRSA, RSW, RGI**
British (1916–92)
Threnody – The Cry
Signed and dated 1970, watercolour
10in (25.5cm) square
£4,000–4,800 / €5,800–7,000
$7,300–8,700 ⚒ B(Ed)

Peter Phillips (b1939)

In early 1960s Peter Phillips gave up studying art at the Royal College to go to television school. He is a Pop Artist who seeks to represent the modern world with relevant image and style. British Pop Art has never reached the prices of American Pop Art and was out of fashion during 1980s and 1990s. However the work of the Pop Artists, and in particular Phillips, is being appreciated once more.

◄ **Peter Phillips**
British (b1939)
Zone II
Oil on acrylic on canvas
82¾ x 61in (210 x 155cm)
£30,000–34,000 / €44,000–50,000
$55,000–62,000 ⊞ PEP

◄ **Peter Phillips**
British (b1939)
Art-O-Matic Riding High
Acrylic on canvas
78¾ x 59in (200 x 150cm)
£106,000–117,000 / €155,000–175,000
$193,000–213,000 ⊞ PEP

Peter Phillips
British (b1939)
Custom Painting II
Oil on canvas on wood
84¼ x 69in (214 x 175.5cm)
£75,000–84,000 / €110,000–121,000
$137,000–151,000 ⊞ PEP

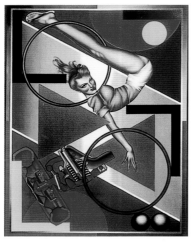

Glyn Philpot, RA
British (1884–1937)
Portrait of Lieutenant Aymes
Signed, oil on canvas
48 x 26¾in (122 x 68cm)
£13,200–15,800 / €19,300–23,000
$24,000–29,000 ➚ S

Le Pho
Vietnamese (1907–2001)
Ladies by the Balcony
Signed, gouache and ink on silk
laid down on paper
25¼ x 16½in (64 x 42cm)
£31,000–37,000 / €45,000–54,000
$56,000–67,000 ➚ S(SI)

Le Pho
Vietnamese (1907–2001)
The Wise Vietnamese
Signed and inscribed, ink on paper
11 x 8in (28 x 20.5cm)
£1,750–2,100
€2,500–3,000
$3,200–3,800 ➚ S(SI)

Pablo Picasso (1881–1973)

Pablo Picasso studied in Barcelona and moved to Paris in 1904 where, along with Georges Braque, he created Cubism. His early paintings in this style are now known as Analytical Cubism. Between 1917 and 1924 Picasso worked on designs for many of Diaghilev's ballets (see Theatre Art pages 196–197). He left Paris in 1946, remaining a prolific artist until his death. His major contribution to modern art, apart from Cubism, is the freedom which characterizes every aspect of his work.

Pablo Picasso
Spanish (1881–1973)
Composition
Lithograph
19½ x 30in (49.5 x 76cm)
£95–110 / €140–160
$175–200 ⚲ DW

Pablo Picasso
Spanish (1881–1973)
The Old King
Signed, lithograph
25¼ x 19½in (64 x 49.5cm)
£550–660 / €800–960
$1,000–1,200 ⚲ BUK

Pablo Picasso
Spanish (1881–1973)
The Horsewoman and the Clowns
Signed, dated 1961 and numbered 16/40, lithograph
22 x 30in (56 x 76cm)
£5,100–6,100 / €7,400–8,900
$9,300–11,100 ⚲ BUK

◄ **Pablo Picasso**
Spanish (1881–1973)
Theatre Scene
Signed and numbered 10/50, aquatint
12¼ x 18½in (31.5 x 47cm)
£2,900–3,450
€4,250–5,100
$5,300–6,300 ⚲ S

Frederick Richard Pickersgill, RA
British (1820–1900)
Christopher Columbus at Lisbon
Oil on canvas
36 x 42in (91.5 x 106.5cm)
£16,600–18,500 / €24,200–27,000
$30,000–34,000 ⊞ FdeL

This is a historical painting. Columbus married an aristocratic Portuguese lady and acquired Portuguese citizenship. On the right is his mother-in-law, who gave him maps that had belonged to her late husband, a master mariner.

William Lamb Picknell
American (1853–97)
Walk on a Country Path
Signed, oil on canvas
29½ x 35¾in (75 x 91cm)
£20,000–24,000
€29,000–34,000
$36,000–43,000 ⚲ S(NY)

Cheong Soo Pieng
Chinese (1917–83)
Harbour scene
Signed and dated 1961, oil on canvas laid on board
23½ x 27in (59.5 x 68.5cm)
£4,700–5,600 / €6,900–8,100
$8,500–10,100 ➚ S(SI)

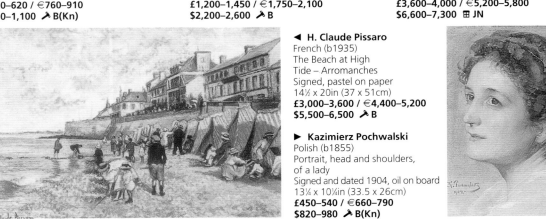

William Henry Pike
British (1846–1908)
Charlestown Harbour, Cornwall
Signed and dated 1883, watercolour
21 x 36in (53.5 x 91.5cm)
£4,000–4,800 / €5,800–7,000
$7,300–8,700 ➚ LAY

Audrey Pilkington
British (b1922)
Portrait of John Minton
Signed, gouache
24¾ x 19¾in (63 x 50cm)
£520–620 / €760–910
$950–1,100 ➚ B(Kn)

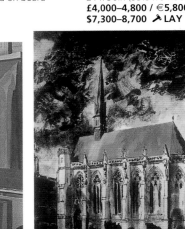

John Piper
British (1903–92)
Exeter College Chapel, Oxford
Signed and inscribed,
edition of 100, silkscreen
31¾ x 23¼in (80.5 x 59cm)
£1,200–1,450 / €1,750–2,100
$2,200–2,600 ➚ B

John Piper
British (1903–92)
Black stockings and high heels
Watercolour
22 x 15in (56 x 38cm)
£3,600–4,000 / €5,200–5,800
$6,600–7,300 ⊞ JN

◄ **H. Claude Pissaro**
French (b1935)
The Beach at High
Tide – Arromanches
Signed, pastel on paper
14½ x 20in (37 x 51cm)
£3,000–3,600 / €4,400–5,200
$5,500–6,500 ➚ B

► **Kazimierz Pochwalski**
Polish (b1855)
Portrait, head and shoulders,
of a lady
Signed and dated 1904, oil on board
13¼ x 10¼in (33.5 x 26cm)
£450–540 / €660–790
$820–980 ➚ B(Kn)

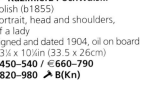

◀ **Jenny Pockley**
British (b1973)
Ghost
Oil and graphite
on gesso
48 x 54in
(122 x 137cm)
£2,950–3,500
€4,300–5,100
$5,400–6,400 ⊞ **SMy**

▶ **Jenny Pockley**
British (b1973)
Jewel
Oil on gesso
48 x 54in
(122 x 137cm)
£3,000–3,300
€4,400–4,800
$5,400–6,000 ⊞ **SMy**

◀ **Nicholas Pocock**
British (1740–1821)
A frigate under tow down the Avon Gorge in light winds
Signed and dated 1787, pen, ink and watercolour
23¼ x 32½in (59 x 82.5cm)
£4,000–4,800 / €5,800–6,900
$7,300–8,700 ⚒ **B**

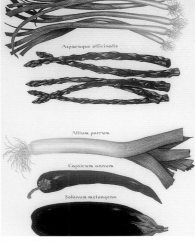

Bryan Poole
New Zealander (b1953)
Common Fig (Ficus carica)
Signed, edition of 100, aquatint etching
20 x 15in (51 x 38cm)
£310–350 / €450–500
$560–620 ⊞ **BrP**

Georges Pogedaieff
Russian (1899–1971)
Still life with vase of lilies
and apples
Signed, oil on board
24 x 15in (61 x 28cm)
£5,000–6,000 / €7,300–8,700
$9,100–10,900 ⚒ **S**

Bryan Poole
New Zealander (b1953)
Mixed Vegetables
Signed, edition of 100, aquatint etching
22½ x 14¾in (57.5 x 37.5cm)
£310–350 / €450–500
$560–620 ⊞ **BrP**

▲ **For further information**
see Botanical & Flower Painting (pages 32–35)

Bernhard Pothast
Dutch (1882–1966)
The Sewing Lesson
Signed, oil on canvas
20¼ x 24¼in (51.5 x 61.5cm)
£6,500–7,800 / €9,500–11,400
$11,800–14,100 ⚒ B

Edward Henry Potthast
American (1857–1927)
Moonlight Campers
Signed, titled and inscribed, oil on canvas
25 x 30in (63.5 x 76cm)
£9,900–11,800 / €14,400–17,200
$18,000–21,500 ⚒ S(NY)

◀ **Mary Potter**
British (1900–81)
Study for the Swans
Watercolour
9½ x 11¾in (24 x 30cm)
£620–740 / €900–1,050
$1,100–1,300 ⚒ B(Kn)

▶ **Marios Prassinos**
Greek (1916–85)
Untitled
Signed and dated 1955, oil on
card laid down on canvas
26 x 19½in (66 x 49.5cm)
£5,400–6,500 / €7,900–9,500
$9,800–11,800 ⚒ B

Maurice B. Prendergast (1859–1924)

Maurice Prendergast was born in Newfoundland and educated in Boston. He
studied in Paris at Julian's and at the Colarossi Academy. Prendergast started his
career as a letterer and show card painter, but painted pictures in his spare time.
He later returned to France, and travelled to Italy and England. In New York he
joined the group of independent artists known as the Eight. Prendergast's
colourful and modern style has been likened to the Post-Impressionists and his
subjects of people at play on the beach and in the park have universal appeal.
His work is held in leading collections throughout the USA, and his paintings
can sell for five- and six-figure sums.

▶ **Maurice B. Prendergast**
American (1859–1924)
Playtime at Salem Park,
Massachusetts
Signed, watercolour, pencil
and black chalk on paper
13¾ x 19½in (35 x 49.5cm)
£78,000–93,000
€114,000–136,000
$142,000–170,000 ⚒ S(NY)

Maurice B. Prendergast
American (1859–1924)
Park Scene
Signed and inscribed, oil on panel
14 x 15¾in (35.5 x 40cm)
£109,000–130,000 / €159,000–190,000
$198,000–237,000 ⚒ S(NY)

◀ **W. M. Prendergast**
American (19thC)
St Vincent, 1879
Titled, watercolour
and pencil
6¾ x 9¾in
(17 x 25cm)
£320–380
€470–560
$580–690 ⤴ GH

▶ **Adam Proctor, RBA**
British (1864–1913)
Turning the Hay
Signed, oil on canvas
9½ x 13½in (24 x 34.5cm)
£3,200–3,800 / €4,650–5,500
$5,800–6,900 ⤴ CGC

Patrick Procktor
British (b1936)
Sacré Coeur from the rue Montalembert
Oil on canvas
53½ x 36¼in (136 x 92cm)
£9,600–11,500 / €14,000–16,800
$17,500–21,000 ⤴ S

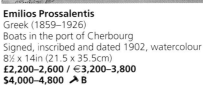

N. D. Prokofiev
Russian (19thC)
View of the River Neva
Signed and dated 1897, watercolour on paper
5¼ x 11¼in (13.5 x 28.5cm)
£2,600–3,100 / €3,800–4,500
$4,750–5,400 ⤴ S

Emilios Prossalentis
Greek (1859–1926)
Boats in the port of Cherbourg
Signed, inscribed and dated 1902, watercolour
8½ x 14in (21.5 x 35.5cm)
£2,200–2,600 / €3,200–3,800
$4,000–4,800 ⤴ B

◀ **Emilios Prossalentis**
Greek (1859–1926)
View of the Parthenon
Signed, watercolour on paper
9½ x 13¾in (24 x 35cm)
£2,700–3,200 / €3,950–4,700
$4,900–5,800 ⤴ B

▶ **James Proudfoot**
British (1908–71)
The Dentist
Signed and dated 1960,
oil on canvas
47½ x 35½in (120 x 90cm)
£420–500 / €610–730
$760–910 ⤴ BR

Margaret Fisher Prout
British (1875–1963)
In the Garden
Signed and dated 1953,
oil on board
22 x 17in (56 x 43cm)
£400–480 / €580–690
$730–870 ⚒ B(B)

Augustus Charles Pugin
French (1769–1832)
Hall of Queens College, Cambridge
Watercolour
7¾ x 10¼in (19.5 x 26cm)
£800–960 / €1,150–1,350
$1,450–1,700 ⚒ B(Kn)

A good provenance can make a huge
difference to the price of a picture.
Collectors like something new to
the market; a good picture that has
been in a family for generations will
fetch more than a picture that has
been in and out of auction houses.

Vicente Puig
Spanish (b1882)
The Masquerade
Signed and dated 1924,
oil on canvas
30¼ x 23¾in (77 x 60.5cm)
£1,600–1,900 / €2,350–2,800
$2,900–3,500 ⚒ B(Kn)

Hovsep Pushman (1877–1966)

Hovsep Pushman was born in Armenia and
studied in Istanbul and China before
emigrating to New York in 1911. He
specialized in atmospheric Oriental still lifes
and was highly regarded in his own lifetime.
Most of his exhibitions sold out within hours.

► **Hovsep Pushman**
Armenian/American
(1877–1966)
Peacock Feathers
Signed, oil on panel
34 x 25in (86.5 x 63.5cm)
£31,000–37,000
€45,000–54,000
$57,000–68,000 ⚒ S(NY)

◄ **Hovsep Pushman**
Armenian/American
(1877–1966)
Turkestan
Signed, oil on panel
25 x 23in
(63.5 x 58.5cm)
£33,000–39,000
€48,000–57,000
$60,000–72,000
⚒ S(NY)

◄ **Hovsep Pushman**
Armenian/American
(1877–1966)
When Autumn Comes
Signed, oil on panel
25 x 19¾in (63.5 x 50cm)
£28,400–34,000
€41,000–49,000
$51,000–61,000 ⚒ S(NY)

◀ **Michael Pybus**
British (b1954)
A Northerly, Whitby Sea Wall
Oil on board
8 x 11in (20.5 x 28cm)
£325–390 / €470–560
$590–700 ⊞ PY

◀ **For further information**
see Urban Art (pages 200–205)

▶ **Patrick Pye, RHA**
Irish (b1929)
Implements of the Passion
Signed, inscribed and dated
1967, tempera on panel
10 x 8in (25.5 x 20.5cm)
£650–780 / €950–1,100
$1,200–1,400 ⤴ WA

◀ **Patrick Pye, RHA**
Irish (b1929)
Agony in the Garden
Signed, inscribed and dated
1968, tempera on panel
24½ x 19in (62 x 48.5cm)
£680–810 / €1,000–1,200
$1,250–1,500 ⤴ WA

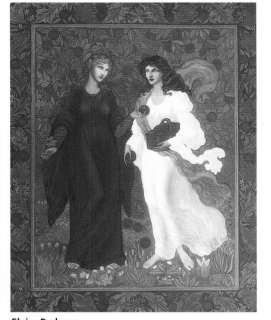

Charles Pyne
British (19thC)
Rabbits in a rural landscape
Signed, watercolour
21¼ x 29in (54 x 73.5cm)
£300–360 / €440–520
$550–660 ⤴ B(Kn)

James Baker Pyne
British (1800–70)
Arona
Inscribed, watercolour
14 x 9½in (35.5 x 24cm)
£500–600 / €730–870
$910–1,100 ⤴ B(Kn)

Elvira Pyrkova
Russian (b1970)
Homage to Burne-Jones
Oil
39 x 31in (99 x 78.5cm)
£2,150–2,400 / €3,150–3,500
$3,900–4,350 ⊞ Dr

◀ **Victor Noble Rainbird**
British (1889–1936)
Rouen Cathedral
Signed and titled, watercolour
9½ x 13½in
(24 x 34.5cm)
£200–240
€ **290–350**
$360–430 ⚺ FHF

▶ **Arnulf Rainer**
Austrian (b1929)
Van Gogh
Oil
23 x 18in
(58.5 x 45.5cm)
£6,900–8,200
€ **10,000–12,000**
$12,600–14,900
⚺ DORO

Mel Ramos
American (b1935)
Hamburger Girl
Signed and dated 1965,
numbered 478/500, print
19 x 14¾in (48.5 x 37.5cm)
£300–360 / € **440–520**
$500–600 ⚺ B(Kn)

Dennis Ramsay
Australian (b1925)
Madonna and Flowers
Signed, tempera on wood
16 x 12in (40.5 x 30.5cm)
£270–320 / € **390–470**
$490–590 ⚺ JAA

▶ **Sarah Raphael**
British (1960–2001)
That Place – Ios (I)
Oil on paper laid on canvas
60 x 48in (152.5 x 122cm)
£54,000–60,000 / € **79,000–88,000**
$98,000–109,000 ⊞ AGN
Dying tragically young, Sarah Raphael was one of the most promising
artists of her generation. Her work is very desirable and recently one
of her large canvases sold for £100,000 / € *146,000 / $182,000.*

◀ **John Rathbone**
British (1750–1807)
View of Rochester, Kent, with figures
Pen, ink and watercolour
11¼ x 16½in (28.5 x 42cm)
£750–900 / € **1,100–1,300**
$1,350–1,600 ⚺ DN

Konstantin Razumov
Russian (b1974)
Nude
Signed, oil on canvas
15 x 24in (38 x 61cm)
£1,400–1,650 / €2,050–2,400
$2,550–3,000 ⚒ JNic

Harold Hope Read, RBA, NS, PS
British (fl1940s)
A Busy Life
Watercolour
9 x 12in (23 x 30.5cm)
£1,100–1,250
€1,600–1,800
$2,000–2,250 ⊞ JN

Josef Rebell
Austrian (1787–1828)
Boats on Lake Como
Signed and dated 1810,
watercolour
11 x 16¼in (28 x 41.5cm)
£2,050–2,450 / €3,000–3,600
$3,700–4,450 ⚒ DORO

A. W. Redgate
British (fl1880–1906)
Hemmington, Leicestershire
Signed and inscribed
11¼ x 17½in (28.5 x 44.5cm)
£1,250–1,500
€1,850–2,200
$2,300–2,750 ⚒ AH

◄ **Paula Rego**
Portuguese (b1935)
Untitled
Signed and inscribed,
edition of 200, silkscreen
30½ x 22¼in (77.5 x 56.5cm)
£420–500 / €610–730
$760–910 ⚒ B

► **Polyklitos Regos**
Greek (1903–84)
Episkopi, Ano volos
Signed and dated 1935, oil on panel
15¾ x 15¼in (40 x 38.5cm)
£3,000–3,600 / €4,400–5,200
$5,500–6,600 ⚒ B

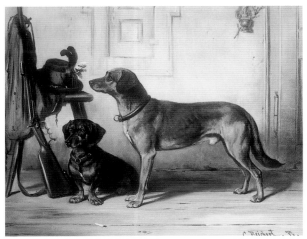

Carl Reichert
Austrian (1836–1918)
The Hunter's Companions
Signed and dated 1877, oil on canvas
16 x 20in (40.5 x 51cm)
£5,500–6,600 / € 8,000–9,600
$10,000–12,000 ⤳ DNY

Nano Reid
Irish (1900–81)
Where Oengus Óg Magnificently Dwells
Signed and inscribed, oil on board
24 x 30in (61 x 76cm)
£8,900–10,700 / € 13,000–15,600
$16,200–19,500 ⤳ WA

◄ **William Reid, Jnr**
Irish (fl1830s–40s)
View of the Giant's
Causeway, County
Antrim
Inscribed, watercolour
with scratching out
7¾ x 11in
(19.5 x 38cm)
£270–320
€ 400–480
$490–580 ⤳ WA

This painting, shown at the Irish Exhibition of Living Art in 1963, is a representative example of the themes and processes which typified the work of Nano Reid at the time. She is best known for her landscapes and, within the genre, she periodically made reference to pre-Christian themes, particularly those associated with the Boyne valley. The title of this painting refers to the traditional link in local folklore between Oengus Óg, a character in Celtic myth, and the megalithic burial site at Newgrange. The characteristic earthy tones and free, expressionistic handling of paint convey the tactile qualities of rich soil and lush growth, and provide the background to the focal point of the image: the entrance to the passage grave with its identifiable entrance stone carved in a swirling geometry and the aperture designed to permit a shaft of sunlight to enter the tomb at the winter solstice.

Frederic Remington (1861–1909)

Frederic Remington did not have a long life but he packed in many adventures. He is acknowledged to be the most important painter who documented the 'Wild West', which he experienced at first hand. He was a cowboy, ran a ranch and worked in a saloon bar and still had time to produce 25 bronzes (reproduced in multiple series), 3,000 paintings and drawings and eight books. He also travelled to North Africa, Russia, Germany, Mexico and Cuba as an artist correspondent.

Frederic Remington
American (1861–1909)
Pony War Dance
Signed, watercolour and gouache on paper
21 x 22¾in (53.5 x 58cm)
£146,000–175,000 € 213,000–256,000
$265,000–318,000 ⤳ S(NY)

◄ **Frederic Remington**
American (1861–1909)
Cowboy Fun in Old Mexico
Signed, oil on panel
18 x 28in (45.5 x 71cm)
£53,000–63,000 / € 77,000–92,000
$96,000–115,000 ⤳ S(NY)

Stephen J. Renard (b1947)

Stephen Renard started his career as a teacher of the sciences, supplementing his income by painting portraits and illustrating children's comics. In 1981 he bought a boat and his love affair with the sea began. He paints English and American sailing boats, some of which are made into posters. Original examples of his work are sought after by a loyal band of collectors, particularly in the USA, and the largest canvases command the highest prices.

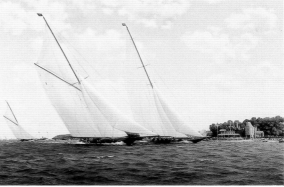

Stephen J. Renard
British (b1947)
Britannia & Shamrock V in the Solent off the Royal Yacht Squadron 1930
Oil on canvas
40 x 60in (101.5 x 152.5cm)
£36,000–40,000 / €52,000–58,000
$66,000–73,000 ⊞ **JS**

Stephen J. Renard
British (b1947)
Britannia, Lulworth and *White Heather* Racing off Norris Castle in the Solent
Oil on canvas
15 x 20in (38 x 51cm)
£4,500–5,000 / €6,600–7,300
$8,200–9,100 ⊞ **JS**

► **Stephen J. Renard**
British (b1947)
Britannia and *Westward* Racing in the Solent
Oil on canvas
30 x 40in (76 x 101.5cm)
£18,000–20,000 / €26,000–29,000
$33,000–37,000 ⊞ **JS**

◄ **Alan Reynolds**
British (b1926)
Nocturne, early October
Signed and dated 1955, watercolour heightened with white
19¾ x 24in (50 x 61cm)
£4,500–5,400
€6,600–7,900
$8,200–9,800 🔨 **B**

► **Alan Reynolds**
British (b1926)
Kentish Hopfield
Watercolour
14¾ x 10¾in (37.5 x 27.5cm)
£1,700–2,000
€2,500–2,900
$3,100–3,650 🔨 **B**

Joshua Reynolds, PRA
British (1723–1812)
Portrait of a gentleman
29¾ x 25in (75.5 x 63.5cm)
£12,000–14,400 / € 17,500–21,000
$22,000–26,000 ⚒ **B**

◄ **Ceri Richards**
British (1903–71)
Cathedrale Englouttie
Signed and dated 1960, oil on canvas
59½ x 24¼in (151 x 61.5cm)
£5,000–6,000 / € 7,300–8,700
$9,100–10,900 ⚒ **B**

Leon Richet
French (1847–1907)
Figure by a Pond
Signed, oil on panel
11½ x 16½in (29 x 42cm)
£800–960 / € 1,200–1,400
$1,450–1,750 ⚒ **Bea**

Philip Rickman
British (1891–1982)
Pheasants in the snow
Signed, gouache
21¼ x 29¾in (54 x 75.5cm)
£2,200–2,600 / € 3,200–3,800
$4,000–4,700 ⚒ **B(NW)**

Herbert Davis Richter, RI, ROI
British (1874–1955)
Room Interior with Still Life
Signed and dated 1943,
oil on canvas
30 x 25in (76 x 63.5cm)
£1,500–1,800 / € 2,200–2,600
$2,700–3,250 ⚒ **L&T**

► **John Ridgewell**
British (b1937)
Townscape with Aquaduct
Oil on canvas
34 x 43¾in (86.5 x 111cm)
£340–400 / € 490–580
$620–730 ⚒ **B(Kn)**

Ernest Higgins Rigg (1868–1947)

Ernest Higgins Rigg was born in Yorkshire and studied at the Bradford School of Art and the Académie Julian, Paris. On his return to England he became a member of the Staithes Group of Artists, painting portraits, animals, landscapes and coastal scenes.

◀ **Ernest Higgins Rigg**
British (1868–1947)
A Roadside Chat
Signed, oil on canvas
19¼ x 26½in
(49 x 67.5cm)
£960–1,150
€1,400–1,650
$1,750–2,100
🔨 B(L)

Ernest Higgins Rigg
British (1868–1947)
Feeding Time
Oil on canvas
13 x 19¾in (33 x 50cm)
£2,200–2,450 / €3,200–3,550
$4,000–4,450 ⊞ PY

▶ **Ernest Higgins Rigg**
British (1868–1947)
The Letter
Oil on canvas
17½ x 15¼in
(44.5 x 38.5cm)
£2,000–2,250
€2,900–3,300
$3,650–4,100 ⊞ PY

Edith Rimmington
British (b1902)
Still Life with Fish
Signed and inscribed, oil on canvas
30 x 39¾in (76 x 101cm)
£1,500–1,800 / €2,200–2,600
$2,700–3,250 🔨 B(Kn)

▶ **Eduard Ritter**
German (1820–92)
Interior of a
Living room
Signed and dated
1846, oil on canvas
15¾ x 19¾in
(40 x 50cm)
£20,000–24,000
€29,000–35,000
$36,000–43,000
🔨 S(NY)

Diego Rivera (1886–1957)

Diego Rivera's life was as colourful as his paintings and murals. He was a showman who had audiences enraptured when he described his art. As a child he spent his time in the company of prostitutes and he was a legendary womanizer. Rivera supported the Communists in Russia, and he depicted the revolutionaries Lenin and Trotsky in a mural in Mexico City. He shared his beliefs with his wife Frida Kahlo, a heroine of the singer Madonna.

◄ **Diego Rivera**
Mexican
(1886–1957)
Choza
Signed, watercolour and charcoal
on paper
4¼ x 7in (11 x 18cm)
£4,450–5,300
€ **6,500–7,700**
$8,100–9,600
⚒ LCM

◄ **Diego Rivera**
Mexican
(1886–1957)
Indian taking a Siesta
Signed, watercolour
on paper
9¼ x 5½in
(23.5 x 14cm)
£4,200–5,000
€ **6,100–7,300**
$7,600–9,100
⚒ LCM

Diego Rivera
Mexician (1886–1957)
Revolutionary Scene
Signed, ink on paper
12¼ x 9½in (31 x 24cm)
£3,500–4,200 / € **5,100–6,100**
$6,400–7,600 ⚒ LCM

Diego Rivera
Mexican (1886–1957)
Stonecutter
Signed, charcoal on rice paper
9½ x 7in (24 x 18cm)
£3,000–3,600
€ **4,400–5,200**
$5,500–6,600 ⚒ LCM

Hugh Goldwin Riviere
British (1869–1956)
Portrait of Rosalind Monica Wagner
Signed and dated 1931, oil on canvas
49¼ x 39⅜in (125 x 100cm)
£3,400–4,100 / € **5,000–6,000**
$6,200–7,500 ⚒ B(Kn)

William George Robb
British (1872–1940)
Frisking Light in Frolick
Oil on canvas
19¾ x 23¾in (50 x 60.5cm)
£2,400–2,900 / € **3,500–4,200**
$4,400–5,300 ⚒ RTo

Landscape views of beautiful and famous places are always more valuable. Portraits of well-known figures fetch more than portraits of unknowns.

Edwin Thomas Roberts
British (1840–1917)
Flirting
Signed, oil on canvas
16¼ x 12¼in (41.5 x 31cm)
£6,300–7,000 / € **9,200–10,200**
$11,500–12,800 ⊞ HFA

Will Roberts
British (b1910)
Man in Red
Signed with initials, oil on board
8½ x 10¼in (21.5 x 26cm)
£1,050–1,250 / €1,550–1,850
$1,900–2,250 ↗ S(O)

Charles Robertson, RWS
British (1844–91)
The Signal Station, Dover, Kent
Signed, watercolour
7 x 10½in (18 x 26.5cm)
£2,500–3,000 / €3,650–4,400
$4,550–5,500 ↗ HN

◀ **Jonathan Robertson**
Scottish (b1947)
The Gleaners
Oil on canvas
22 x 20in (56 x 51cm)
£1,700–1,900 / €2,500–2,750
$3,100–3,450 ⊞ CFAG

▶ **Saul Robertson**
Scottish (20thC)
On a Summer Evening
Oil on board
9 x 7in (23 x 18cm)
£720–800 / €1,050–1,200
$1,300–1,450 ⊞ CFAG

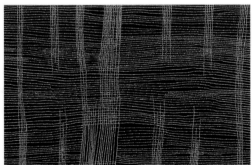

Dorothy Napangardi Robinson
Australian (b1956)
Salt Crystals of Mina Mina
Inscribed, synthetic polymer paint on linen
54 x 84in (137 x 213.5cm)
£24,000–29,000 / €35,000–42,000
$44,000–53,000 ↗ SHSY

Markey Robinson
Irish (1918–99)
The Avenue
Signed, oil on board
24 x 32in (61 x 81.5cm)
£6,700–8,100 / €9,800–11,800
$12,200–14,700 ↗ WA

Michel Rodde
French (b1913)
Coastal Scene
Signed, oil on canvas
21½ x 18in (54.5 x 45.5cm)
£380–450 / €550–660
$690–820 ↗ JAA

Patsy Dan Rodgers
Irish (b1945)
Gale Force Nine,
Tory Island
Signed and inscribed,
oil on board
18 x 23½in
(45.5 x 59.5cm)
£1,150–1,350
€1,700–2,000
$2,100–2,450 ↗ WA

◄ **Fred Roe**
British (1864–1947)
The Ghost Story
Signed and dated
1898, oil on canvas
18 x 24in
(45.5 x 61cm)
£11,700–13,000
€17,100–19,000
$21,000–24,000
⊞ HFA

Walter Roessler
Russian (19th/20thC)
A Discerning Chap
Signed, oil on panel
7 x 5¼in (18 x 13.5cm)
£4,500–5,000 / €6,600–7,300
$8,200–9,100 ⊞ HFA

B. H. Rogers
British (20thC)
Keeping watch over the cradle
Signed, watercolour and bodycolour
14¾ x 19¾in (37.5 x 50cm)
£250–300 / €370–440
$460–550 ↗ B(Kn)

Georgios N. Roilos
Greek (1867–1928)
Portrait of a gentleman
Signed, oil on canvas
26 x 23½in (66 x 59.5cm)
£2,800–3,350 / €4,100–4,900
$5,100–6,100 ↗ B

Georgios N. Roilos
Greek (1867–1928)
Coastal landscape with pine trees
Signed, oil on board
8 x 14in (20.5 x 35.5cm)
£900–1,050 / €1,300–1,550
$1,600–1,900 ↗ B

◄ **George Romney**
British (1734–1802)
Studies of a young woman
Pen and ink
6¼ x 8in (16 x 20.5cm)
£300–360 / €440–520
$550–660 ✦ GH

► **Marcel Ronay**
German (b1910)
Lady in Boots
Ink and wash
11 x 7in (28 x 18cm)
£360–400 / €520–580
$660–730 ⊞ JDG

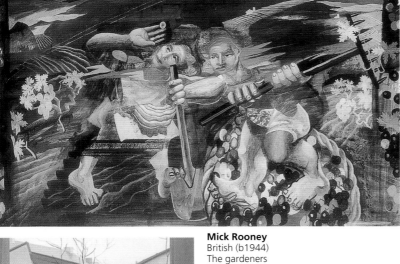

Mick Rooney
British (b1944)
The gardeners
Acrylic and watercolour
30¾ x 50in (78 x 127cm)
£3,800–4,550 / €5,500–6,600
$6,900–8,300 ✦ B

Johann Heinrich Roos
German (1631–85)
Resting rider with his dog in the
Roman Campagna
Oil on canvas
12 x 15½in (30.5 x 39.5cm)
£6,200–7,400 / €9,000–10,800
$11,300–13,500 ✦ DORO

◄ **Carlo de Roover**
Belgian (1900–86)
Portrait
Signed, titled and
dated 1941,
oil on canvas
39½ x 23¾in
(100.5 x 59.5cm)
£310–370
€450–540
$560–670 ✦ BERN

► **Carlo de Roover**
Belgian (1900–86)
Orpheus
Signed and dated
1964, oil on canvas
41¼ x 31½in
(105 x 80cm)
£95–110
€140–165
$170–200 ✦ BERN

◄ **Charles Rosenberg**
British (fl1844–48)
South West View of St Nicholas Church,
Lower Tooting, Surrey
Aquatint with hand colouring
18½ x 21in (47 x 53.5cm)
£210–250 / € 310–370
$380–450 ⚹ BBA

◄ **Lucius Rossi**
Italian (1846–1913)
Portrait of a girl wearing a
feathered hat
Signed, oil on panel
14¼ x 10½in (36 x 26.5cm)
£1,500–1,800 / € 2,200–2,600
$2,700–3,200 ⚹ B(Kn)

Percival Leonard Rosseau
American (1859–1937)
Master's Sons
Signed and dated 1913, oil on canvas
26 x 32in (66 x 81.5cm)
£45,000–54,000 / € 66,000–79,000
$81,000–97,000 ⚹ S(NY)

► **Charles Rossiter**
British (b1827)
Sewing by Daylight
Signed, oil on canvas
10 x 8in (25.5 x 20.5cm)
£6,300–7,000 / € 9,200–10,200
$11,500–12,800 ⊞ HFA

◄ **Michael Rothenstein**
British (1908–93)
Aberayron
Signed and inscribed, linocut
17 x 24¼in (43 x 61.5cm)
£300–360 / € 440–520
$550–660 ⚹ B

Franz Alexeevich Roubaud
Russian (1856–1928)
Cossack leading his horse
Signed and dated 1915, oil on canvas
13¾ x 25½in (35 x 65cm)
**£9,000–10,800 / €13,100–15,700
$16,400–19,600** ⚒ S

Gaston Roullet
French (1847–1925)
Barges on a Dutch Canal
Signed and inscribed, oil on canvas
15¼ x 21½in (38.5 x 54.5cm)
**£1,500–1,800 / €2,200–2,600
$2,700–3,200** ⚒ B(Kn)

◄ **Theodore Rousseau**
French (1812–67)
Lakeside
Signed, pastel
6½ x 8¼in
(16.5 x 21cm)
**£5,800–7,000
€8,500–10,200
$10,500–12,700**
⚒ L&T

Theodore Roussel
French/British (1847–1926)
The Snow, My Front Garden,
March 2nd 1909
Signed, edition of 40, softground
etching and aquatint
9 x 7in (23 x 18cm)
**£320–380 / €470–550
$580–690** ⚒ B

Tom Rowden
British (1842–1926)
Highland cattle by a stream
Signed, watercolour heightened
with bodycolour
7 x 18¼in (18 x 46.5cm)
**£500–600 / €730–870
$910–1,100** ⚒ CHTR

► **Thomas Rowlandson**
British (1756–1827)
St James's Courtship; St Giles's Courtship
A pair, 1799, etchings
12¾ x 10¼in (32.5 x 26cm)
**£700–840 / €1,000–1,200
$1,300–1,550** ⚒ B

Herbert Royle (1870–1958)

Henry Royle was born in Manchester and trained at the Harris Institute, Preston and School of Art, Southport. He was a member of the Manchester Academy of Fine Arts, the Liverpool Academy of Art and the Sandon Studios Society. Royle exhibited in London from 1893, including the Royal Academy, and at the Liverpool Autumn Exhibition.

Herbert Royle
British (1870–1958)
Farmyard scene
Signed, oil on board
19 x 23¼in (48.5 x 59cm)
**£2,800–3,350 / € 4,100–4,900
$5,100–6,100** ↗ AH

Herbert Royle
British (1870–1958)
On the Nevern, Pembrokeshire
Signed, oil
15½ x 23½in (29 x 59.5cm)
**£3,000–3,600 / € 4,400–5,200
$5,500–6,600** ↗ AH

► **Herbert Royle**
British (1870–1958)
Cattle Watering at Bolton Abbey
Signed, oil
11½ x 15½in (29 x 39.5cm)
**£7,700–9,200 / € 11,200–13,400
$14,000–16,700** ↗ AH
This painting was given to the vendor's father, a tailor in Addingham, in payment for a tweed suit.

Carl Rungus
American (1869–1959)
Moose in the Woods
Signed and inscribed, oil on canvas
24 x 32in (61 x 81.5cm)
**£53,000–63,000 / € 77,000–92,000
$96,000–115,000** ↗ S(NY)

George Russell (AE)
Irish (1867–1935)
Two girls by the shore
Signed, oil on canvas
20 x 26in (51 x 66cm)
**£15,100–17,800 / € 22,000–26,000
$28,000–33,000** ↗ WA

Thomas Ryan, PPRHA
Irish (b1929)
Still life with apples
Signed, oil on board
14½ x 18½in (37 x 47cm)
£2,050–2,450 / €3,000–3,600
$3,750–4,450 ✗ WA

Thomas Ryan, PPRHA
Irish (b1929)
Edge of Wood, Mornington, County Meath
Signed and inscribed, oil on canvas board
17½ x 13½in (44.5 x 34.5cm)
£1,500–1,800 / €2,200–2,600
$2,700–3,250 ✗ WA

Dey de Rybcowsky
Bulgarian (1880–1936)
Sunrise
Oil on canvas
24 x 40in (61 x 101.5cm)
£960–750 / €1,400–1,650
$1,750–2,100 ✗ DORO

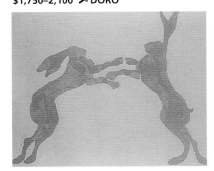

Sophie Ryder
British (b1963)
Boxing Hares
Signed and numbered 53/70, screenprint
30¾ x 40½in (78 x 103cm)
£700–840 / €1,000–1,200
$1,250–1,500 ✗ B(Kn)

Susan Ryder
British (b1944)
Interior Scene with Yellow Armchair
Signed, oil on board
23¾ x 17¾in (60.5 x 45cm)
£650–780 / €950–1,150
$1,200–1,400 ✗ B(Kn)

Jenny Ryrie
British (20thC)
Falls
Watercolour on paper
21 x 24in (53.5 x 61cm)
£810–900 / €1,150–1,300
$1,500–1,650 ⊞ BRID

Using the fluidity and translucency of water-based media, Jenny Ryrie explores the energy of the landscape, especially the life-generating force of light, and symbolizes light, water and life to help explore the mystical dimensions of the natural world.

◀ **Yrjö Saarinen**
Finnish (1899–1958)
Riku Sarkola
Signed, oil on canvas
25½ x 2¼in
(65 x 54cm)
£1,600–1,900
€2,300–2,750
$2,900–3,500
⚒ **BUK**

▶ **Richard St Clair**
American (b1943)
Bike show
Signed, oil on line
18 x 15in
(45.5 x 38cm)
£2,200–2,450
€3,200–3,550
$4,000–4,400
⊞ **GALG**

Prices for works by well-known artists depend on condition and the period in which they were painted. Work from certain periods of an artist's life is often acknowledged to be better than that from another. Paintings in good condition always achieve higher prices.

Kikuo Saito
Japanese (b1939)
Untitled
Acrylic on canvas
18 x 200in (45.5 x 508cm)
£630–740 / €920–1,100
$1,150–1,350 ⚒ **LHA**

Sofia Saklikovskaya
Russian (1899–1975)
Country village scene; from the series Old and New Ways of Life
Signed, watercolour, pencil and ink on paper
17½ x 15¾in (44.5 x 40cm)
£7,200–8,600 / €10,500–12,500
$13,100–15,600 ⚒ **S**

Sofia Saklikovskaya
Russian (1899–1975)
A reveling table; from the series Old and New Ways of Life
Signed, watercolour, pencil and ink on paper
15¾ x 11¾in (40 x 30cm)
£6,000–7,200 / €8,700–10,500
$10,900–13,100 ⚒ **S**

Rémi Salin
French (b1954)
The Colourer of Nightmares
Oil on canvas
24 x 15in (61 x 38cm)
£1,250–1,400 / €1,800–2,050
$2,250–2,500 ⊞ **GALG**

Max Salmi
Finnish (1931–95)
On the beach
Signed, oil
15¾in (40cm) square
£1,450–1,700 / € 2,100–2,500
$2,650–3,100 ↗ BUK

Santeri Salokivi
Finnish (1886–1940)
View from the mountains, Åland
Oil on canvas
18½ x 22in (47 x 56cm)
£9,900–11,900 / € 14,500–17,400
$18,000–21,600 ↗ BUK

Santeri Salokivi
Finnish (1886–1940)
Summer's day on the beach
Signed, oil on board
8½ x 12¼in (21.5 x 31cm)
£7,200–8,600 / € 10,500–12,600
$13,100–15,600 ↗ BUK

Frederick Sands
British (1820–1904)
East Coast Scene
Signed, watercolour
15¾ x 23¾in (40 x 60.5cm)
£1,200–1,450
€ 1,750–2,100
$2,200–2,600 ↗ B&L

◄ **Birger Sandzen**
American (1871–1954)
Landscape
Signed and dated 1919,
oil on canvas
24 x 34in (61 x 86.5cm)
£36,000–43,000
€ 53,000–63,000
$66,000–79,000 ↗ S(NY)

Birger Sandzen
American (1871–1954)
At River's Edge
Oil on panel
20 x 24in (51 x 61cm)
£17,000–20,000 / € 25,000–29,000
$30,000–35,000 ↗ S(NY)

◄ **Rubens Santoro**
Italian (1859–1942)
A woman carrying
water beside a
Venetian canal
Signed, oil on canvas
15¾ x 11¼in
(40 x 28.5cm)
£35,000–42,000
€ **51,000–61,000**
$64,000–76,000 ↗ B

Paul Turner Sargent
American (1880–1946)
River Landscape
Oil on canvas
10 x 13in (25.5 x 33cm)
£360–430 / € **530–630**
$650–780 ↗ TREA

Paul Turner Sargent
American (1880–1946)
Wildflowers
Oil on canvas
10 x 13in (25.5 x 33cm)
£360–430 / € **530–630**
$650–780 ↗ TREA

Takezo Sato
Japanese
(1891–1972)
A Devon Shore
Signed, watercolour
13 x 17in
(33 x 43cm)
£550–660
€ **800–960**
$1,000–1,200 ↗ B

◄ **Attributed to
Hattie Saussy**
American
(1890–1978)
Quiet Waters
Inscribed and titled,
oil on canvas board
12 x 16in
(30.5 x 40.5cm)
£630–750
€ **910–1,100**
$1,150–1,350 ↗ JAA

Georgy Savitsky
Russian (1887–1949)
Meeting at the Masquerade
Signed, 1917, mixed media
9¼ x 10in (23.5 x 25.5cm)
£620–720 / € **900–1,050**
$1,100–1,300 ↗ BUK

Henry Thomas Schäfer
British (1873–1915)
A Reclining Pose
Signed and dated 1879, oil on canvas
19 x 31in (48.5 x 78.5cm)
£17,900–19,900 / €26,000–29,000
$32,000–36,000 ⊞ HFA

◄ **Richard Schmid**
American (b1934)
Nude
Signed, inscribed and dated 1963,
oil on masonite
15½ x 11½in (39.5 x 29cm)
£3,100–3,750 / €4,500–5,400
$5,700–6,800 ⚒ JAA

Petrus van Schendel
Belgian (1806–70)
Whilst Baby Sleeps
Signed and dated 1836, oil on canvas
23 x 18in (58.5 x 45.5cm)
£67,000–74,000 / €98,000–108,000
$122,000–135,000 ⊞ HFA

Petrus van Schendel is a master of the night
scene and inspired Atkinson Grimshaw and
Whistler. He painted on board and during
his lifetime he was considered to be avante-
garde. His large street scenes can fetch
around £500,000 / €730,000 / $910,000 if
in good condition. Condition is important
because paint on board can crack

► **Richard Schmid**
American (b1934)
Manhattan Street Scene Near Penn Station
Signed, inscribed and dated 1964, oil on masonite
12 x 20in (30.5 x 51cm)
£2,250–2,700 / €3,250–3,900
$4,150–4,950 ⚒ JAA

Kershaw Schofield
British (fl1900–38)
River Meadow with Cattle Grazing
Signed, oil
18½ x 23½in (47 x 59.5cm)
£360–430 / €520–620
$660–780 ⚒ AH

► **Rodolphe**
Schönberg
Belgian (20thC)
Sandbank
Signed and dated
1923, oil on canvas
23¾ x 31½in
(60.5 x 80cm)
£310–370
€450–540
$560–670 ⚒ BERN

George F. Schultz
American (1869–1934)
Rocky Cove – Monhegan Island
Signed, oil on canvas
24 x 32in (61 x 81.5cm)
£310–370 / €450–540
$570–680 ⚒ JAA

Henri Schouten
Belgian (1857–1927)
A turkey; A cockerel
A pair, signed, oil on canvas
39¼ x 32in (99.5 x 81.5cm)
£6,700–7,400 / €9,100–10,800
$11,300–13,500 ⚒ B

Joannes Frederick Schutz
Dutch (1817–88)
Dutch small craft and a brig drying their sails in a calm
Signed and dated 1878, oil on canvas
27½ x 41½in (70 x 105.5cm)
£8,500–10,200 / €12,400–15,000
$15,500–18,600 ⚒ B

Claude Schurr
French (b1921)
Harbour Scene
Signed, oil on canvas
21½ x 18in (54.5 x 45.5cm)
£340–400 / €490–580
$630–750 ⚒ JAA

◄ **Tom Scott, RSA**
British (1854–1927)
The Border
Widow's Lament
Signed, inscribed
and dated 1901,
watercolour and
scratching out
25 x 31in
(63.5 x 78.5cm)
£11,000–13,200
€16,100–19,300
$20,000–24,000
⚒ B(Ed)

William Scott, RA
British (1913–89)
Street scene, Ruabon
Signed and dated 1944, watercolour
9¼ x 13¼in (23.5 x 33.5cm)
£2,800–3,350 / €4,100–4,900
$5,100–6,100 ⚒ B

Glen Scouller
Scottish (b1950)
Fishing Boats, Hastings
Signed, watercolour
6 x 8½in (15 x 21.5cm)
£630–700 / € 920–1,050
$1,150–1,300 ⊞ WrG
Glen Scouller was born in Glasgow and studied at the Glasgow School of Art, where he later taught. He was elected to the Royal Glasgow Institute of Fine Arts in 1989 and has exhibited widely, both in mixed and one-man shows.

Sean Scully
Irish (b1945)
Enter 6
Set of six, plate six signed and numbered 37/40,
1993, aquatints
17¾ x 13½in (45 x 34.5cm)
£7,000–8,400 / € 10,200–12,300
$12,700–15,300 ⤴ B

▶ **Elliot Seabrooke**
British (1886–1950)
Summer Landscape
Signed and dated
1943, oil on canvas
20 x 24in (51 x 61cm)
£600–720
€ 880–1,050
$1,100–1,300
⤴ B(Kn)

Gaston Sebire
French (b1920)
Seaside
Signed, oil on canvas
10 x 14in (25.5 x 35.5cm)
£470–550 / € 680–890
$860–1,000 ⤴ JAA

**Alexander Borisovich
Serebriakov**
Russian (1907–95)
Grand drawing room interior
Signed, watercolour on paper
24¼ x 18½in (61.5 x 47cm)
£10,200–12,200
€ 14,900–17,800
$18,600–22,200 ⤴ S

Jean Pierre Serrier
French (1934–89)
Solitude en commun
Signed, inscribed and dated 1966, oil on canvas
29 x 36in (73.5 x 91.5cm)
**£720–860 / € 1,050–1,250
$1,300–1,550** ➚ WW

► **Duncan Shanks, ARSA**
Scottish (b1937)
Shower over the Clyde Valley
Signed, inscribed and dated 1978, oil on canvas
60 x 48in (152.5 x 122cm)
**£3,700–4,400 / € 5,400–6,400
$6,700–8,000** ➚ TEN
*This painting was exhibited at the Royal Scottish
Academy in 1979.*

Dorothea Sharp (1874–1955)

Dorothea Sharp painted the pleasant things in life such as flowers
and children playing on the beach in the sunshine. Although some
people consider her beach scenes not to be as good as her flower
paintings, her work saw renewed popularity in the 1980s with the
publishing of her small monograph *Painting in Oils*, and she is still
popular today. Her paintings are held in many public collections
in Britain and she has been called an English Impressionist.

The difference in size of the two paintings shown here is reflected
by the prices achieved at auction.

Dorothea Sharp
British (1874–1955)
Children playing in the sea
Signed, oil on panel
12½ x 16in (32 x 40.5cm)
**£4,500–5,400 / € 6,600–7,900
$8,200–9,800** ➚ B

◄ **Dorothea Sharp**
British (1874–1955)
Gathering daisies
Signed, oil on canvas
20 x 24in (51 x 61cm)
**£18,000–21,000 / € 26,000–30,000
$33,000–38,000** ➚ B

Joseph Henry Sharp
American (1859–1953)
Chief Washakie
Signed, oil on canvas
18 x 12in (45.5 x 30.5cm)
£49,000–59,000 / €72,000–86,000
$90,000–108,000 ♣ S(NY)

Ellen Sharples
British (1769–1849)
Portrait of John Claremont Whiteman
Pastel
9 x 8¼in (23 x 21cm)
£1,650–1,950 / €2,400–2,850
$3,000–3,550 ♣ S

Clare E. Shaw
American (1866–1951)
California Spring Landscape with Figures
Signed, oil on canvas board
11¼ x 14½in (28.5 x 37cm)
£280–330 / €410–490
$510–610 ♣ JAA

Ernest Howard Shepard
British (1876–1976)
Pooh singing on a stepping stone
Inscribed, pen, ink and watercolour
8in (20.5cm) square
£18,000–21,000 / €26,000–30,000
$33,000–38,000 ♣ B

◄ **Ernest Howard Shepard**
British (1876–1976)
Piglet digging a hole
Inscribed, pen, ink and watercolour
2¼ x 2¾in (5.5 x 7cm)
£6,500–7,800 / €9,500–11,400
$11,800–14,200 ♣ B

Brian Shields (Braaq)
British (1951–97)
An Industrial Street Scene
Signed, inscribed and dated 1976,
oil on board
23½ x 17¼in (59.5 x 44cm)
£1,350–1,600 / €1,950–2,350
$2,450–2,900 ♣ B(L)

◄ **John Shinnors**
Irish (b1950)
Female still life
calendar, April
Signed, oil on canvas
24in (61cm) square
£7,500–9,000
€ 11,000–13,600
$13,200–16,400
⚒ WA

► **Frederick
Golden Short**
British (1863–1936)
A river landscape in
a forest
Signed, oil on panel
6 x 8in (15 x 20.5cm)
£240–290
€ 350–420
$440–520 ⚒ WW

◄ **David Shrigley**
British (b1968)
Untitled (Do not flinch)
Marker on cardboard
10¾ x 8½in
(27.5 x 21.5cm)
£620–690
€ 900–1,000
$1,100–1,250
⊞ GNW

► **David Shrigley**
British (b1968)
Untitled (Milk)
Acrylic, poster
colour on paper
16¾ x 18½in
(42.5 x 47cm)
£860–960
€ 1,250–1,400
$1,550–1,750
⊞ GNW

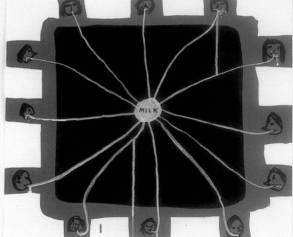

Adolph R. Shulz
American (1869–1963)
Autumn Landscape
Oil on canvas laid down on board
6½ x 9¾in (16.5 x 25cm)
£230–270 / € 330–390
$420–500 ⚒ TREA

► **Adolph R. Shulz**
American
(1869–1963)
Jackson's Branch
Signed, etching
9 x 6in (23 x 15cm)
£180–210
€ 260–310
$320–380 ⚒ TREA

◀ **Alberta Rehm Schulz**
American (b1892)
Clear Creek
Train Station
Signed, drawing
11 x 13½in
(28 x 34.5cm)
£190–230
€280–330
$350–420 ⌁ TREA

▶ **Walter Richard Sickert, RA**
British (1860–1942)
Bust portrait of a lady
Signed, oil on canvas
20 x 16in (51 x 40.5cm)
£4,500–5,400
€6,600–7,900
$8,200–9,800 ⌁ B

◀ **Richard Simkin**
British (1840–1926)
Band of the Royal
Welsh Fusiliers (23rd)
Signed, watercolour
8½ x 14½in
(21.5 x 37cm)
£380–450
€550–650
$690–820 ⌁ WW

Walter Richard Sickert, RA
British (1860–1942)
Reclining nude
Signed, oil on canvas
14¾ x 18in (37.5 x 45.5cm)
£24,000–29,000 / €35,000–42,000
$44,000–53,000 ⌁ B

Simon Simonsen
Danish (1841–1928)
A dispute
Signed, oil on canvas
20½ x 27½in (52 x 70cm)
£2,050–2,400 / €3,000–3,500
$3,700–4,400 ⌁ DNY

◀ **Charles Simpson**
British (b1952)
Dark & Light
Signed, oil on board
30 x 36in (76 x 91.5cm)
£3,400–3,800 / €5,000–5,500
$6,200–6,900 ⊞ P&H

If possible, it is advisable to sell a landscape in a gallery or auction house that is near to the place depicted in the picture – it will have a greater chance of achieving a good price. However, this does not apply to works by famous artists: you will get better results in a larger city as there will be a considerably higher number of potential buyers.

Wilho Sjöström
Finnish (1873–1944)
View over the lake
Signed, oil
25¾ x 21¾in (65.5 x 55.5cm)
£1,250–1,500 / €1,800–2,150
$2,300–2,750 ↗ BUK

John Rattenbury Skeaping, RA
British (1901–80)
Greyhound
Signed and dated, pencil and
coloured chalks
12 x 22½in (48.5 x 57cm)
£1,750–2,100 / €2,550–3,050
$3,200–3,800 ↗ DNY

◄ **John Falconar
Slater**
British (1857–1937)
A garden scene
with lupins and
other flowers in
the foreground,
cold frames and
trees beyond
Signed, oil on board
24 x 36in
(61 x 91.5cm)
£3,100–3,700
€4,500–5,400
$5,600–6,700
↗ TEN

A. A. Slusser
American (19thC)
Portrait of a Lion
Signed and inscribed, ink on paper
20 x 27in (51 x 68.5cm)
£320–380 / €460–550
$590–700 ↗ LHA

► **Gustave de Smet**
Belgian (1877–1943)
Garden at Laethem-Saint-Martin
Oil on canvas
12½ x 17½in (32 x 44.5cm)
£18,000–20,000 / €26,000–29,000
$33,000–37,000 ⊞ WoF

*Gustave de Smet studied at the Académie des Beaux-Arts in Ghent
from 1889 to 1896. In 1901 he, his brother Leon de Smet, Frits van
den Berghe and Constant Permeke settled in Laethem-Saint-Martin
where they founded the Second Laethem Group, drawing their
inspiration from the rural surroundings of the river Leie. In 1911 he
moved to Ghent and, on the outbreak of WWI, to the Netherlands
where he joined up again with Frits van den Berghe. His early work is
Impressionist in style, influenced by the work of Emile Claus. Through
contacts with modern Dutch painters such as Jan Sluyters and the
Frenchman Henri le Fauconnier, he came into contact with German
Expressionism and Cubism. After the war he returned to Belgium
where he forged a reputation as one of the country's most important
Expressionist artists.*

◄ **David Smith**
Scottish (b1957)
Fishing Boats and Cornfields
Acrylic and mixed media
31½in (80cm) square
£2,250–2,500 / €3,300–3,650
$4,100–4,600 ⊞ WrG

► **Dorothea Smith**
British (20thC)
Portrait of a gentleman
Signed, oil on canvas
24 x 20in (61 x 51cm)
£150–180 / €220–260
$270–320 ⋌ WW

G. R. Smith
British (fl1847–73)
Cowes
Signed, inscribed and dated 1866, watercolour heightened with white
6½ x 9¼in (16.5 x 23.5cm)
£1,400–1,650 / €2,050–2,400
$2,550–3,000 ⋌ B
*This mid-Victorian view of the waterfront at Cowes includes the Royal
Yacht Squadron's headquarters at the Castle, before the extensive
redevelopment resulting from the Prince of Wales's (later King
Edward VII's) enthusiastic patronage of the annual regatta week.*

James Burrell Smith
British (1822–97)
Alnwick
Signed, titled and dated 1856, watercolour heightened with white
10½ x 16½in (26.5 x 42cm)
£2,900–3,450 / €4,250–5,000
$5,300–6,300 ⋌ HN

James Burrell Smith
British (1822–97)
Rushing Waters
Signed and dated 1884, oil on canvas
15½ x 20in (39.5 x 51cm)
£6,100–6,800 / €8,900–9,900
$11,100–12,400 ⊞ HFA

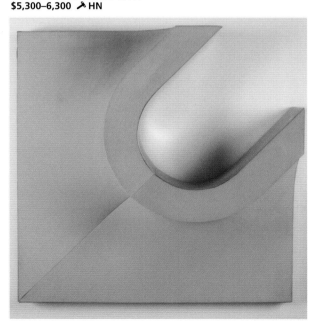

► **Richard Smith**
British (b1931)
You Was Never
Lovlier
Acrylic on canvas
construction
36in (89cm) square
£1,550–1,800
€2,250–2,650
$2,800–3,300
⋌ LHA

Han Snel
Dutch (1928–98)
Two Balinese women
Signed and dated 1989, oil on canvas
19¾ x 23½in (50 x 59.5cm)
£3,500–4,200 / €5,100–6,100
$6,400–7,600 ⚒ S(SI)

Orlando Sobalvarro
Nicaraguan (b1943)
The Circensians
Oil on canvas
45 x 70¼in (114.5 x 178.5cm)
£370–440 / €540–640
$670–800 ⚒ LCM

Henri Somm
French (1844–1907)
Elegant on the beach in the wind
Signed and dated 1883, watercolour
12 x 7in (30.5 x 18cm)
£2,100–2,500 / €3,100–3,650
$3,800–4,550 ⚒ B

Charles Spencelayh, RMS, HRBSA
British (1865–1958)
Happy Memories
Signed and inscribed, oil on panel
9¾ x 7¾in (25 x 19.5cm)
£62,000–74,000
€91,000–108,000
$113,000–135,000 ⚒ B

Charles Spencelayh started out as a miniaturist, hence his talent for fine detail, and he often painted on ivory to achieve the quality he required. His subject matter was usually interior scenes in which a grandfatherly figure is surrounded by clutter: those with the most clutter and the more appealing central male character achieve the highest prices. Collectors have been known to pay up to £300,000 / €438,000 / $546,000 for a finely detailed example of this work.

► **Vera Spencer**
British (b1926)
Awaiting the Connection, Ruabon
Signed and inscribed, watercolour
14½ x 19in (37 x 48.5cm)
£200–240 / €290–350
$360–430 ⚒ B(Kn)

Charles Spencelayh, RMS, HRBSA
British (1865–1958)
In the Bluebell Wood
Signed, oil on canvas
15 x 12in (38 x 30.5cm)
£10,700–11,900 / €15,600–17,400
$19,500–22,000 ⊞ HFA

Georges Spiro
Italian (1909–94)
The Tree of Life
Signed, oil on canvas
24¾ x 19¾in (63 x 50cm)
£1,550–1,850 / €2,250–2,700
$2,800–3,350 ⚲ BUK

Jan Jacob Spohler
Dutch (1811–66)
Summer Landscape, Holland
Signed, oil on canvas
17 x 24½in (43 x 62cm)
£17,000–18,500 / €24,000–27,000
$30,000–33,000 ⊞ BuP

Stuart Stanley
British (20thC)
Evening Friday Street
Oil on canvas
16 x 30in (40.5 x 76cm)
£360–400 / €520–580
$660–730 ⊞ ST

Arthur Spooner
British (1873–1962)
St Malo
Signed, oil on board
11¾ x 15½in (30 x 39.5cm)
£260–310 / €380–450
$470–560 ⚲ CGC

▶ **Stuart Stanley**
British (20thC)
Beachy Head II
Acrylic on paper
23½ x 15½in (59.5 x 42cm)
£310–350 / €450–510
$560–640 ⊞ ST

▶ **James Stark**
British (1794–1859)
The Woodland Shoot
Signed, oil on canvas
12 x 9in (30.5 x 23cm)
£6,300–7,000
€9,200–10,200
$11,500–12,800
⊞ HFA

Hans Staudacher
Swiss (b1923)
Untitled
Signed, watercolour on paper
20½ x 14¼in (52 x 36cm)
£1,350–1,600 / €2,000–2,400
$2,450–2,900 ↗ DORO

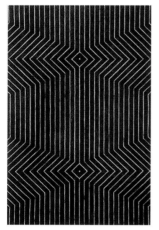

◄ Frank Stella
American (b1936)
Gavotte
Signed and dated 1967,
numbered 54/100, lithograph
15in (38cm) square
£400–480 / €580–700
$730–870 ↗ B(Kn)

Ralph Steadman
British (b1936)
The Smoker's Dream of Paradise
Signed and dated 1991, pen and ink
with watercolour washes
32½ x 23in (82.5 x 58.5cm)
£550–660 / €800–960
$1,000–1,700 ↗ B

Willem Steelink
Dutch (1826–1913)
The Sheep Pool
Signed, oil on board
4½ x 6¾in (11.5 x 17cm)
£600–720 / €880–1,050
$1,100–1,300 ↗ B(B)

**◄ Marie Spartali
Stillman**
British (1844–1927)
Study of an angel
holding a white lily
Signed and dated
1891, watercolour
11 x 21in
(28 x 53.5cm)
£2,400–2,850
€3,500–4,150
$4,350–5,200
↗ FHF

Dorothy Stirling
Scottish (b1939)
Summer Pond
Acrylic on board
19¾ x 23¾in (50 x 60.5cm)
£1,750–1,950 / €2,550–2,850
$3,200–3,550 ⊞ CAMB

Konstantin Stoilov
Russian (1850–1924)
Siberian Gold Convoy
Signed, oil on canvas
27 x 41¾in (68.5 x 106cm)
£7,800–9,300 / €11,400–13,600
$14,200–16,900 ↗ S

Arthur Claude Strachan
British (1885–1938)
A country cottage
Signed, watercolour heightened with bodycolour
17¼ x 23½in (44 x 59.5cm)
£1,500–1,800
€2,200–2,600
$2,700–3,200 ➤ B

► **William Strang**
British (1859–1921)
Portrait of Edward Pryor
Signed and dated 1907, pencil
9¾ x 8½in (25 x 21.5cm)
£450–540 / €660–790
$820–980 ➤ WW

Marcus Stone, RA
British (1840–1921)
Summer fruit; Winter berries
A pair, signed and inscribed, oil on canvas
37 x 12½in (94 x 32cm)
£15,000–18,000 / €22,000–26,000
$27,000–32,000 ➤ B

George Stratemeyer
American (19thC)
A traveller on horseback on the Pali Road, Hawaii
Inscribed, oil on canvas
14¼ x 20in (36 x 51cm)
£10,200–12,200 / €14,900–17,800
$18,600–22,200 ➤ S

Robert Street
American (1796–1865)
Village in winter
Signed, oil on canvas
30 x 36in (76 x 91.5cm)
£20,000–24,000 / €29,000–35,000
$36,000–43,000 ➤ S(NY)

Philip Eustace Stretton
British (fl1884–1919)
The Harvester's Companions
Signed and dated 1892, oil on canvas
16 x 20in (40.5 x 51cm)
£13,700–16,500 / €20,000–24,000
$25,000–30,000 ⚲ DNY

Charles Stuart
British (1880–1904)
A Scottish mountain viewed from across a river
Signed, oil on canvas
23½ x 17¾in (59.5 x 45cm)
£1,400–1,650 / €2,000–2,400
$2,500–3,000 ⚲ B(B)

◀ **Srihadi Sudarsono**
Indonesian (b1931)
Penari
Signed, titled and dated 1989,
oil on canvas
51 x 39½in (129.5 x 100.5cm)
£23,000–27,000
€34,000–40,000
$42,000–49,000 ⚲ S(SI)

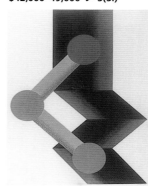

Kumi Sugai
Japanese (1919–96)
Sun
Signed and dated 1970,
numbered 36/190, lithograph
30 x 21in (76 x 53.5cm)
£360–430 / €520–620
$660–780 ⚲ B

◀ **David Macbeth
Sunderland, RSA**
British (1883–1973)
Plockton, Lochcarron
Double sided, signed, oil on board
14¼ x 17¼in (36 x 44cm)
£1,350–1,600 / €1,950–2,350
$2,450–2,900 ⚲ B(Ed)

George Ernest Studdy
British (1878–1948)
Up To My Eyes Just Now!
Signed and inscribed,
watercolour and gouache over
pencil on artboard
8¾ x 6½in (22.5 x 16.5cm)
£330–390 / €480–570
$600–710 ⚲ BBA

Rowland Suddaby
British (1912–72)
Cottage by the Pond
Signed, oil on canvas
25½ x 29½in (65 x 75cm)
£800–960 / €1,200–1,400
$1,450–1,750 ⚲ B(Kn)

David Macbeth Sunderland, RSA
British (1883–1973)
Figures bathing in a harbour by a quayside
Signed, oil on panel
9½ x 11¼in (24 x 28.5cm)
£1,200–1,400 / €1,750–2,050
$2,200–2,550 ⚲ TEN

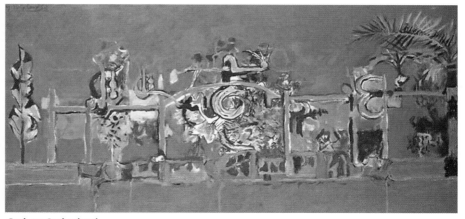

Graham Sutherland
British (1903–80)
The Rock II
Signed, numbered,
limited edition of 75,
lithograph on wove paper
24¾ x 18½in (63 x 47cm)
£1,100–1,250
€ 1,600–1,800
$2,000–2,250 ⊞ JLx
*Sutherland has had
many exhibitions over
the past years,
contributing to the
rise in prices of his
canvases. However,
affordable lithographs
can still be bought.*

Graham Sutherland
British (1903–80)
Vine Pergola
Signed and dated 1952,
oil on canvas
18 x 36in (45.5 x 91.5cm)
£58,000–65,000
€ 85,000–95,000
$105,000–118,000 ⊞ AGN

Locate the source

The source of each illustration in can be found by checking the code letters below each caption with the Key to Illustrations, pages 234–236.

Fedor Vasilievich Sychkov
Russian (1870–1958)
The Happy Mushroom Gatherers
Signed, oil on canvas
32¼ x 39in (82 x 99cm)
£33,000–39,000 / € 48,000–57,000
$60,000–71,000 ⚒ S

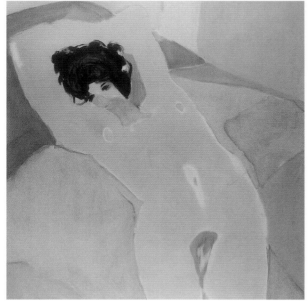

Philip Sutton
British (b1928)
Zadadier nude, number two
Inscribed and dated 1967,
oil on canvas
50in (127cm) square
£2,200–2,650 / € 3,200–3,850
$4,000–4,800 ⚒ B

▶ **Frederick Oakes Sylvester**
American (1869–1915)
Summer Landscape
Oil on board
5½ x 6¾in (14 x 17cm)
£380–450 / € 550–650
$700–840 ⚒ TREA

◄ **Len Tabner**
British (b1946)
Mapfra
Gouache
28¼ x 41¼in (72 x 105cm)
£2,800–3,350 / €4,100–4,900
$5,100–6,100 ⚹ B(Kn)

Romeo V. Tabuena
Mexican (b1922)
Rooster and water buffalo
Signed and dated 1967, acrylic on masonite
19½ x 15¼in (49.5 x 38.5cm)
£2,350–2,800 / €3,450–4,100
$4,300–5,100 ⚹ S(SI)

Algernon Talmage
British (1871–1939)
Sheep grazing in a meadow
Signed, oil on panel
5½ x 9in (14 x 23cm)
£650–780 / €950–1,000
$1,200–1,400 ⚹ HYD

Robin Tanner
British (1904–88)
Autumn
Signed, titled, inscribed and dated 1933, etching
13¼ x 12½in (33.5 x 32cm)
£550–660 / €800–960
$1,000–1,200 ⚹ B

Robin Tanner
British (1904–88)
Barn interior
Signed, inscribed and dated 1970, etching
7 x 5in (18 x 12.5cm)
£190–230 / €290–340
$350–420 ⚹ B

Edmund Tarbell
American (1862–1938)
Study of a girl with sailboat
Oil on canvas
18 x 14in (45.5 x 35.5cm)
£53,000–64,000 / €78,000–93,000
$96,000–115,000 ⚹ S(NY)

Eugen Taube
Finnish (1860–1913)
Sunset in Skärgården
Signed, oil on canvas
15½ x 24¾in (39 x 63cm)
£1,350–1,600 / €1,950–2,300
$2,450–2,900 ↗ **BUK**

John Tenniel
British (1820–1914)
Mr Birrell as Gulliver
Signed, pencil
6¼ x 8in
(16 x 20.5cm)
£260–310
€380–450
$470–560 ↗ **B(Kn)**

▶ **Fred Thieler**
German (1916–99)
St M – 12/58
Signed and dated
1958, oil on board
mounted on cellutex
37¾ x 26¾in
(96 x 68cm)
£4,000–4,800
€5,900–7,000
$7,300–8,700 ↗ **B**

Victor Tempest
British (b1913)
North Woolwich
Signed, oil on board
15¾ x 19¾in (40 x 50cm)
£550–660 / €800–960
$1,000–1,200 ↗ **B(Kn)**

Donald Teskey
Irish (b1956)
Grand Canal Place II
Signed, titled and
dated 1998,
oil on canvas
12 x 15in
(30.5 x 38cm)
£4,250–5,100
€6,200–7,400
$7,700–9,300
↗ **WA**

▶ **Edgar Herbert
Thomas**
British
(fl1888–1926)
The River Bend
Signed and dated
1926, oil on board
9 x 6in (23 x 15cm)
£420–500
€610–730
$760–910 ↗ **S(O)**

H. Thomas
British (20thC)
Portrait of an elegant lady
Signed and dated 1920,
watercolour
15½ x 12in (39.5 x 30.5cm)
£240–290 / € 350–420
$440–530 ⚘ B(Kn)

André Thomkins
German (1930–85)
Untitled
1982, lackskin on paper
9½ x 18in (24 x 45.5cm)
£3,850–4,300 / € 5,600–6,300
$7,000–7,800 ⊞ H&W

*André Thomkins developed the
technique known as lackskin,
whereby enamel paint is poured
on top of water in a basin. The
form required is produced by
blowing and 'cutting' (by using a
thin thread). The image is left
floating on the water and is
removed using a sheet of paper.*

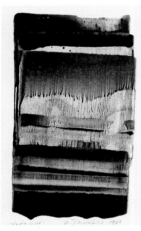

◄ André Thomkins
German (1930–85)
Haute Lisse
1960, distemper on paper
8 x 5¼in (20.5 x 13.5cm)
£2,500–2,800 / € 3,700–4,100
$4,600–5,100 ⊞ H&W

Epaminondas Thomopoulos
Greek (1878–1974)
In the Country, near Patras
Signed and dated 1905, oil on canvas
17½ x 25in (44.5 x 63.5cm)
£11,000–13,200 / € 16,100–19,300
$20,000–24,000 ⚘ B

Edward Horace Thompson
British (1879–1949)
Passing Gleams, Derwent Water and the
Borrowdale Fells from Friar's Crag
Signed, inscribed and dated 1921, pencil and watercolour
11¼ x 17¼in (28.5 x 44cm)
£1,900–2,300 / € 2,750–3,300
$3,500–4,200 ⚘ TEN

Patricia Thompson
British (b1945)
Cowes Parade Isle of Wight
Signed, watercolour
14 x 18in (35.5 x 45.5cm)
£580–650 / € 850–950
$1,050–1,200 ⊞ LAW

◄ **Adam Bruce Thomson, RSA, PRSW, HRSW**
British (1855–1976)
Autumn, Peeblesshire
Signed and inscribed, watercolour
19¼ x 24in (49 x 61cm)
£1,500–1,800 / €2,200–2,650
$2,750–3,300 ⚒ B(Ed)

Archibald Thorburn
British (1860–1935)
Flushed pheasants, autumn
Signed and dated 1899, watercolour and bodycolour
21 x 29¼in (53.5 x 74.5cm)
£7,200–8,650 / €10,500–12,600
$13,100–15,700 ⚒ B(Kn)

◄ **Esaias Thorén**
Swedish (1901–81)
Still life
Signed and dated 1948
21 x 25½in (53.5 x 65cm)
£3,150–3,800 / €4,600–5,500
$5,750–6,900 ⚒ BUK

Hubert Thornley
British (19thC)
Warships, a tug and
other vessels in
an estuary
Signed, oil on canvas
9¾ x 15¾in
(25 x 40cm)
£1,800–2,150
€2,600–3,100
$3,300–3,950
⚒ B(B)

► **William Thornley**
British (fl1858–98)
Scarborough
Signed, oil on canvas
14 x 12in (35.5 x 30.5cm)
£6,300–7,000 / €9,200–10,200
$11,500–12,700 ⊞ HFA

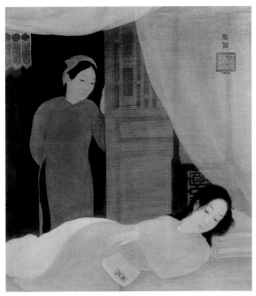

Mai Trung Thu
Vietnamese
(1906–80)
The Sleep
Signed and dated
1938, gouache and
ink on silk
26¼ x 22in
(66.5 x 56cm)
£14,900–17,900
€ 18,000–26,100
$27,100–32,600 ♠ S(SI)

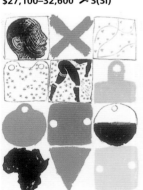

◀ **Joe Tilson**
British (b1928)
Against Apartheid
Signed and dated
1983, numbered
51/100, screenprint
32¾ x 23in
(83 x 58.5cm)
£260–310
€ 380–450
$470–560 ♠ B(Kn)

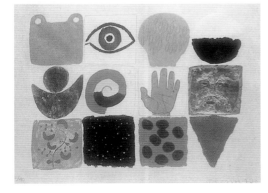

◀ **Joe Tilson**
British (b1928)
Signatures
Set of six, signed, edition of 40, etchings
with aquatint and hand-applied gold leaf
on Khadi paper
Largest 22½ x 31in (57 x 78.5cm)
£1,600–1,900 / € 2,350–2,800
$3,000–3,500 ♠ B(Kn)

▶ **H. E. Tidmarsh**
British (fl1880–1918)
Shipping on the Thames with the
Houses of Parliament beyond
Signed, inscribed and dated
1922, watercolour
9 x 15in (23 x 38cm)
£600–720 / € 870–1,050
$1,100–1,300 ♠ B(Kn)

▶ **William Tillyer**
British (b1938)
Untitled English
landscape
Signed, acrylic
on canvas
30 x 35¾in (76 x 91cm)
£5,000–6,000
€ 7,400–8,800
$9,100–10,900 ♠ B

Walasse Ting
Chinese (b1929)
Catch Me a Grasshopper
Signed, titled and dated 1979,
acrylic on canvas
40½ x 50¼in (103 x 127.5cm)
£7,000–8,400
€ 10,300–12,300
$12,700–15,300
♠ S(SI)

◄ **Alexander Grigorievich Tishler**
Russian (1898–1980)
Theatre Woman
Signed and dated
1971, oil on canvas
29½in (75cm) square
£84,000–101,000
€ 123,000–147,000
$153,000–184,000 ✎ S
Alexander Grigorievich Tishler was considered to be a deviant artist in Stalinist Russia (1922–53), when the only acceptable form of art was Socialist Realism. During the 1960s, Tishler's gentle lyrical Modernism inspired artists who wanted to paint more than just tractors and smiling workers. He was invited to show at the Manezh building in Red Square during a short-lived liberation of the arts when Leonid Brezhnev was in power (1964–82). Tishler's early paintings, executed in secret, fetch more than his later works.

James Jacques Joseph Tissot
French (1836–1902)
A Sadduccee
Signed, watercolour and bodycolour
7 x 3in (18 x 7.5cm)
£3,600–4,300 / € 5,300–6,300
$6,600–7,800 ✎ B

◄ **Kaapa Mbitjna Tjampitjinpa**
Australian (c1920–1989)
Untitled
Inscribed, synthetic polymer paint on canvas
31¼ x 78¼in (79.5 x 199cm)
£3,850–4,600 / € 5,600–6,700
$7,000–8,400 ✎ SHSY

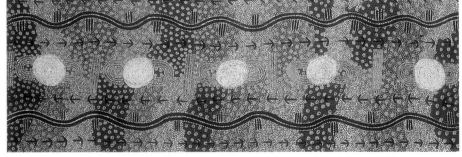

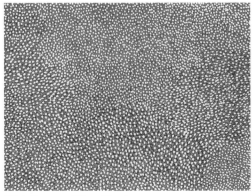

Mick Namarari Tjapaltjarri
Australian (1916–98)
Mouse Dreaming
Synthetic polymer paint on canvas
51¼ x 68½in (130 x 174cm)
£7,900–9,500 / € 11,500–13,800
$14,400–17,300 ✎ SHSY

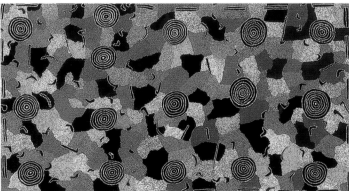

Johnny Warngkula Tjupurrula
Australian (1925–2001)
Untitled (events associated with the soakage site of Tjikari)
Synthetic polymer paint on linen
48 x 72in (122 x 183cm)
£5,400–6,500 / € 7,900–9,500
$9,800–11,800 ✎ SHSY

Ralph Todd
British (1856–1932)
Evening reverie
Signed, oil on canvas
14 x 9½in (35.5 x 24cm)
£1,700–2,050 / €2,500–3,000
$3,100–3,700 ⚒ LAY

Max Todt
British (1847–90)
Serenading
Signed and dated 1880, oil on panel
14 x 11in (35.5 x 28cm)
£7,200–8,000 / €10,500–11,700
$13,100–14,600 ⊞ HFA

Ralph Todd
British (1856–1932)
Hosking's old dairy
Oil on canvas
20 x 27in (51 x 68.5cm)
£1,450–1,750 / €2,100–2,500
$2,650–3,200 ⚒ LAY

Francis William Topham, RA, OWS
Irish (1808–77)
Late Again!
Signed, titled and dated 1856,
watercolour heightened with white
10½ x 7¾in (26.5 x 19.5cm)
£3,300–3,900 / €4,800–5,700
$6,000–7,100 ⚒ WA

▶ **Kenn Torno(w)**
American (20thC)
Winter Landscape
Signed, oil on canvas
16 x 20in
(40.5 x 51cm)
£520–620
€760–900
$920–1,100
⚒ TREA

Feliks Topolski
Polish (1907–89)
Rome, Cappella Sistina – Allied
soldiers in Italy
Signed and dated 1944, pen,
ink and wash
30 x 21¼in (76 x 54cm)
£1,500–1,800 / €2,200–2,650
$2,750–3,300 ⚒ B

Wenzel Ulrik Tornoe
Danish (1844–1907)
A wistful thought
Oil on canvas
21½ x 13¾in (54.5 x 35cm)
£650–780 / €950–1,100
$1,200–1,400 ♪ B(Kn)

Julian Trevelyn
British (1910–88)
Reading Sartre before a harbour
Signed and dated 1939, ink and wash
11½ x 15½in (29 x 39.5cm)
£1,900–2,250 / €2,750–3,300
$3,450–4,100 ♪ LAY

◄ **Theofrastos Triantafyllidis**
Greek (1881–1955)
Bathers on the boat
Signed, oil on cardboard
11¾ x 7¼in (30 x 18.5cm)
£18,000–21,600 / €26,600–32,000
$33,000–39,000 ♪ B

Sarah Thompson Townsend
British (fl1910–30)
Spring Fair
Signed, oil on canvas
10 x 14in (25.5 x 35.5cm)
£6,300–7,000 / €9,200–10,200
$11,500–12,700 ⊞ PGB

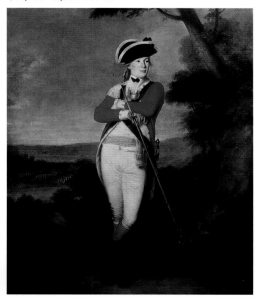

► **William Henry Hamilton Trood**
British (1860–99)
Come and Get It!
Signed, oil on canvas
12 x 16¼in
(30.5 x 41.5cm)
£3,300–3,950
€4,850–5,800
$6,000–7,200
♪ DNY

John Trotter
British (fl1756–92)
Portrait of Captain John Alston (1762–83) wearing the
uniform of the 100th Regiment
Oil on canvas
49½ x 40in (125.5 x 101.5cm)
£66,000–79,000 / €96,000–115,000
$120,000–144,000 ♪ S

*Irish-born John Trotter was a portrait painter. He studied
in Italy and returned to his native land in 1773. Prices for
his works have risen owing to the recent upturn in the
Irish economy.*

Jonathan Truss
British (b1960)
Head of a tiger
Signed, oil on canvas
17½ x 21½in
(44.5 x 54.5cm)
£800–960
€ **1,200–1,400**
$1,500–1,750
↗ WW

Konstantin Alexandrovich Trutovsky
Russian (1826–93)
Flirting at the well
Signed and dated 1888, oil on canvas
18¾ x 26in (47.5 x 66cm)
£13,200–15,800 / € **19,300–23,100**
$24,000–28,800 ↗ S

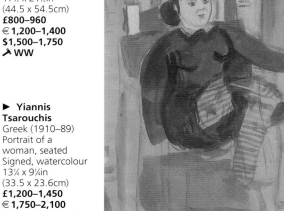

► **Yiannis
Tsarouchis**
Greek (1910–89)
Portrait of a
woman, seated
Signed, watercolour
13¼ x 9¼in
(33.5 x 23.6cm)
£1,200–1,450
€ **1,750–2,100**
$2,200–2,600 ↗ B

Stavros Tsikoudakis
Greek (1945–2003)
Trojan I
Signed, oil on canvas
35¼ x 43in (89.5 x 109cm)
£4,800–5,800 / € **7,000–8,400**
$8,800–10,500 ↗ B

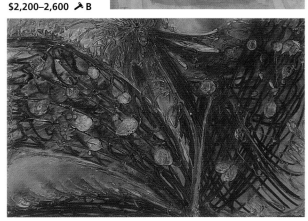

Thanassis Tsingos
Greek (1914–65)
Fleurs
Signed, oil on canvas
34½ x 51in (87.5 x 129.5cm)
£7,000–8,400 / € **10,200–12,300**
$12,700–15,300 ↗ B

► **Costas Tsoclis**
Greek (b1930)
Space with
wooden plank
Signed and
numbered 40/50,
wood and nails on
print, plexiglass
42 x 32 x 2¾in
(106.5 x 81.5 x 7cm)
£1,600–1,900
€ **2,350–2,750**
$2,900–3,450 ↗ B

◄ **Allen Tucker**
American (1866–1939)
Woman in a Pom Pom Hat
Signed and dated 1913,
oil on canvas
72 x 25in (183 x 63.5cm)
£24,700–27,500
€36,000–40,000
$45,000–50,000 ⊞ **FBH**

**Joseph Mallord William
Turner, RA**
British (1775–1851)
Saltwood Castle, Hythe, Kent
Pencil, grey and blue wash
7 x 5¼in (18 x 13.5cm)
£3,600–4,300 / €5,300–6,300
$6,500–7,800 ⚲ **B**

*J. M. W. Turner produced
paintings of many English
castles, mostly in watercolour.
This pencil drawing of Saltwood
Castle is rather small, and this is
reflected in the price, proving
that it is possible to own a work
by such a master.*

Desmond Turner, RUA
Irish (b1923)
Farm by a river, County Down
Signed, oil on canvas
14 x 18in (35.5 x 45.5cm)
£680–820 / €1,000–1,200
$1,250–1,500 ⚲ **WA**

◄ **Charles Frederick Tunnicliffe, RA, RE**
British (1901–79)
The Diver
Signed, oil on canvas
24 x 11in (61 x 28cm)
£5,200–5,800 / €7,700–8,500
$9,500–10,500 ⊞ **Bne**

Charles Frederick Tunnicliffe, RA, RE
British (1901–79)
Mistlethrush
Signed, inscribed and dated 1980, bodycolour and pencil
on tracing paper
15¾ x 11¾in (40 x 30cm)
£280–340 / €420–500
$520–620 ⚲ **B(B)**

Ken Turner
British (20thC)
Pheasants in a Cabbage Field
Signed, oil on board
35½ x 23½in (90 x 151cm)
£150–180 / €220–260
$280–330 ⚲ **WW**

Theatre Art

The theatre, opera and ballet are magnets to those who paint and many artists designed sets or costumes as a sideline to their other work. Cecil Beaton is best known as a photographer, but he also did some theatre/stage design. Some artists use the theatre as a stepping stone to further their art careers, enjoying the guaranteed income and the camaraderie by being involved with actors, dancers and singers. Other artists such as David Hockney are asked to design sets after their art reputation is established. It is an extra pull for Glyndebourne opera house, for instance, if they can advertise sets by this famous painter. Walter Richard Sickert and countless other artists attended the theatre regularly and made sketches, although not necessarily of anything to do with the production.

In Russia at the turn of the 20th century, the St Petersburg theatre and ballet was a very exciting place to be. Theatre impresario Sergei Diaghilev was beginning to gather around him some of the most famous names in the arts, such as composers Tchaikovsky and Stravinsky and ballet dancer Nijinsky, as well as firebrand intellectual Alexander Nicholaevich Benois, who had founded a group of thinkers and art critics called the Artistic World. Benois' paintings were considered crude and amateurish but it is his theatre designs that show some talent in the field of visual arts. The ballet attracted Russia's intelligentsia, the aristocratic, the rich and the influential as well as beautiful and glamorous women.

The new and exciting ballet productions often attracted artists who felt they could not fit in with the establishment, such as Léon Samoilovich Bakst who was expelled from St Petersburg Academy of Fine Arts for depicting the Virgin Mary as a sobbing old woman. Sudekin was asked to leave the Moscow College of Painting for exhibiting works with intimate subjects not contained in the teaching programme of the college. His best known and desired paintings come from Diaghilev's Russian Season in Paris from 1912 to 1914. Golovin took part in exhibitions proclaiming the new Russian art but produced his best work for the ballet and became the official decorator of the Imperial theatres between 1899 and 1917.

Of all the artists surrounding Diaghilev, Boris Nikhailovich Kustodiev was not just a theatre artist but exhibited widely with the New Society of Artists a generation after Léon Bakst. Bakst is the most well known theatre artist and is sought after especially by affluent Russians who are keen to invest in Russian art. Interestingly, the Baksts that fetch the most are of women in extraordinary dresses. Whether or not a production was a resounding success makes no difference to the price of theatre art. Theatre art is sold mostly on the decorative quality of the work.

Romain de Tertoff, who called himself Erté after the French pronunciation of his initials, was born in Russia at a time when Diaghilev's artists were getting into their stride. Much more flamboyant and decorative are his drawings for costumes and stage sets for the Folies-Bergère in Paris and George White's *Scandals* in New York. While living in Paris from 1912, he became a fashion illustrator for *Harpers Bazaar* and these drawings are becoming increasingly collectable. He also designed for the musical *Stardust*.

Frenchman Alexandra Alexandrovna Exter's work fetches high prices because his work is radical and incorporates elements of modern art. As for English theatre designers, prices for Cecil Beaton's work will pick up thanks to an exhibition dedicated to his work at the National Portrait Gallery in London. His set designs fetch more money than his sketches for costumes.

Edward Gordon Craig was one of Britain's most influential theatre designers of the early 20th century. The son of actress Ellen Terry, he wrote books such as *The Art of the Theatre*, designed for the playwright Ibsen and worked alongside the artist Stanislavski.

Karl von Appen
German (1900–81)
Helena Wiegal as Mother Courage, Berliner Ensemble, Palace Theatre
Signed and dated 1956, pencil
13 x 17½in (33 x 44.5cm)
£290–350 / € 430–510
$530–630 ✑ S

Further information
Artists mentioned in the introduction above may have works appearing elsewhere in this Guide. Consult the index for page numbers.

▶ **Léon Samoilovich Bakst**
Russian (1866–1924)
Costume design for Madame Trouhanova in *La Peri*
Signed, titled and dated 1911, numbered 54/100, hand-coloured lithograph
19 x 13¾in (48.5 x 35cm)
£7,800–9,400
€ 11,400–13,700
$14,200–17,100 ✑ S

Cecil Beaton
British (1904–80)
Costume design
Pencil and gouache
14 x 10in (35.5 x 25.5cm)
£260–310 / €380–450
$470–560 ⚒ G(L)

▶ **Edward Gordon Craig**
British (1872–1966)
Countryside Lane
Signed and inscribed, wood engraving
7¾ x 5¼in (19.5 x 13.5cm)
£310–370 / €450–540
$560–670 ⚒ S

▶ **Alexander Nikolaevich Benois**
Russian
(1870–1960)
Set design for
Il Trovatore
Signed and dated
1948, watercolour
over pencil on paper
10¾ x 15¾in
(27.5 x 40cm)
£4,800–5,800
€7,000–8,400
$8,800–10,500 ⚒ S

▶ **Alexandra Alexandrovna Exter**
French (1882–1949)
Costume design
for a dancer
Gouache on paper
19¾ x 13½in
(50 x 34.5cm)
£34,000–41,000
€50,000–60,000
$63,000–75,000 ⚒ S

▶ **Boris Mikhailovich Kustodiev**
Russian (1878–1927)
Costume design for Dash, the merchant's wife
Signed, inscribed and dated 1919, watercolour over
pencil on paper
13 x 8¼in (33 x 21cm)
£4,800–5,800 / €7,000–8,400
$8,600–10,300 ⚒ S

Alexander Yakovlevich Golovin
Russian (1863–1930)
Costume design for Fyodor Chaliapin in
the role of Tonio the Clown from the
opera *Pagliacci*
Signed, inscribed and dated 1918, pen and
ink and watercolour heightened with
gouache and pencil on paper
15 x 11in (38 x 28cm)
£14,400–17,300 / €21,000–25,300
$26,200–31,500 ⚒ S

Sergei Yurievich Sudeikin
Russian (1882–1946)
Stage set design of a
rainbow above a grotto
Signed and inscribed,
gouache on card
12 x 19¼in
(30.5 x 49cm)
£14,400–17,300
€21,000–25,300
$26,200–31,500 ⚒ S

▶ **Romain de Tirtoff (Erté)**
Russian (1892–1990)
Four costume designs
for the Tiller Girls
Signed, bodycolour
and ink
14 x 10in (35.5 x 25.5cm)
£1,500–1,800
€2,200–2,600
$2,700–3,250 ⚒ LAY

◄ **Alice Wright Uhlman**
Amercian (20thC)
Composition with Red
Signed, oil on canvas
32 x 48in (81.5 x 122cm)
£210–250 / €300–360
$380–450 ⚒ LHA

Fred Uhlman (1901–85)

Fred Uhlman was a self-taught artist who moved from Stuttgart to Paris in 1933, and then to London where he married. His still life paintings and views of the Welsh valleys where he spent his summers are particularly popular. Uhlman's first solo exhibition was in Paris in 1935, and he had regular one-man and mixed media shows throughout Britain. Examples of his paintings are held at the Fitzwilliam Museum in Cambridge and the Victoria & Albert Museum, London.

▶ **Fred Uhlman**
British (1901–85)
Landscape near Auribeau
Signed and titled, oil on board
10¼ x 15in (26 x 38cm)
£1,000–1,200
€1,450–1,750
$1,800–2,150 ⚒ B

Fred Uhlman
British (1901–85)
The Red Church
Signed and titled, oil on canvas
19 x 23in (48.5 x 58.5cm)
£1,100–1,300 / €1,600–1,900
$2,000–2,350 ⚒ B(B)

Fred Uhlman
British (1901–85)
Night Scene
Signed, oil on board
15½ x 19¼in (39.5 x 49cm)
£1,500–1,800 / €2,200–2,600
$2,750–3,250 ⚒ B

Leon Underwood
British (1890–1975)
Charterhouse Square, London
Signed and dated 1939,
watercolour
21¼ x 30in (54 x 76cm)
£3,800–4,450 / € 5,500–6,600
$6,900–8,300 ⚒ L&T

J. C. Uren
British (1845–1932)
Wreckers at work
Signed, watercolour
10 x 17½in (25.5 x 44.5cm)
£1,100–1,300 / € 1,600–1,900
$2,000–2,350 ⚒ LAY

► **Maurice Utrillo**
French (1883–1955)
Rue de Versailles
Signed and dated 1919,
gouache on board
19¾ x 25½in (50 x 65cm)
£18,200–21,800
€ 26,600–32,000
$34,000–40,000 ⚒ LHA

Storing your paintings

If you buy a picture with flaking paint store
it horizontally in a damp dark place to stop
further deterioration. Never store a picture
in an outbuilding or below freezing point as
damage will occur very quickly. Keep pictures,
especially watercolours, away from direct
sunlight. Do not attempt to clean a good
picture yourself but enlist the help of a
specialist – contact a museum or reputable
gallery to recommend a good restorer.

◄ **Victor Uytterschault**
Belgian (1847–1917)
The Windmills
Signed, watercolour with touches of graphite
12½ x 18½in (32 x 47cm)
£360–430 / € 530–630
$650–780 ⚒ B(B)

Urban Art – London & New York

The British Empire in the 19th century and the growing power of America in the 20th century made London and New York two of the most important cities in the world. Artists' impressions have helped bolster the image of these places for their citizens and also for visitors. However, there are perceptible differences in the way American and English artists view their cities.

English artists tend to romanticize London as a huge neighbourly village whereas American artists celebrate the urban dynamism of New York with its impressive buildings or, as in the case of the work by Eliot Clark shown here, the destruction of them. British artist Maxwell Ashby Armfield spent seven years in New York just after WWI and was overwhelmed by the beauty of the place. The huge towering buildings sparked his interest in architectural symmetry as expounded by the Greeks and the Egyptians. The American experience gave him confidence and breadth which he later reflected in his work. Swedish artist Agnes Cleve was also interested in the modern buildings of New York: they appealed to her interest in Cubism. American artists do not always show New York in its best light. In the early 20th century, many strove for realism and artists such as Robert Henri and Jerome Myers showed the flip side of the American dream – the urban poor.

Stylistically, artists in both cities were influenced by French Impressionism. Painters such as Camille Pissarro and Claude Monet visited London and their influence can be seen in other artists' work such as Paul Fordyce Maitland and Frederick Gore, son of the artist Spencer Gore. Frederick's brightly coloured palette owes more to the French art of the south than the English tradition of more muddy tones.

The river Thames is a focal point for many British artists and it is interesting to see how the development of the river's role in the city's industrial development is recorded in artists' work. Artists celebrated this, particularly American-born James Abbott McNeill Whistler (see page 204), whose work will always be a good investment. His larger oils seldom come up for sale but his beautiful etchings are at the moment available at an affordable price for such a master. The first state or creation of an etching is often rarer than subsequent states when the artist may have made alterations to the copperplate. Whistler rarely signed these etchings, but this does not detract from the price as, in his case, it is the quality of the images that count.

Artists whose work flourishes in other spheres may be inspired to paint scenes of London and New York and these pictures can be bought for less than work created within their specialist areas. Ken Howard, for instance, is known more for his interiors, nudes and war pictures but painted a little vignette of London (see page 204). Likewise, paintings of London by Edward Seago, better known for his circus scenes and watercolours of East Anglia, are a good inexpensive starting point for Seago fans. Works by John Piper, an architectural and landscape painter, and Julian Trevelyan, a more off-beat and very interesting artist, are worth looking out for.

Maxwell Ashby Armfield, RWS
British (1882–1972)
Madison Square Park, New York
Signed and inscribed, oil on canvas
34 x 30in (86.5 x 76cm)
£67,000–81,000 / €98,000–108,000
$122,000–147,000 ⚒ S
Maxwell Armfield spent seven years in America immediately following WWI, just as New York City began to acquire its famous skyline. It was at this time that he solved, in his own mind, the problem of composition. He became profoundly interested in the concept of Dynamic Symmetry, taking a course of lectures in the lost canon of proportion of the ancient Greeks and Egyptians given by Professor Jay Hambridge.

Further information
Artists mentioned in the introduction above may have works appearing elsewhere in this Guide. Consult the index for page numbers.

▶ **John Betlam**
British (fl1914–41)
Piccadilly
Signed, oil on canvas
27¼ x 35½in (69 x 90cm)
£3,600–4,300 / €5,300–6,300
$6,600–7,800 ⚒ B(Kn)

◀ **Arthur George Bell**
British (1849–1916)
The Thames at Richmond Bridge
Signed, oil on panel
14 x 21in (35.5 x 53.5cm)
£3,100–3,450 / €4,550–5,000
$5,600–6,300 ⊞ Bne

Robert Buhler
British (1916–89)
The Albert Bridge at Night
Signed, oil on canvas
25 x 30in (63.5 x 76cm)
£2,500–3,000 / € **3,650–4,350**
$4,600–5,500 ⚒ **B**

▶ **Anne Bull**
British (b1940)
Battersea Square
Oil
34 x 39in (86.5 x 99cm)
£1,750–1,950 / € **2,550–2,850**
$3,200–3,550 ⊞ **Stl**

◀ **Trevor Chamberlain**
British (b1933)
Stormy Weather, Putney
Signed, titled, inscribed and
dated 1986, oil on canvas
14¼ x 20in (36 x 51cm)
£750–900 / € **1,100–1,300**
$1,350–1,600 ⚒ **B(Kn)**

Eliot Clark
American (1883–1980)
The Hotel Windsor Fire
Signed, inscribed and dated 1899, oil on canvas
29¾ x 39¾in (75.5 x 101cm)
£21,400–25,100 / € **32,000–38,000**
$40,000–47,000 ⚒ **S(NY)**

Agnes Cleve
Swedish (1876–1951)
New York
Signed and dated 1936, mixed media
20½ x 26½in (52 x 67.5cm)
£2,250–2,700 / € **3,300–3,950**
$4,100–4,900 ⚒ **BUK**

◀ **Paul Cornoyer**
American
(1864–1923)
Madison Square in
New York
Signed, oil on canvas
18 x 20in
(45.5 x 51cm)
£35,000–42,000
€ **51,000–61,000**
$63,000–75,000
⚒ **LHA**

◀ **William F. Draper**
American (b1912)
View of New York
City looking south
Signed, oil on canvas
44 x 42in
(112 x 106.5cm)
£19,800–23,800
€ **28,900–34,000**
$36,000–43,000
⚒ **S(NY)**

Thomas Easley
British (b1949)
View of London from Westminster Bridge
Signed and dated 1988, oil on board
30¾ x 49¾in (78 x 126.5cm)
£1,000–1,200
€ **1,450–1,700**
$1,800–2,100 🔨 B(Kn)

◀ **Frederick Gore, RA**
British (b1913)
River Thames at
Battersea Bridge 1962
Signed, oil on canvas
28 x 48in
(71 x 122cm)
£8,100–9,000
€ **11,800–13,000**
$14,800–16,400
⊞ CARL

Jack L. Gray
American (1927–1981)
New York Harbour at Sunset
Signed, oil on canvas
26¼ x 40¼in (66.5 x 102cm)
£19,800–23,800
€ **28,900–34,000**
$36,000–43,000 🔨 S(NY)

Ken Howard, RA, RWA, NEAC
British (b1932)
Mornington Crescent
Signed, oil on canvas
20 x 24in (51 x 61cm)
£1,850–2,200 / € **2,700–3,200**
$3,400–4,000 🔨 B(NW)

Paul Fordyce Maitland
British (1863–1909)
Mills and Barges, Chelsea
Signed and titled, oil on canvas
10 x 14in (25.5 x 35.5cm)
£1,500–1,800
€ **2,200–2,650**
$2,750–3,300 🔨 B

Herbert Menzies Marshall, RWS
British (1841–1913)
Tower Bridge from the North Bank
Signed and dated 1909, watercolour
19 x 28½in (48.5 x 72.5cm)
£7,700–8,500 / € **11,200–12,400**
$14,000–15,500 ⊞ Bne

Paul Maze
British (1887–1979)
St Paul's from the River
Signed, pastel
14½ x 21in (37 x 53.5cm)
£1,800–2,150 / €2,650–3,150
$3,300–3,900 ➴ B

Hubert James Medleycott
British (1841–1920)
The Thames at Blackfriars
Signed and dated 1894, watercolour
13¾ x 20¼in (35 x 51.5cm)
£1,800–2,150 / €2,650–3,150
$3,300–3,900 ➴ B

John Piper
British (1903–93)
Five Gates of London
Signed and inscribed, 1978,
silkscreen on Cuve wove
16¾ x 63in (42.5 x 160cm)
£2,500–3,000 / €3,700–4,400
$4,500–5,400 ➴ B

► **Michael Pybus**
British (b1954)
A Winter Evening, Lambeth Bridge
Watercolour
8 x 11in (20.5 x 28cm)
£250–280 / €360–400
$450–500 ⊞ PY

Orlando Rouland
American (1871–1945)
When Night Comes On, Central Park, NY
Signed, oil on canvas
38 x 35in (96.5 x 89cm)
£22,600–27,100 / €33,000–39,000
$41,000–49,000 ➴ SK

David Sawyer
British (b1961)
Sunset, St Nicholas' Church, Tooting
Oil on board
6 x 8in (15 x 20.5cm)
£400–450 / €600–660
$740–820 ⊞ P&H

Frederick William Scarborough
British (d1939)
Blackwall Reach, London
Signed and inscribed, watercolour
6¾ x 20½in (17 x 52cm)
£4,500–5,400 / € 6,600–7,900
$8,200–9,800 🔨 L&T

► **Josiah Sturgeon**
British (20thC)
Autumn evening, Chelsea
Signed and titled, oil on board
12¼ x 16¼in (31 x 41.5cm)
£450–540 / € 660–790
$820–980 🔨 B(Kn)

Edward Seago, RWS
British (1910–74)
The Tall House, Park Lane
Signed, watercolour and pencil
11 x 14in (28 x 35.5cm)
£3,800–4,550 / € 5,500–6,600
$6,900–8,300 🔨 B

Julian Trevelyan
British (1910–88)
Kew Gardens
Signed, titled and numbered 13/75, aquatint
13¾ x 19in (35 x 48.5cm)
£200–240 / € 300–350
$360–430 🔨 B

Patricia Thompson
British (20thC)
Sloane Square, London
Watercolour
18 x 25in (45.5 x 63.5cm)
£580–650 / € 850–950
$1,050–1,200 ⊞ LAW

James Abbott McNeill Whistler
American (1834–1903)
Thames Warehouses
1859, etching
7 x 8in (18 x 20.5cm)
£900–1,100 / € 1,350–1,600
$1,700–2,000 🔨 B

◄ **James Abbott McNeill Whistler**
American (1834–1903)
Eagle Wharf
1859, etching
5¼ x 8½in (13.5 x 21.5cm)
£1,300–1,550 / € 1,900–2,250
$2,350–2,800 🔨 B

Michelle Williams
British (b1978)
New York – New York
Mixed media
37¾ x 26in (96 x 66cm)
**£1,100–1,250 / €1,600–1,800
$2,000–2,200** ⊞ ArW

Guy Wiggins
American (1883–1962)
Fifth Avenue at 55th Street
Signed and titled, oil on canvas board
16 x 12in (40.5 x 30.5cm)
**£31,000–37,000 / €45,000–54,000
$56,000–67,000** ➚ S(NY)

▶ **William Lionel Wyllie**
British (1851–1931)
The Opening of Tower Bridge, 30th June 1894
Oil on canvas
31 x 53in (78.5 x 134.5cm)
**£21,000–25,200 / €31,000–37,000
$38,000–45,000** ➚ B
*The original version of this painting is held in
the collection of London's Guildhall Art Gallery.
This example was painted at a slightly later date.
While there are differences to the foreground
of this picture, it is essentially the same as
that exhibited at the Royal Academy in 1895.*

◀ **John Yardley**
British (b1933)
St Martin's and
Trafalgar Square
Watercolour
5½ x 8¾in
(14 x 22cm)
**£170–200
€250–300
$310–370** ➚ B(Kn)

▶ **Markino Yoshio**
Japanese (1869–1956)
The Embankment, London
Signed, watercolour
5½ x 6¾in (14 x 17cm)
**£7,000–8,400 / €10,200–12,200
$12,700–15,300** ➚ B

Adolph Valette
French (1876–1942)
Bailey Bridge
Oil on canvas
13 x 16in (33 x 40.5cm)
£14,500–17,400 / €21,200–25,400
$26,500–32,000 ⚒ CDC

This urban scene depicts Bailey Bridge, more correctly known as Albert Bridge, over the River Irwell in the centre of Manchester, at dusk.

Sam Vanni
Finnish (1908–92)
Composition
Signed, gouache
30¾ x 22in (78 x 56cm)
£3,700–4,450 / €5,400–6,500
$6,700–8,000 ⚒ BUK

◀ **Edgar John Varley**
British (1839–88)
Markbeech Church – Evening
Signed, inscribed and dated 1886, watercolour
5½ x 7in (14 x 18cm)
£1,000–1,200 / €1,500–1,750
$1,850–2,200 ⚒ HN

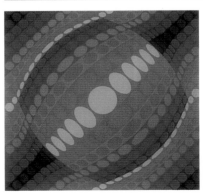

◀ **Victor Vasarely**
Hungarian (1906–97)
Composition
Signed and numbered 58/175, silkscreen
22¼in (56.5cm) square
£190–230 / €290–340
$350–420 ⚒ B

▶ **Pierre de Vaucleroy**
Belgian (1892–1969)
Reclining nude
Signed and dated 1925, oil on canvas
31½ x 25¾in (80 x 65.5cm)
£5,400–6,500 / €7,900–9,500
$9,800–11,800 ⚒ S

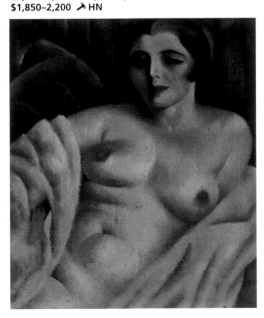

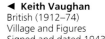

◄ **Keith Vaughan**
British (1912–74)
Village and Figures
Signed and dated 1943, mixed media, pencil, pen, ink, watercolour
and bodycolour
8½ x 12¼in (21.5 x 31cm)
£6,400–7,700 / €9,300–11,200
$11,700–14,000 ✐ B(B)

Mary Howey Murray Vawter
American (1871–1950)
Indiana Landscape
Signed, pencil
12 x 16in (30.5 x 40.5cm)
£440–530 / €640–770
$800–960 ✐ TREA

Landscape views of beautiful and
famous places are always more
valuable. Portraits of well-known
figures fetch more than portraits
of unknowns.

◄ **Vasili Vasilievich
Vereschagin**
Russian (1842–1904)
Military Road to Tiflis
Signed, oil on canvas
8¾ x 6¾in (22 x 17cm)
£7,400–8,900
€10,800–13,000
$13,500–16,200 ✐ S

► **John Verney**
British (1913–43)
Concarneau
Signed and titled,
black conté crayon
and white chalk on
light brown-tinted
paper with grey
wash, one figure
heightened in ink
13½ x 16¼in
(34.5 x 41.5cm)
£150–180
€220–260
$270–320 ✐ DW

Theodore Joseph Verschaeren
Belgian (1874–1937)
The meal
Signed and dated 1928, oil on canvas
48½ x 39½in (123 x 100.5cm)
£1,350–1,600 / €2,000–2,350
$2,450–2,900 ✐ BERN

Frank Vietor
American (b1919)
Train with City in
the Distance
Signed, watercolour
and gouache
on paper
7¼ x 12in
(19 x 30.5cm)
£470–570
€690–830
$850–1,000
TREA

► **François
Etienne Villeret**
French (1800–66)
Antwerp Cathedral
Signed, watercolour
8¾ x 6in (22 x 15cm)
£280–340
€420–500
$520–620 B(Kn)

André Vignoles
French (b1920)
Still life with flowers
Signed and dated 1959, oil on canvas
24 x 19½in (61 x 49.5cm)
£500–600 / €730–870
$920–1,100 JAA

▲ **For further information**
see Botanical & Flower Painting
(pages 32–35)

◄ **Ejnar Vindfeldt**
Danish (1905–53)
Out of Reach
Signed, oil on canvas
17 x 14¾in (43 x 37.5cm)
£3,300–3,950 / €4,850–5,800
$6,000–7,200 DNY

George Vivian
British (1798–1873)
The Rialto Bridge and Grand
Canal, Venice, with figures and
gondolas in the foreground
Signed, oil on canvas
23½ x 41½in (59.5 x 105.5cm)
£8,000–9,600
€11,700–14,000
$14,600–17,500 MCA

Edouard Vuillard (1868–1940)

Edouard Vuillard's early influences came from the Nabis and the Intimistes – the movements that bridged the gap between Post-Impressionism and Modernism. The Nabis, a band of Parisian art school rebels, took their name from the Hebrew word for profit. They did away with shading, perspective and tonal progression in favour of simplified outlines filled with inlays of pure colour. Abstract paintings from this period are extremely rare and Vuillard's work became less avant-garde as he grew older. His interiors are the most prized, particularly as they depict real scenes and act as visual diaries of his life. These can fetch six-figure sums but preparatory sketches are affordable and could well rise in price.

▶ **Edouard Vuillard**
French (1868–1940)
Three women in an interior
Black crayon
6¾ x 4in (17 x 10cm)
£7,350–8,200 / €10,700–11,900
$13,400–14,900 ⊞ WoF

Edouard Vuillard
French (1868–1940)
Village street 1935
Pastel on paper
14½ x 18¼in (37 x 46.5cm)
£19,800–22,000 / €28,900–32,000
$36,000–40,000 ⊞ WoF

Edouard Vuillard
French (1868–1940)
Woman reading
Pen, ink and pencil on paper
8 x 4½in (20.5 x 11.5cm)
£3,500–3,900 / €5,100–5,700
$6,400–7,100 ⊞ WoF

◀ **Edouard Vuillard**
French (1868–1940)
Nude study
Charcoal on paper
12¼ x 7½in (31 x 19cm)
£4,300–4,800 / €6,300–7,000
$7,800–8,700 ⊞ WoF

Many artists donate their paintings to auction for charity and it is often possible to buy good pictures at low prices, although artists sometimes submit inferior work for which you could be overcharged. Therefore check as to which is the artist's favourite charity – artists who give to a particular charity are likely to give better work than those who give indiscriminately. However, whatever you pay you will be supporting a good cause.

▶ **Pericles Vyzantios**
Greek (1893–1972)
At the exhibition
Signed, oil on canvas
19½ x 29in (49.5 x 73.5cm)
£10,500–12,600 / €15,300–18,400
$19,100–22,900 ➶ B

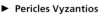

Fritz Wagner
German (20thC)
Awaiting his Verdict
Signed, oil on canvas
19¾ x 24in (50 x 61cm)
**£11,600–12,900 / € 16,900–18,800
$21,100–23,400** ⊞ HFA

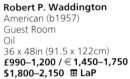

Robert P. Waddington
American (b1957)
Guest Room
Oil
36 x 48in (91.5 x 122cm)
**£990–1,200 / € 1,450–1,750
$1,800–2,150** ⊞ LaP

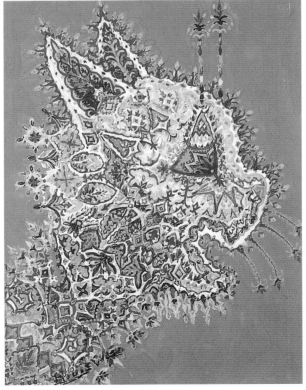

John Cheltenham Wake
British (fl1855–78)
Shipping off Dover
Signed and dated 1878, oil on canvas
14 x 21in (35.5 x 53.5cm)
**£3,400–3,800 / € 4,950–5,500
$6,200–6,900** ⊞ Bne

Louis Wain
British (1860–1939)
Untitled
Gouache
9 x 7in (23 x 18cm)
**£4,000–4,500 / € 5,900–6,500
$7,400–8,200** ⊞ BOX

Ernest Charles Walbourn
British (1872–1927)
Gleaning the Catch
Signed, oil on canvas
20 x 30in (51 x 76cm)
**£8,900–9,900 / € 13,000–14,500
$16,200–18,000** ⊞ HFA

Ernest Walbourn
British (fl1897–1904)
Feeding Time
Signed, oil on canvas
18 x 12in (45.5 x 30.5cm)
£5,400–6,000 / € 7,900–8,800
$9,800–10,900 ⊞ HFA

Thomas Walch
Austrian (1867–1943)
The view in the distance (shepherd with sheep)
Oil on canvas
25½ x 35½in (65 x 90cm)
£2,450–2,950 / € 3,600–4,300
$4,500–5,400 ↗ DORO

▶ **Alfons Walde**
Austrian (1891–1958)
Solitary mountain farm
Signed, oil on board
13 x 20½in (33 x 52cm)
£38,000–45,000 / € 55,000–66,000
$69,000–82,000 ↗ B

James Wallace
British (fl1899–1910)
A coastal scene with three children in a small boat,
hills beyond
Signed, oil on canvas
20 x 26¾in (51 x 68cm)
£2,000–2,400 / € 2,900–3,500
$3,650–4,350 ↗ TEN

James Charles Ward
British (fl1830–59)
Looking across the Woodland Gate
Signed, oil on canvas
9 x 15in (23 x 38cm)
£2,050–2,300 / € 3,000–3,350
$3,750–4,200 ⊞ HFA

Leslie Matthew Ward (Spy)
British (1851–1922)
The Very Rev'd Armitage Robinson,
Dean of Westminster 1905
Signed, watercolour heightened in white
14¼ x 10½in (36 x 26.5cm)
£3,600–4,300 / €5,300–6,300
$6,600–7,800 ⚹ B(O)

William H. Ward
British (fl1860–76)
The Riverbank
Signed, oil on canvas
14 x 10in (35.5 x 25.5cm)
£6,100–6,800 / €8,900–9,900
$11,100–12,400 ⊞ HFA

Andy Warhol
American (1928–87)
Campbell's Soup can on shopping bag
Silkscreen
19¼ x 17in (49 x 43cm)
£700–840 / €1,000–1,200
$1,250–1,500 ⚹ B

Andy Warhol
American (1928–87)
Mao
Signed, silkscreen
40¼ x 29¼in (102 x 74.5cm)
£1,950–2,350 / €2,850–3,400
$3,550–4,250 ⚹ BUK

◄ **Edmund George Warren,
RI, ROI**
British (1834–1909)
Harvest Time near
Ashburton, Devon
Signed and dated 1884,
watercolour and gouache
18¾ x 26½in (47.5 x 67.5cm)
£7,600–8,500
€11,100–12,400
$13,800–15,500 ⊞ Bne

▶ **Edmund George Warren, RI, ROI**
British (1834–1909)
Harvest Showers
Signed, oil on canvas
24 x 36in (61 x 91.5cm)
£13,000–14,500 / €19,000–21,000
$24,000–27,000 ⊞ Bne

◄ **Billie Waters**
British (1896–1979)
Seal Pup
Signed, oil on board
14 x 20in (35.5 x 51cm)
£2,000–2,400 / €2,900–3,500
$3,600–4,350 ⚘ B(Kn)

Donald Watson
British (20thC)
Short-eared owls in flight
Signed and dated 1973, watercolour
8¼ x 9¾in (21 x 25cm)
£200–240 / €290–350
$370–440 ⚘ B(Kn)

◄ **Frederick Judd Waugh**
American (1861–1940)
Morning light on breaking surf
Signed, oil on board
25 x 30in (63.5 x 76cm)
£3,800–4,500 / €5,500–6,600
$6,900–8,200 ⚘ B

George Weatherill
British (1810–90)
Whitby Abbey by Moonlight
Watercolour
9 x 5in (23 x 12.5cm)
£2,700–3,000
€3,900–4,400
$4,900–5,400 ⊞ PY

► **Mary Weatherill**
British (1834–1913)
Moonlight off Whitby Harbour
Watercolour
3¼ x 6in (8.5 x 15cm)
£570–630 / €830–920
$1,050–1,150 ⊞ PY

T. Weaver
British (19thC)
Miranda, 6 years old, herd book
Signed, inscribed and dated 1822, oil on canvas
21¾ x 26½in (55.5 x 67.5cm)
£5,200–6,200 / €7,600–9,100
$9,500–11,300 ⚒ WW

John Sanderson
Wells
British (1872–1911)
Setting to depart;
Onward bound
A pair, signed,
oil on canvas
16 x 24in (40.5 x 61cm)
£27,000–30,000
€39,000–43,000
$49,000–54,000
⊞ HFA

Thomas Weaver
British (1774–1843)
Portrait of a boy on a donkey in a park with a terrier
Signed, inscribed and dated 1833, oil on canvas
22 x 27¼in (56 x 69cm)
£2,600–3,100 / €3,800–4,550
$4,750–5,700 ⚒ DN

◄ **James Webb**
British (1825–95)
On the Scheldt
Oil on canvas
8 x 12in (20.5 x 30.5cm)
£2,700–3,200 / €3,900–4,650
$4,900–5,800 ⚒ B

Otto Weber
German (1832–88)
Changing Pastures, children beside
a wooden gate with cattle and
sheep nearby, a collie dog beyond
Signed, inscribed and dated 1869,
pencil and watercolour
19½ x 28½in (49.5 x 72.5cm)
£4,800–5,700 / €7,000–8,300
$8,700–10,400 ⚒ TEN

► **Joseph Werner**
Swiss (1637–1710)
Two Bacchantes
Gouache on vellum laid down
on wood
5½ x 4¼in (14 x 11cm)
£13,200–15,900 / €19,300–23,000
$24,000–29,000 ⚒ S(NY)

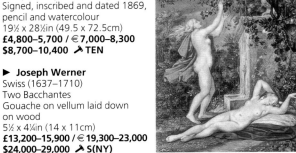

Tom Wesselmann
American (b1931)
Lulu
Signed, numbered 16/25, lithograph
16¾ x 25in (42.5 x 63.5cm)
£1,200–1,450 / €1,750–2,100
$2,200–2,600 ↗ **B(Kn)**

Konstantin Alexandrovich Westchilov
Russian (1878–1945)
Golden Autumn
Signed, oil on board
21 x 28in (53.5 x 71cm)
£16,800–20,000 / €24,000–29,000
$31,000–37,000 ↗ **S**

◄ **Julius Weyde**
German (1822–60)
Visit to Grandpa
Signed, oil on canvas
26 x 19½in (66 x 49.5cm)
£27,000–30,000
€39,000–43,000
$49,000–54,000 ⊞ **HFA**

► **James Abbott McNeill Whistler**
American (1834–1903)
La Vielle aux Loques
Etching
8 x 5¾in (20.5 x 14.5cm)
£750–900 / €1,100–1,300
$1,400–1,650 ↗ **B**

▲ **For further information**
on Whistler see Urban Art
(pages 200–205)

► **James Abbott McNeill Whistler**
American
(1834–1903)
Landscape with
the horse
Etching
5 x 8in
(12.5 x 20.5cm)
£950–1,100
€1,400–1,600
$1,750–2,000 ↗ **B**

Ethelbert White
British (1891–1972)
The Haycart
Signed, oil on canvas
19¾ x 30in (60.5 x 76cm)
£800–960 / €1,150–1,400
$1,450–1,750 ↗ **B(Kn)**

Michael J. Whitehand
British (b1941)
Whiteheather leading *Britannia*, Isle of White
Oil on canvas
36 x 50in (91.5 x 127cm)
£2,750–3,050 / € 4,000–4,450
$5,000–5,500 ⊞ NFA

Frederick Whitehead
British (1853–1938)
Study of a French peasant
Signed and inscribed, oil on board
8½ x 13in (21.5 x 33cm)
£600–720 / € 880–1,050
$1,100–1,300 ⚒ B(Kn)

► **Frederick Whitehead**
British (1853–1938)
A view down High West Street,
Dorchester, with a horse and
cart and a formation of
infantrymen marching
towards barracks
Signed, oil on panel
7 x 11in (18 x 28cm)
£2,400–2,900 / € 3,500–4,200
$4,400–5,300 ⚒ HYD

John William Whiteley
British (1859–1936)
Three-quarter length study
of a male nude from behind
Signed and dated 1900,
oil on canvas
19 x 9¾in (48.5 x 25cm)
£800–960 / € 1,150–1,400
$1,450–1,700 ⚒ B(Kn)

Charles Whymper
British (1853–1941)
Grey partridge in undergrowth
Signed, watercolour
10¼ x 6¾in (26 x 17cm)
£480–570 / € 700–830
$880–1,050 ⚒ B(Kn)

◄ **Samuel de Wilde**
British (c1748–1832)
Head and shoulders profile
portrait of Mrs Siddons
Monochrome watercolour
on tinted paper
6¼ x 4¾in (16 x 12cm)
£260–310 / € 380–450
$470–560 ⚒ GH

◄ Maurice Canning Wilks
British/Irish (1910–84)
The Errigal Range, Co Donnegal
Signed and inscribed, oil on canvas
21½ x 28in (54.5 x 71cm)
£3,600–4,300 / € 5,300–6,300
$6,600–7,800 ⚹ WW

Maurice Canning Wilks
British/Irish (1910–84)
Glenarm, Antrim
Signed, watercolour
11 x 14½in (28 x 37cm)
£1,000–1,200 / € 1,450–1,750
$1,800–2,150 ⚹ CHTR

► Ernst Willers
German (1803–80)
A wooded landscape with goats
on a path near Ariccia
Inscribed and dated 1837, oil on
paper laid down on canvas
15½ x 19¾in (39.5 x 50cm)
£4,900–5,900 / € 7,200–8,600
$9,000–10,800 ⚹ S(NY)

Arthur Willett
British (fl1883–92)
Huntsman and hounds in a
meadow, with sheep beside a
stream in the foreground
Signed and inscribed, pencil and
watercolour heightened with white
21½ x 15in (54.5 x 38cm)
£1,100–1,300 / € 1,600–1,900
$2,000–2,350 ⚹ TEN

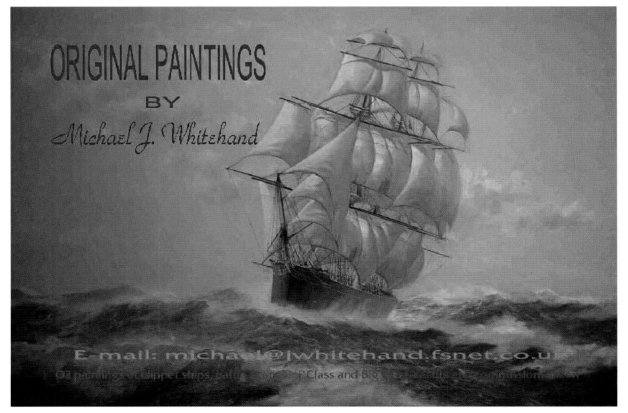

ORIGINAL PAINTINGS
BY
Michael J. Whitehand

E-mail: michael@jwhitehand.fsnet.co.uk

Edward Charles Williams (1807–81)

Edward Charles Williams came from a family of painters. His father was Edward, his brothers were Alfred Arthur, who changed his surname to Gilbert, and Henry who changed his surname to Boddington in order to avoid being mistaken for his brother and father. It is Edward Charles who painted views of the River Thames and coastal scenes and sometimes collaborated with William Shayer on large village or gypsy subjects. He is the most highly-regarded artist of the family, and his paintings are the most valuable.

The prices of the pictures shown here are influenced by the sizes of the two works, the painting entitled *Rest from the Harvest* is twice the size of *Fishing in a Mountain Lake*.

◀ **Edward Charles Williams**
British (1807–81)
Rest from the Harvest
Signed and dated 1881, oil on canvas
24 x 42in (61 x 106.5cm)
£16,600–18,500 / € 24,200–27,000
$30,000–34,000 ⊞ HFA

Edward Charles Williams
British (1807–81)
Fishing in a Mountain Lake
Signed and dated 1863,
oil on canvas
10 x 14in (25.5 x 35.5cm)
£6,300–7,000 / € 9,200–10,200
$11,500–12,700 ⊞ HFA

▶ **Terrick Williams, RA**
British (1860–1936)
Net mending, Cassis
Signed and titled, oil on canvas
15¼ x 21in (38.5 x 53.5cm)
£8,200–9,800 / € 12,000–14,300
$14,900–17,800 🔨 B

Terrick Williams, RA
British (1860–1936)
St Tropez
Pastels
8¼ x 11in (21 x 28cm)
£1,300–1,550
€ 1,900–2,250
$2,350–2,800 🔨 B

▶ **Walter Williams**
British (1835–1906)
On Watch
Oil on canvas
5½ x 8in (14 x 20.5cm)
£7,900–8,800 / € 11,600–12,800
$14,400–16,000 ⊞ HFA

Warren Williams, ARCA
British (1863–1918)
A still morning on the Dart looking south at Dittisham, Devon
Signed, titled and inscribed, watercolour
23 x 34¾in (58.5 x 88.5cm)
£6,700–7,500 / €9,800–10,900
$12,200–13,600 ⊞ JC

Frederick Williamson
British (1856–1900)
A summer landscape with a boy seated beside a sandy lane,
sheep and cottage nearby
Signed, watercolour
5¼ x 8¼in (13.5 x 21cm)
£1,300–1,550 / €1,900–2,250
$2,350–2,800 ↗ TEN

Henry Brittan Willis, RWS
British (1810–84)
Sheep and cattle in a landscape
Oil on canvas
30 x 47in (76 x 119.5cm)
£15,800–17,500 / €23,000–26,000
$29,000–32,000 ⊞ JN

Thorton Willis
American (b1938)
Wall
Signed, acrylic on canvas
90 x 72in (228.5 x 183cm)
£1,150–1,350 / €1,650–1,950
$2,100–2,450 ↗ LHA

Eric Wilson
British (1911–46)
Street Corner, Montmartre, Paris
Signed, oil on canvas
11¾ x 15½in (30 x 39.5cm)
£6,800–8,200 / €9,900–11,900
$12,400–14,900 ↗ LJ

John James Wilson
British (1818–75)
Near Brabourne, East Kent
Signed and dated 1864, oil on canvas
11½ x 19½in (29 x 49.5cm)
£3,800–4,200 / €5,500–6,100
$6,900–7,600 ⊞ Bne

◄ **Paul G. Wilson**
British (b1956)
Untitled
Oil on canvas
20 x 30in (51 x 76cm)
£580–700 / € 850–1,000
$1,050–1,250 🔨 **RTo**

William Wilson, RSA, RSW
Scottish (1905–72)
Olive Trees, San Gimignano
Signed and dated 1952, pencil and watercolour
18 x 24in (45.5 x 61cm)
£1,300–1,550
€ 1,900–2,250
$2,350–2,800 🔨 **L&T**

A good provenance can make a huge difference to the price of a picture. Collectors like something new to the market; a good picture that has been in a family for generations will fetch more than a picture that has been in and out of auction houses.

Hans Wilt
Austrian (1867–1917)
Fountain at Schönbrunn
Signed and dated 1912, oil on canvas
28½ x 39in (72.5 x 99cm)
£3,400–4,100 / € 5,000–6,000
$6,200–7,400 🔨 **DORO**

William Frederick Witherington, RA
British (1785–1865)
The Ferry Crossing
Signed, oil on panel
8 x 11½in (20.5 x 29cm)
£4,800–5,400 / € 7,000–7,900
$8,700–9,800 ⊞ **HFA**

Grant Wood
American (1891–1942)
Quetzal in Flight
Signed, oil on fibreboard
31 x 35in (78.5 x 89cm)
£11,000–13,000 / € 16,000–19,000
$20,000–24,000 🔨 **JAA**

Robert William Wood
American (1901–77)
Fall Landscape with Distant Mountains
Signed, oil on canvas
25 x 30in (63.5 x 76cm)
**£1,300–1,550 / € 1,900–2,250
$2,350–2,800** ⚘ **LHA**

Christine Woodside, RSW, RGI
British (b1945)
Palazzo Dario
Mixed media
15 x 14in (38 x 35.5cm)
**£1,100–1,300 / € 1,600–1,900
$2,000–2,350** ⊞ **P&H**

Edmund Henry Wuerpel
American (1866–1958)
Evening on the Mississippi River
Oil on canvas laid down on board
12 x 8in (30.5 x 20.5cm)
**£550–660 / € 800–960
$1,000–1,200** ⚘ **TREA**

◄ **Andrew Wyeth**
American (b1917)
Low Tide
Signed and inscribed, watercolour on paper
17¾ x 21½in (45 x 54.5cm)
**£28,000–33,000 / € 41,000–48,000
$51,000–61,000** ⚘ **S(NY)**

Andrew Wyeth is the son of Newell Convers Wyeth, the well-known illustrator of children's books. He did not receive a formal eductation but was tutored at home by his father, who also taught him to paint. Andrew works primarily in watercolour and egg tempera, and his pieces vary from strikingly realistic to surrealistic. Andrew is considered a national living treasure and is often referred to as 'the painter of the people'. His work is held in high regard by museums and galleries, and in 1964 the Farnsworth Museum in Rockwood, Maine paid what was then the highest price ever by a gallery for the work of a living artist. Andrew's son Jamie is also a successful painter.

◄ **Newell Convers Wyeth**
American (1882–1945)
The Story of Glass
Signed, oil on panel
27 x 25in (68.5 x 63.5cm)
**£39,000–47,000
€ 57,000–68,000
$72,000–86,000** ⚘ **S(NY)**

► **Newell Convers Wyeth**
American (1882–1945)
The Story of Furs
Signed and inscribed, oil on panel
27 x 25in (68.5 x 63.5cm)
**£66,000–79,000
€ 96,000–115,000
$120,000–144,000** ⚘ **S(NY)**

Steve Yabsley
British (20thC)
Flower Donkey
Acrylic on canvas
23¾ x 19¾in (60.5 x 50cm)
£850–950 / € 1,250–1,400
$1,550–1,700 ⊞ WrG

Alexander Evgenievich Yakovlev
Russian (1887–1938)
Lake Alberta, Africa
Signed and dated 1925,
gouache on board
20½ x 29¾in (52 x 75.5cm)
£9,600–11,500
€ 14,000–16,800
$17,500–21,000 ⚒ S

▶ **John Yardley, RI**
British (b1933)
The Smart Black Suit
Signed, watercolour
9¼ x 13¼in (23.5 x 33.5cm)
£750–830 / € 1,050–1,200
$1,350–1,500 ⊞ Bne

Vladimir Igorevich Yakovlev
Russian (1934–98)
White Flower
Signed, gouache on paper
23¾ x 16¾in (60.5 x 42.5cm)
£4,200–5,000 / € 6,100–7,300
$7,600–9,100 ⚒ S

◀ **John Yardley, RI**
British (b1933)
Grand Canal: Venice
Signed, watercolour
12½ x 18½in
(32 x 47cm)
£1,300–1,450
€ 1,900–2,100
$2,350–2,650
⊞ Bne

▶ **Fred Yates**
British (b1922)
Beach on Sunday
morning
Signed and dated
1967, oil on board
19¾ x 71¾in
(50 x 182.5cm)
£1,100–1,300
€ 1,600–1,900
$2,000–2,350 ⚒ Bea

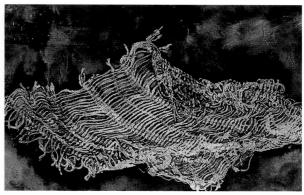

Anne Yeats
Irish (1919–2001)
Shawl
14 x 21in (35.5 x 53.5cm)
£1,400–1,650 / € 2,000–2,400
$2,550–3,000 ↗ **WA**

◄ **Anne Yeats**
Irish (1919–2001)
Balloon Face
Signed, oil on canvas
18 x 16in (45.5 x 41cm)
£2,050–2,450 / € 3,000–3,600
$3,750–4,450 ↗ **WA**

Dina Yeltseva
Russian (b1965)
The Apple
Signed, oil on canvas
9¾ x 11¾in (25 x 30cm)
£220–260 / € 320–380
$400–470 ↗ **JNic**

Pavel Yermolov
Russian (b1971)
Ancient Shelf
Signed, oil on canvas
11¾ x 15¾in (30 x 40cm)
£350–420 / € 510–610
$640–760 ↗ **JNic**

John Butler Yeats
Irish (1839–1922)
Lady Gregory
Inscribed, pencil
7 x 5in (18 x 12.5cm)
£4,450–5,300 / € 6,500–7,800
$8,100–9,600 ↗ **JAd**

▶ **Alexander Young**
British (1865–1923)
The harbour at Scarborough, a paddle
steamer and other boats in the foreground,
a view of the town in the distance
Signed and dated 1893, oil on canvas
24 x 18¼in (61 x 46.5cm)
£1,900–2,300 / € 2,800–3,350
$3,500–4,200 ↗ **TEN**

Blamire Young
Australian (1862–1935)
The Doom of Hellas
Signed, watercolour
29¼ x 43in (74.5 x 109cm)
£5,000–6,000 / € 7,400–8,800
$9,100–10,900 ↗ **LJ**

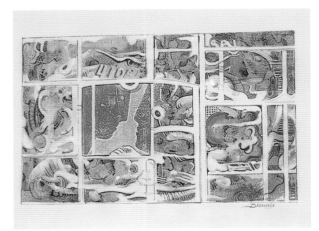

Dionissis Zaverdinos
Greek (b1954)
Abstract
Signed, oil on canvas
19½ x 27½in (49.5 x 70cm)
£2,100–2,500 / €3,100–3,650
$3,800–4,550 🔨 B

Theodore Zimmerman
British (20thC)
A Lovely Day on the Beach at Le Touquet, France
Signed and inscribed, pastel
7 x 8½in (18 x 21.5cm)
£2,300–2,750 / €3,350–4,000
$4,200–5,000 🔨 TEN

▶ **Leopold Zinnögger**
Austrian (1811–72)
Still life with melon
Signed and dated, watercolour on paper
39 x 20in (39 x 51cm)
£410–490
€600–720
$750–890 🔨 DORO

Anna Katrina Zinkeisen, RP, ROI
Scottish (1901–76)
Portrait of Lady Dunn
Signed and dated 1961, oil on canvas
64 x 33in (162.5 x 84cm)
£1,400–1,700 / €2,100–2,500
$2,600–3,100 🔨 B(WM)

Anatoly Timoffeevich Zverev
Russian (1931–86)
A beauty
Signed, oil on board
26 x 18½in (66 x 47cm)
£960–1,150 / €1,450–1,700
$1,750–2,100 🔨 BUK

Anatoly Timoffeevich Zverev
Russian (1931–86)
Cockerel
Signed and dated, oil on board
19¾ x 26¾in (50 x 68cm)
£3,600–4,300 / €5,300–6,300
$6,600–7,800 🔨 S

Directory of Auctioneers

Auctioneers who hold frequent sales should contact us by January 2005 for inclusion in the next edition.

UNITED KINGDOM

Berkshire
Dreweatt Neate, Donnington Priory, Donnington, Newbury RG14 2JE
Tel: 01635 553553
donnington@dnfa.com
www.dnfa.com/donnington

Buckinghamshire
Bourne End Auction Rooms, Station Approach, Bourne End SL8 5QH
Tel: 01628 531500

Cambridgeshire
Cheffins, Clifton House, Clifton Road, Cambridge CB1 7EA
Tel: 01223 213343
www.cheffins.co.uk

Channel Islands
Bonhams and Langlois, Westaway Chambers, 39 Don Street, St Helier, Jersey JE2 4TR Tel: 01534 722441
www.bonhams.com

Cheshire
Bonhams, New House, 150 Christleton Road, Chester CH3 5TD Tel: 01244 313936
www.bonhams.com

Cornwall
David Lay (ASVA), Auction House, Alverton, Penzance TR18 4RE
Tel: 01736 361414
david.lays@btopenworld.com

Cumbria
Thomson, Roddick & Medcalf Ltd, Coleridge House, Shaddongate, Carlisle CA2 5TU Tel: 01228 528939
www.thomsonroddick.com

Devon
Bearnes, St Edmund's Court, Okehampton Street, Exeter EX4 1DU
Tel: 01392 207000
enquiries@bearnes.co.uk
www.bearnes.co.uk

Michael J Bowman, 6 Haccombe House, Nr Netherton, Newton Abbott TQ12 4SJ Tel: 01626 872890

Dreweatt Neate formerly Honiton Galleries. Incorporating Robin A. Fenner, 205 High Street, Honiton EX14 1LQ Tel: 01404 42404
honiton@dnfa.com
www.dnfa.com/honiton

Dorset
Charterhouse, The Long Street Salerooms, Sherborne DT9 3BS
Tel: 01935 812277
enquiry@charterhouse-auctions.co.uk
www.charterhouse-auctions.co.uk

Hy Duke & Son, The Dorchester Fine Art Salerooms, Weymouth Avenue, Dorchester DT1 1QS
Tel: 01305 265080
www.dukes-auctions.com

Essex
Sworders, 14 Cambridge Road, Stansted Mountfitchet CM24 8BZ
Tel: 01279 817778
auctions@sworder.co.uk
www.sworder.co.uk

Gloucestershire
Dreweatt Neate formerly Bristol Auction Rooms, St John's Place, Apsley Road, Clifton, Bristol BS8 2ST
Tel: 0117 973 7201
bristol@dnfa.com
www.dnfa.com/bristol

Greater Manchester
Capes Dunn & Co, The Auction Galleries, 38 Charles Street, Off Princess Street M1 7DB
Tel: 0161 273 6060/1911
capesdunn@yahoo.co.uk

Herefordshire
Brightwells Fine Art, The Fine Art Saleroom, Easters Court, Leominster HR6 0DE Tel: 01568 611122
fineart@brightwells.com
www.brightwells.com

Hertfordshire
Tring Market Auctions, The Market Premises, Brook Street, Tring HP23 5EF Tel: 01442 826446
sales@tringmarketauctions.co.uk
www.tringmarketauctions.co.uk

Kent
Bonhams, 49 London Road, Sevenoaks TN13 1AR
Tel: 01732 740310
www.bonhams.com

The Canterbury Auction Galleries, 40 Station Road West, Canterbury CT2 8AN Tel: 01227 763337
auctions@thecanterburyauctiongalleries.com
www.thecanterburyauctiongalleries.com

Mervyn Carey, Twysden Cottage, Scullsgate, Benenden, Cranbrook TN17 4LD Tel: 01580 240283

Dreweatt Neate formerly Bracketts Fine Art Auctioneers, The Auction Hall, The Pantiles, Tunbridge Wells TN2 5QL Tel: 01892 544500
tunbridgewells@dnfa.com
www.dnfa.com/tunbridgewells

Ibbett Mosely, 125 High Street, Sevenoaks TN13 1UT
Tel: 01732 456731
auctions@ibbettmosely.co.uk
www.ibbettmosely.co.uk

London
Bloomsbury Auctions Ltd, Bloomsbury House, 24 Maddox Street W1S 1PP Tel: 020 7495 9494
info@bloomsburyauctions.com
www.bloomsburyauctions.com

Bonhams, Montpelier Street, Knightsbridge SW7 1HH
Tel: 020 7393 3900
www.bonhams.com

Bonhams, 10 Salem Road, Bayswater W2 4DL Tel: 020 7229 9090
www.bonhams.com

Bonhams, 101 New Bond Street W1S 1SR Tel: 020 7629 6602
www.bonhams.com

Bonhams, 65-69 Lots Road, Chelsea SW10 0RN Tel: 020 7393 3900
www.bonhams.com

Christie's, 8 King Street, St James's SW1Y 6QT Tel: 020 7839 9060
www.christies.com

Christie's, 85 Old Brompton Road SW7 3LD Tel: 020 7930 6074
www.christies.com

Sotheby's, 34-35 New Bond Street W1A 2AA Tel: 020 7293 5000
www.sothebys.com

Sotheby's Olympia, Hammersmith Road W14 8UX Tel: 020 7293 5555
www.sothebys.com

Merseyside
Cato Crane & Co, Liverpool Auction Rooms, 6 Stanhope Street, Liverpool L8 5RF Tel: 0151 709 5559
johncrane@cato-crane.co.uk
www.cato-crane.co.uk

Norfolk
Keys, Off Palmers Lane, Aylsham NR11 6JA Tel: 01263 733195
www.aylshamsalerooms.co.uk

Northern Ireland
John Ross & Company, 37 Montgomery Street, Belfast, Co Antrim BT1 4NX
Tel: 028 9032 5448

Nottinghamshire
Neales, 192 Mansfield Road, Nottingham NG1 3HU Tel: 0115 962 4141 fineart@neales.co.uk
www.neales-auctions.com

Oxfordshire
Bonhams, 39 Park End Street, Oxford OX1 1JD Tel: 01865 723524
www.bonhams.com

Simmons & Sons, 32 Bell Street, Henley-on-Thames RG9 2BH
Tel: 01491 612810
www.simmonsandsons.com

Scotland
Bonhams, 65 George Street, Edinburgh EH2 2JL Tel: 0131 225 2266
www.bonhams.com

Lyon & Turnbull, 33 Broughton Place, Edinburgh EH1 3RR Tel: 0131 557 8844
info@lyonandturnbull.com

Sotheby's, 112 George Street, Edinburgh EH2 4LH Tel: 0131 226 7201
www.sothebys.com

Thomson, Roddick & Medcalf Ltd, 60 Whitesands, Dumfries DG1 2RS
Tel: 01387 279879
trmdumfries@btconnect.com
www.thomsonroddick.com

Thomson, Roddick & Medcalf Ltd, 20 Murray Street, Annan DG12 6EG
Tel: 01461 202575
www.thomsonroddick.com

Thomson, Roddick & Medcalf Ltd, 43/4 Hardengreen Business Park, Eskbank, Edinburgh EH22 3NX
Tel: 0131 454 9090
www.thomsonroddick.com

Somerset
Bonhams, 1 Old King Street, Bath BA1 2JT Tel: 01225 788 988
www.bonhams.com

Gardiner Houlgate, The Bath Auction Rooms, 9 Leafield Way, Corsham, Nr Bath SN13 9SW Tel: 01225 812912
auctions@gardiner-houlgate.co.uk
www.invaluable.com/gardiner-houlgate

Greenslade Taylor Hunt Fine Art, Magdelene House, Church Square, Taunton TA1 1SB Tel: 01823 332525

Lawrences Fine Art Auctioneers, South Street, Crewkerne TA18 8AB
Tel: 01460 73041
www.lawrences.co.uk

Staffordshire
Wintertons Ltd, Lichfield Auction Centre, Fradley Park, Lichfield WS13 8NF Tel: 01543 263256
enquiries@wintertons.co.uk
www.wintertons.co.uk

Suffolk
Bonhams, 32 Boss Hall Road, Ipswich IP1 5DJ Tel: 01473 740494
www.bonhams.com

Surrey
John Nicholson, The Auction Rooms, Longfield, Midhurst Road, Fernhurst GU27 3HA Tel: 01428 653727

East Sussex
Gorringes Auction Galleries, Terminus Road, Bexhill-on-Sea TN39 3LR Tel: 01424 212994
bexhill@gorringes.co.uk
www.gorringes.co.uk

Gorringes Inc Julian Dawson, 15 North Street, Lewes BN7 2PD
Tel: 01273 478221
auctions@gorringes.co.uk
www.gorringes.co.uk

West Sussex
Sotheby's Sussex, Summers Place, Billingshurst RH14 9AD
Tel: 01403 833500
www.sothebys.com

Rupert Toovey & Co Ltd, Spring Gardens, Washington RH20 3BS
Tel: 01903 891955
auctions@rupert-toovey.com
www.rupert-toovey.com

Tyne & Wear
Anderson & Garland (Auctioneers), Marlborough House, Marlborough Crescent, Newcastle-upon-Tyne NE1 4EE Tel: 0191 232 6278

Wales
Bonhams, 7–8 Park Place, Cardiff CF10 3DP Tel: 029 2072 7980
cardiff@bonhams.com
www.bonhams.com

West Midlands
Bonhams, The Old House, Station Road, Knowle, Solihull B93 0HT
Tel: 01564 776151
www.bonhams.com

Fellows & Sons, Augusta House, 19 Augusta Street, Hockley, Birmingham B18 6JA Tel: 0121 212 2131
info@fellows.co.uk www.fellows.co.uk

Wiltshire
Dominic Winter Book Auctions, The Old School, Maxwell Street, Swindon SN1 5DR Tel: 01793 611340
info@dominicwinter.co.uk
www.dominicwinter.co.uk

Woolley & Wallis, Salisbury Salerooms, 51-61 Castle Street, Salisbury SP1 3SU
Tel: 01722 424500/411854
junebarrett@woolleyandwallis.co.uk
www.woolleyandwallis.co.uk

Yorkshire
Bonhams, 17a East Parade, Leeds LS1 2BH Tel: 0113 2448011
www.bonhams.com

Dee, Atkinson & Harrison, The Exchange Saleroom, Driffield YO25 6LD Tel: 01377 253151
info@dahauctions.com
www.dahauctions.com

David Duggleby, The Vine St Salerooms, Scarborough YO11 1XN
Tel: 01723 507111
auctions@davidduggleby.com
www.davidduggleby.com

Andrew Hartley, Victoria Hall Salerooms, Little Lane, Ilkley LS29 8EA Tel: 01943 816363
info@andrewhartleyfinearts.co.uk
www.andrewhartleyfinearts.co.uk

Morphets of Harrogate, 6 Albert Street, Harrogate HG1 1JL
Tel: 01423 530030

Richardson & Smith, 8 Victoria Square, Whitby YO21 1EA
Tel: 01947 602298

Tennants, The Auction Centre, Harmby Road, Leyburn DL8 5SG
Tel: 01969 623780
enquiry@tennants-ltd.co.uk
www.tennants.co.uk

AUSTRALIA
Leonard Joel Auctioneers, 333 Malvern Road, South Yarra,

Victoria 3141 Tel: 03 9826 4333
decarts@ljoel.com.au or
jewellery@ljoel.com.au
www.ljoel.com.au

Shapiro Auctioneers, 162 Queen
Street, Woollahra, Sydney NSW 2025
Tel: 612 9326 1588

Sotheby's Australia, 118-122 Queen
Street, Woollahra, New South Wales
2025 Tel: 61 2 9362 1000
www.sothebys.com

AUSTRIA
Dorotheum, Palais Dorotheum,
A-1010 Wien, Dorotheergasse 17,
1010 Vienna Tel: 515 60 229
client.services@dorotheum.at

BELGIUM
Bernaerts, Verlatstraat 18-22, 2000
Antwerpen/Anvers
Tel: +32 (0)3 248 19 21
edmond.bernaerts@ping.be
www.auction-bernaerts.com

CANADA
Ritchies Inc., Auctioneers & Appraisers
of Antiques & Fine Art, 288 King
Street East, Toronto, Ontario
M5A 1K4 Tel: (416) 364 1864
auction@ritchies.com
www.ritchies.com

Sotheby's, 9 Hazelton Avenue, Toronto,
Ontario M5R 2EI Tel: 416 926 1774
www.sothebys.com

Waddington's Auctions, 111
Bathurst Street, Toronto MSV 2RI
Tel: 001 416 504 9100
vb@waddingtonsauctions.com
www.waddingtonsauctions.com

CHINA
Sotheby's, 5/F Standard Chartered
Bank Building, 4–4A Des Voeux
Road, Central Hong Kong
Tel: 852 2524 8121
www.sothebys.com

FRANCE
Sotheby's France SA, 76 rue du
Faubourg, Saint Honore, Paris 75008
Tel: 33 1 53 05 53 05
www.sothebys.com

HONG KONG
Christie's Hong Kong, 2203-8
Alexandra House, 16-20 Chater Road
Tel: 852 2521 5396
www.christies.com

ITALY
Christie's, Palazzo Massimo,
Lancellotti, Piazza Navona 114,
00186 Rome Tel: 39 06 686 3333
www.christies.com

Sotheby's Rome, Piazza d'Espana 90,
Rome 00186 Tel: 39(6)
6841791/6781798
www.sothebys.com

MEXICO
Galeria Louis C. Morton, GLC
A7073L IYS, Monte Athos 179,
Col. Lomas de Chapultepec CP11000
Tel: 52 5520 5005
glmorton@prodigy.net.mx
www.lmorton.com

NETHERLANDS
Sotheby's Amsterdam, De Boelelaan
30, Amsterdam 1083 HJ
Tel: 31 20 550 2200
www.sothebys.com

REPUBLIC OF IRELAND
James Adam & Sons,
26 St Stephen's Green, Dublin 2
Tel: 00 353 1 6760261
www.jamesadam.ie/

Thomas P Adams & Co, 38 Main
Street, Blackrock, Co Dublin
Tel: 00 353 1 288 5146

Hamilton Osborne King, 4 Main
Street, Blackrock, Co. Dublin
Tel: 00 353 1 288 5011
blackrock@hok.ie www.hok.ie

Whyte's Auctioneers,
38 Molesworth Street, Dublin 2
Tel: 00 353 1 676 2888
info@whytes.ie www.whytes.ie

SINGAPORE
Sotheby's (Singapore) Pte Ltd,
1 Cuscaden Road, 01-01 The Regent
249715 Tel: 65 6732 8239
www.sothebys.com

SWEDEN
Bukowskis, Arsenalsgatan 4,
Stockholm Tel: +46 (8) 614 08 00
info@bukowskis.se
www.bukowskis.se

SWITZERLAND
Galerie Koller, Hardturmstrasse 102,
8031 Zurich Tel: +41 (1) 445 63 31
hochuli@galeriekoller.ch

U.S.A.
The Coeur d'Alene Art Auction,
PO Box 310, Hayden ID 83835
Tel: 208 772 9009
drumgallery@nidlink.com
www.cdaartauction.com

Rachel Davis Fine Arts, 1301 West
79th Street, Cleveland OH 44102
Tel: 216 939 1191 rdavis@en.com
www.racheldavisfinearts.com

Doyle New York, 175 East 87th
Street, New York NY 10128
Tel: 212 427 2730
info@doylenewyork.com
www.doylenewyork.com

Leslie Hindman, Inc., 122 North
Aberdeen Street, Chicago, Illinois
60607 Tel: 001 312 280 1212
www.lesliehindman.com

Jackson's Auctioneers & Appraisers,
2229 Lincoln Street, Cedar Falls IA
50613 Tel: 319 277 2256

James D Julia, Inc., P O Box 830,
Rte.201 Skowhegan Road,
Fairfield ME 04937

Tel: 207 453 7125
jjulia@juliaauctions.com
www.juliaauctions.com

Kimball M Sterling, Inc., 125 West
Market Street, Johnson City,
Tennessee 37601 Tel: 423 928 1471
kimsold@tricon.com
www.outsiderartauctions.com

New Orleans Auction Galleries, Inc.,
801 Magazine Street, AT 510 Julia,
New Orleans, Louisiana 70130
Tel: 504 566 1849

Phillips, de Pury & Co., 3 West 57
Street, New York NY 10019
Tel: 212 570 4830 phillips-auctions.com

Phillips New York, 406 East 79th
Street, New York NY10021
Tel: 212 570 4830

Shannon's, 354 Woodmont Road,
Milford, Connecticut 06460
Tel: 203 877 1711
www.shannons.com

Skinner Inc., The Heritage On The
Garden, 63 Park Plaza, Boston MA
02116 Tel: 617 350 5400

Skinner Inc., 357 Main Street, Bolton
MA 01740 Tel: 978 779 6241

Sloan's & Kenyon, 4605 Bradley
Boulevard, Bethesda, Maryland
20815 Tel: 301 634 2330
info@sloansandkenyon.com
www.sloansandkenyon.com

Sotheby's, 1334 York Avenue at
72nd St, New York NY 10021
Tel: 212 606 7000
www.sothebys.com

Treadway Gallery, Inc., 2029
Madison Road, Cincinnati, Ohio
45208 Tel: 001 513 321 6742
www.treadwaygallery.com

Directory of Museums

If you wish to be included in next year's directory, or if you have a change of address or telephone number, please contact Miller's advertising department by January 2005. We advise readers to telephone first to check opening times before visiting a museum.

UNITED KINGDOM
Aberdeen Art Gallery, Schoolhill,
Aberdeen AB10 1FQ
Tel:0122 452 3700

Ashmolean Museum, Beaumont
Street, Oxford OX1 2PH
Tel: 01865 278010

Barbican Art Gallery, Silk Street,
London EC2 Tel: 020 7382 7043

British Museum,
Great Russell Street, London
WC1B 3DC Tel: 020 7323 8299

Courtauld Institute,
Somerset House, Strand,
London WC2R 0RN
Tel: 020 7848 2508

Dulwich Picture Gallery, College
Road, London, SE21 7BG
Tel: 020 8693 5254

Hayward Gallery, Royal Festival Hall,
Belvedere Road, London SE1 8XX
Tel: 020 7960 4242

Laing Art Gallery, New Bridge
Street, Newcastle, NE1 8AG
Tel: 0191 232 7734

Leeds City Art Gallery,
The Headrow, Leeds
LS1 3AA Tel: 0113 247 8248

The Lowry, Pier 8, Salford Quays,
Manchester M50 3AZ
Tel: 0161 876 2020
www.thelowry.com

Manchester City Art Galleries,
City Art Gallery, Mosley Street,
Manchester M2 3JL
Tel: 0161 236 5244

National Gallery, Trafalgar Square,
London WC2N 5DN
Tel: 020 7747 2885

National Gallery of Scotland,
The Mound,
Edinburgh EH2 2EL
Tel: 0131 624 6200

National Portrait Gallery,
St Martin's Place,
London WC2H 0HE
Tel: 020 7306 0055

National Museum of Wales,
Cathay's Park,
Cardiff CF10 3NP

Royal Academy of Arts,
Burlington House,
Piccadilly, London W1J 0BD
Tel: 020 7300 8000

Saatchi Gallery, 98A Boundary
Road, St John's Wood, London
NW8 0RH Tel: 020 7624 3798

Scottish National Gallery of Modern
Art, 75 Belford Road, Edinburgh
EH4 3DR Tel: 0131 624 6200

Scottish National Portrait Gallery,
1 Queen Street,
Edinburgh EH2 1JD
Tel: 0131 624 6200

Tate Britain, Millbank,
London SW1P 4RG
Tel: 020 7887 8000

Tate Liverpool, Albert Dock,
Liverpool L3 4BB
Tel: 0151 702 7400

Tate Modern, Bankside,
London SE1 9TG Tel: 020 7887 8000

Tate St Ives, Porthmeor Beach,
St Ives, Cornwall TR26 1TG
Tel: 01736 796226

Ulster Museum, Botanic Gardens,
Belfast BT9 5AB
Tel 0232 381 251

Walker Art Gallery,
William Brown Street, Liverpool
L3 8EL Tel: 0151 478 4199

Wallace Collection,
Hertford House,
Manchester Square,
London W1U 3BN
Tel: 020 7563 9500

Whitechapel Art Gallery,
80–82 Whitechapel High Street,
London E1 7GX
Tel: 020 7247 6924

Whitworth Art Gallery,
The University of Manchester,
Oxford Road,
Manchester M15 6ER
Tel: 0161 275 7450

AUSTRALIA
Art Gallery of New South Wales,
Art Gallery Road, The Domain,
Sydney NSW 2000
Tel: 612 9225 1700

Art Gallery of South Australia,
North Terrace, Adelaide,
South Australia 5000
Tel: 618 8207 7000

National Gallery of Australia,
Parkes Place,
Canberra ACT 2601
Tel: 612 6240 6502

AUSTRIA
Academy of Fine Arts Vienna,
A–1010 Vienna, Schillerplatz 3
Tel: 43 158 816

Galerie Welz Ges.m.b.H,
Sigmund-Haffner-Gasse 16,
A–5020 Salzburg
Tel: 0662 841 771

BELGIUM
Palais des Beaux-Arts Bruxelles,
23 rue Ravenstein,
B–1000 Brussels
Tel: 322 5078211

CANADA
Art Gallery of Ontario,
317 Dundas Street West, Ontario
Tel: 416 979 6648

Montreal Museum of Fine Arts,
PO Box 3000, Station H, Montreal,
Quebec H3G 2T9
Tel: 514 285 1600
webmaster@mbamtl.org
www.mmfa.qc.ca

National Gallery of Canada,
380 Sussex Drive, Box 427,
Station A, Ottawa,
Ontario K1N 9N4
Tel: 613 990 1985

DENMARK
The National Museum of Fine Art,
Solvgade 48–50,
1307 Copenhagen
Tel: 33 74 84 94
smk@smk.dk

FINLAND
Finnish National Gallery,
Kaivokatu2/Brunnsgaten 2,
00100 Helskinki/Helsingfors
Tel: 358 (0)9 17 33 61

FRANCE
Centre National d'Art et de Culture
Georges Pompidou, Place Georges
Pompidou, 75004 Paris
Tel: 01 44 78 12 33

The Louvre, 36 Quai du Louvre,
75058 Paris www.louvre.fr

Musée d'Orsay Museum of Fine
Arts, 63 rue de Lille, 75343 Paris
Tel: 01 40 49 48

GERMANY
Deutsche Guggenheim Berlin,
Unter den Linden 13–15,
10117, Berlin
Tel: 49 (0) 30 20 20 93 0

Hamburger Kunsthalle,
Stifung öffenlichen Rechts,
Glockengießerwall,
20095 Hamburg
Tel: 49 40 428 131 200
info@hamburger-kunsthalle.de
www.hamburger-kunsthalle.de

Neue Pinakothek,
Barer Straße 29,
D–80799, Munich
Tel: 089 23805195
info@pinakothek.de

New National Gallery,
Potsdamerstraße 50,
10785 Berlin-Tiergarten
Tel: 030 266 2651
nng@smb.spk-berlin.de

HOLLAND
Rijksmuseum, Stadhouderskade 42,
1071 20 Amsterdam
Tel: 020 6747 047

HUNGARY
Hungarian National Gallery, Buda
Castle, The Royal Palace, Building B,
C, D, 2 Szent Ghörgy Square,
Budapest Tel: (36–1) 1757 533

ICELAND
National Gallery of Iceland,
Frikirkjuvegur 7,
101 Reykjavik
Tel: 354 515 9600

ITALY
National Gallery of Modern Art,
Viale delle Belle Arti 131, Rome
Tel: 06 322 4151

Peggy Guggenheim Collection,
Palazzo Venier dei Leoni,
701 Dorsoduro, 30123 Venice
Tel: 041 2405 411

Uffizi Gallery, Via della Ninna 5,
50121 Florence
Tel: 055 2388 651/652
info@uffizi-firenze.it

JAPAN
National Museum of Modern Art,
3 Kitanomaru Koen,
Chiyoda-ku, Tokyo 102–8322
Tel: 03 5777 8600

National Museum of Western Art,
7–1 Ueno-Koen, Taito-ku,
Tokyo 110–0007
Tel: 03 3828 5131

NEW ZEALAND
Auckland Art Gallery,
Corner Wellesley & Kitchener
Streets, Auckland
Tel: 649 379 1349

Christchurch Art Gallery
Te Puna o Waiwhetu,
PO Box 2626,
Christchurch 8015
Tel: (64–3) 9417970
art.gallery@ccc.govt.nz

Dunedin Public Art Gallery,
30 The Octagon,
PO Box 566, Dunedin,
Tel: 64 3 4774000
dpagmail@dcc.govt.nz

Museum of New Zealand
Te Papa Tongarewa,
Cable Street, PO Box 467,
Wellington Tel: 04 381 7000

NORWAY
National Museum of Contemporary
Art, Bankplassen 4, PB8191 dep.,
N–0034, Oslo
Tel: 223 35 820
info@mfs.museum.no

REPUBLIC OF IRELAND
National Gallery of Ireland,
Merrion Square, Dublin 2
Tel: 010 661 5133

National Print Museum,
Gavison Chapel, Beggar's Bush,
Haddington Road, Dublin 4
Tel: 010 660 3770

RUSSIA
Ivangorod Fortress Museum,
1/6 Kingiseppskoye Shosse,
Ivangorod, Leningrad
Tel: (275) 51792

Moscow Museum of Outsider Art,
105043 Russia, Moscow,
Izmallovski Boulevard, 30
Tel: 095 465 6304
outsider@cityline.ru
www.museum.ru/outsider/

Pushkin State Museum of Fine Arts,
121019 Moscow,
12 Volkhonka Street
Tel: 203 79 98

Sosnovy Bor Museum of Modern
Art, 56–a Leningradskaya ul,
Sosnovy Bor, Leningrad
Tel: (269) 69065

State Hermitage Museum,
34 Dvortsovaya Naberezhnaya
(Palace Embankment),
St Petersburg 190000
Tel: 812 110 96 25

Tretyakov State Gallery,
Lavrushinskii Lane, 10
Tel: 231 13 62

SOUTH AFRICA
Durban Art Gallery,
Second Floor, City Hall,
Smith Street, Durban
Tel: 27 31 3006238

Johannesburg Art Gallery,
King George Street,
Joubert Park,
2044 Johannesburg
Tel: 27 (011) 725 3130/80

South African National Gallery,
Government Avenue, Gardens,
Cape Town
Tel: 021 465 1628

SPAIN
Guggenheim Museum Bilbao,
Abandoibarra Et. 2,
48001 Bilbao
Tel: 34 94 435 9080

Museo del Prado,
P del Prado s/n,
28014 Madrid
Tel: 330 28 00

SWEDEN
Nationalmuseum, Södra
Blasieholmshamnen, Stockholm
Tel: 08 5195 4300

SWITZERLAND
Musée d'art et d'histoire,
2 rue Charles-Galland
CH1206 Geneva
Tel: 41 22 418 2600
mah@ville-ge.ch

Museum Rietberg Zürich,
Gablerstraße 15, CH 8002 Zürich
Tel: 01 206 3131

USA
Arthur Sackler Museum,
485 Broadway, Cambridge,
MA 02138 Tel: 617 495 9400

Busch-Reisinger Museum,
6 Prescott Street, Cambridge,
MA 02138 Tel: 617 495 9400

Fogg Art Museum,
32 Quincy Street, Harvard,
Cambridge, MA 02138
Tel: 617 495 9400

Institute of Contemporary Art,
955 Boylston Street,
Boston Tel: 617 266 5152

Museum of Fine Arts,
465 Huntingdon Avenue, Boston
Tel: 617 267 9300

The Art Institute of Chicago,
111 South Michigan Avenue,
Chicago, Illinois 60603
Tel: 312 443 3600

Cincinnati Art Museum,
953 Eden Park Drive, Cincinnati,
Ohio 45202
Tel: 513 639 2984

Contemporary Arts Museum,
5216 Montrose Boulevard,
Houston TX 77006–6598
Tel: 713 284 8250

The Museum of Fine Arts,
1001 Bissonnet Street,
Houston TX 77005–713639
Tel: 713 284 8250

Guggenheim Hermitage Museum,
The Venetian, 3355 Las Vegas
Boulevard South, Las Vegas,
NV 89109 Tel: 702 414 2440

Brooklyn Museum of Art,
200 Eastern Parkway,
Brooklyn,
New York
Tel: 718 638 5000

Metropolitan Museum of Art,
1000 Fifth Avenue at 82nd Street,
New York, NY 10028–7710
Tel: 212 570 3828
www.metmuseum.org

National Academy Museum,
1083 Fifth Avenue at 89th Street,
New York, NY 10128
Tel: 212 369 4880
www.nationalacademy.org

Solomon R. Guggenheim Museum,
1071 Fifth Avenue at 89th Street,
New York Tel: 212 423 3500
www.guggenheim.org

National Cowboy & Western
Heritage Museum,
1700 N E 63rd Street,
Oklahoma City, Oklahoma 73111
Tel: 405 478 2250

Philadelphia Museum of Art,
Benjamin Franklin Parkway,
26th Street, Philadelphia, PA19130
Tel: 215 763 8100

De Young Art Center, 2501 Irving
Street, San Francisco, CA 94122
Tel: 415 682 2484

Fine Arts Museum of San Francisco,
Legion of Honor, 100 34th Avenue,
San Francisco, CA 94121
Tel: 415 863 3330

San Francisco Museum of Modern
Art, 151 3rd Street, San Francisco,
CA 94103–3159
Tel: 415 357 4000
www.sfmoma.org

The Seattle Art Museum,
100 University Street,
Corner 1st Avenue, Seattle
Tel: 654 3100

National Portrait Gallery,
Smithsonian Institution,
8th and F Streets, NW Washington,
DC 20560 Tel: 202 275 1738

Directory of Galleries

If you wish to be included in next year's directory, or if you have a change of address or telephone number, please contact Miller's advertising department by January 2005. We advise readers to telephone first to check opening times before visiting a gallery.

UNITED KINGDOM

Berkshire
The Contemporary Fine Art Gallery, 31 High Street, Eton, Windsor SL4 6AX Tel: 01753 854315
mail@cfag.co.uk
www.cfag.co.uk

Buckinghamshire
Penn Barn Gallery, By The Pond, Elm Road, Penn HP10 8LB
Tel: 01494 815691

Cambridgeshire
Byard Art, 4 St. Mary's Passage, Cambridge CB2 3PQ
Tel: 01223 464646
info@byardart.co.uk
www.byardart.co.uk

Cambridge Contemporary Art, 6 Trinity Street, Cambridge CB2 1SU
Tel: 01223 324 222
info@cambridgegallery.co.uk
www.cambridgegallery.co.uk

Cambridge Fine Art, Priesthouse, 33 Church Street, Little Shelford, Nr Cambridge CB2 5HG
Tel: 01223 842866

Cheshire
Baron Fine Art, 68 Watergate Street, Chester CH1 2LA Tel: 01244 342520

Cleveland
T B & R Jordan (Fine Paintings), Aslak, Aislaby, Eaglescliffe, Stockton-on-Tees TS16 0QN Tel: 01642 782599

Cornwall
Belgrave Gallery, Fore Street, St. Ives TR26 1HE Tel: 01736 794888
sales@belgravegallery.com
www.belgravegallery.com

The Net Loft Gallery and The Old Customs House Studio, The Harbour, Porthleven TR13 9JD
Tel: 01326 564010
www.cornwall-art.co.uk

New Millennium Gallery, Street-an-Pol, St. Ives TR26 2DS Tel: 01736 793121
stives@dircon.co.uk
www.stives.dircon.co.uk

Penzance Gallery, 14 Chapel Street, Penzance TR14 4AW Tel: 01736 66620

Shears Fine Art, 58 Chapel Street, Penzance TR18 4AE
Tel: 01736 350501/361359
dianashears@exchange.uk.com

St Ives Society of Artists, Norway Gallery, Norway Square, St Ives TR26 1NA Tel: 01736 795582
www.stivessocietyofartists.com

Devon
J Collins & Son, The Studio, 28 High Street, Bideford EX39 2AN
Tel: 01237 473103
biggs@collinsantiques.co.uk
www.collinsantiques.co.uk

Gordon Hepworth Fine Art, Hayne Farm, Newton St. Cyres, Exeter EX5 5DE Tel: 01392 851351
www.gordonhepworthfineart.co.uk

Somerville Gallery, 25 Mayflower Street, Plymouth PL1 1QJ
Tel: 01752 221 600
paul.somerville@tiscali.co.uk

Dorset
Alpha House Gallery, South Street, Sherborne DT9 3LU Tel: 01935 814 944
artatalpha@aol.com
www.dorsetartweek.com/alphahouse

The Swan Gallery, 51 Cheap Street, Sherborne DT9 3AX Tel: 01935 814465

Essex
Brandler Galleries, 1 Coptfold Road, Brentwood CM14 4BN
Tel: 01277 222269
john@brandler-galleries.com
www.brandler-galleries.com

Gloucestershire
Benton Fine Art, Regent House, High Street, Moreton-in-Marsh GL56 0AX
Tel: 01608 652153
bentonfineart@excite.com

Kenulf Fine Arts Ltd, Digbeth Street, Stow-on-the-Wold GL54 1BN
Tel: 01451 870878
kenulf.finearts@virgin.net

Heather Newman Gallery, Milidduwa, Mill Lane, Cranham, Nr Painswick GL6 6TX Tel: 01452 812230
info@heathernewmangallery.co.uk
www.heathernewmangallery.co.uk

Jonathan Poole, Compton Cassey House, Nr Withington, Cheltenham GL54 4DE Tel: 01242 890224
jonathanpoole@comptoncassey.demon.co.uk

Nina Zborowska, Damsels Mill, Paradise, Painswick GL6 6UD
Tel: 01452 812460
enquiries@ninazborowska.com
www.ninazborowska.com

Hampshire
The Studio Bookshop, 17 Broad Street, Alresford SO24 9AW Tel: 01962 732 998
aoxley@freenet.co.uk

Kent
Artworks, Innshoes House, Pye Corner ME17 1EF Tel: 07754 386 891
ArtworksUK@AOL.com
www.art-works.co.uk

Graham Clarke Ltd, White Cottage, Green Lane, Boughton Monchelsea, Maidstone ME17 4LF
Tel: 01622 743938

The Hunt Gallery, 33 Strand Street, Sandwich CT13 9DS Tel: 01304 612792
huntgallery@hotmail.com
www.thehuntgallery.com

Lotus House Studios, 25 Station Road, Lydd, Romney Marsh TN29 9ED
Tel: 01797 320585

Ingrid Nilson, Newenden TN18 5PL
Tel: 01797 252030
ingrid@ingridnilson.com
www.ingridnilson.com

London
Abbott & Holder, 30 Museum Street WC1A 1LH Tel: 020 7637 3981
abbott.holder@virgin.net

Arthur Ackermann & Peter Johnson Ltd, 27 Lowndes Street SW1X 9HY
Tel: 020 7235 6464
ackermannjohnson@btconnect.com

John Adams Fine Art Ltd, 200 Ebury Street SW1W 8UN Tel: 020 7730 8999

Agnew's, 43 Old Bond Street W1S 4BA Tel: 020 7290 9250
christopherkingzett@agnewsgallery.co.uk

Ainscough Contemporary Art, Drayton Gardens SW10 9QS
Tel: 020 7341 9442
art@acag.co.uk

Archeus Fine Art, 3 Albemarle Street W1S 4HE Tel: 020 7499 9755
art@archeus.co.uk

Art Space Gallery, 84 St Peter's Street N1 8JS Tel: 020 7359 7002
mail@artspacegallery.co.uk
www.artspacegallery.co.uk

Artinform, 23 Bloemfontein Avenue W12 7BJ Tel: 020 8932 5142
mikelp@artinform.com
www.artinform.com

ArtLondon.Com, Suite 958, 28 Old Brompton Road SW7 3SS
Tel: 020 7402 2897
info@artlondon.com
www.artlondon.com

Artware Fine Art, 18 La Gare, 51 Surrey Row SE1 0BZ
Tel: 020 7921 9704
greg@artwarefineart.com

Austin/Desmond Fine Art, Pied Bull Yard, 68/69 Great Russell Street WC1B 3BN Tel: 020 7242 4443
gallery@austindesmond.com
www.austindesmond.com

George Babbington, 134 Addison Gardens W14 0DS
Tel: 020 7602 5454
george.babbington@btinternet.com
www.babbington.net

Chris Beetles Ltd, 8 & 10 Ryder Street, St James's SW1Y 6QB
Tel: 020 7839 7551

Belgrave Gallery, 53 Englands Lane NW3 4YD Tel: 020 7722 5150
sales@belgravegallery.com
www.belgravegallery.com

Belgravia Gallery, 59 Ebury Street SW1W 0NZ Tel: 020 7730 1511
laura@belgraviagallery.com
www.belgraviagallery.com

John Bennett Fine Art, 206 Walton Street SW3 2JL Tel: 020 7225 2223

James Birch Gallery, 22 Laystall Street EC1R 4PA Tel: 0207 837 1595

The Blue Gallery, 28/29 Great Sutton Street EC1V 0DS Tel: 020 7490 3833
bluegallery@compuserve.com
www.bluegallery.co.uk

Lena Boyle Fine Art, 40 Drayton Gardens SW10 9SA Tel: 020 7259 2700 or 020 7373 8247
lena.boyle@btinternet.com
www.lenaboyle.com

Browse & Darby Gallery, 19 Cork Street W1S 3LP Tel: 020 7734 7984
art@browseanddarby.co.uk

The Bruton Street Gallery Ltd, 28 Bruton Street W1J 6QW
Tel: 020 7499 9747
art@brutonstreetgallery.com
www.brutonstreetgallery.com

Burlington Paintings Ltd, 10 & 12 Burlington Gardens W1S 3EY
Tel: 020 7734 9984
pictures@burlington.co.uk
www.burlington.co.uk

Caelt Gallery, 182 Westbourne Grove W11 2RH Tel: 020 7229 9309
art@caeltgallery.com
www.caeltgallery.com

Carlyle Gallery, 62 Old Church Street SW3 6DP Tel: 020 7352 8686
stephen.bartley@ukgateway.net

Keith Chapman (Marine Art), 91 Raymouth Road SE16 2DA
Tel: 020 7232 1885
keithchapman@talk21.com

Jonathan Clark Fine Art, 18 Park Walk SW10 0AQ Tel: 020 7351 3555
clark@jc-art.com www.jc-art.com

Jonathan Cooper, Park Walk Gallery, 20 Park Walk SW10 0AQ
Tel: 020 7351 0410
mail@jonathancooper.co.uk
www.jonathancooper.co.uk

Coskun Fine Art, 93 Walton Street SW3 2HP Tel: 020 7581 9056
gulgallery@aol.com
www.coskunfineart.com

Counter Editions Ltd, 5–9 Hatton Wall EC1N 8HX Tel: 020 7692 0000
www.countereditions.com

Alan Cristea Gallery, 31 Cork Street W1X 2NU Tel: 020 7439 1866

Curwen Gallery, 4 Windmill Street, off Charlotte Street W1P IHF
Tel: 020 7636 1459
pryle@curwengallery.com
www.curwengallery.com

Davies & Tooth, 32 Dover Street W1S 4NE Tel: 020 7409 1516
art@davies-tooth.com
www.davies-tooth.com

William Drummond (Convent Garden Gallery Ltd), 8 St. James's Chambers, 2 Ryder Street, St. James's SW1Y 6QA
Tel: 020 7930 9696

Eaton Gallery, 34 Duke Street, St James's SW1Y 6DF Tel: 020 7930 5950

Fine Art Commissions, 107 Walton Street SW3 2HP
Tel: 020 7589 4111
info@fineartcommissions.com
www.fineartcommissions.com

Fleur de Lys Gallery, 227A Westbourne Grove W11 2SE Tel: 020 7727 8595
fleurdelysgallery@yahoo.com
www.fleur-de-lys.com

Flowers East, 82 Kingsland Road E2 8DP Tel: 020 7920 7777/020 7920 7770
gallery@flowerseast.com
www.flowerseast.com

Frost & Reed Ltd, 2–4 King Street, St James's SW1Y 6QP
Tel: 020 7839 4645
www.frostandreed.co.uk

Gallery K, 101-103 Heath Street, Hampstead NW3 6SS
Tel: 020 7794 4949
art@galleryk.co.uk

Gallery Niklas von Bartha, First Floor, 136b Lancaster Road W11 1QU
Tel: 020 7985 0015
info@vonbartha.com
www.vonbartha.com

Martyn Gregory Gallery, 34 Bury Street, St James's SW1Y 6AU
Tel: 020 7839 3731

Grosvenor Prints, 28-32 Shelton Street, Covent Garden WC2H 9HP
Tel: 020 7836 1979

Paul Hahn, 5 Lower Grosvenor Place SW1W 0EJ Tel: 020 7592 0224
paulhahn@hahngallery.co.uk

Laurence Hallett (LAPADA)
Tel: 020 7798 8977
DST104KEY@cwctv.net

Hanina Gallery, 180 Westbourne Grove W11 2RH
Tel: 020 7243 8877
hanina@globalnet.co.uk
www.hanina-gallery.co.uk

Benjamin C. Hargreaves, 90 Kenyon Street, Fulham SW6 6LB Tel: 020 7385 7757

Hart Gallery, 113 Upper Street, Islington N1 1QN Tel: 020 7704 1131 www.hartgallery.co.uk

Angela Hone Watercolours Tel: 01628 484170 honewatercolours@aol.com

Rebecca Hossack, 35 Windmill Street W1P 1HH Tel: 020 7436 4899 rebecca@r-h-g.co.uk www.r-h-g.co.uk

Kate Howe Fine Art, 32 Sumner Place SW7 3NT Tel: 020 7225 5272 kate.howe@lineone.net

James Hyman Fine Art, 9 North Square NW11 7AB Tel: 020 8455 7882 jameshymanart@aol.com www.artnet.com/jhyman.html

Independent Gallery, 3a Compton Avenue N12XD Tel: 020 7704 2297 pop.art@btinternet.com

Gillian Jason Modern & Contemporary Art, 40 Inverness Street NW1 7HB Tel: 020 7267 4835 art@gillianjason.com www.gillianjason.com

Mark Jason Fine Art, 71 New Bond Street W1S 1DE Tel: 020 7629 4080 info@jasonfineart.com www.jasonfineart.com

Kings Road Gallery, 436 King's Road SW10 0LJ Tel: 020 7351 367 tanya@kingsroadgallery.com www.kingsroadgallery.com

Julian Lax, 37–39 Arkwright Road, Hampstead NW3 6BJ Tel: 020 7794 9933

Frederic Leris, 25 Yoakley Road N16 0BH Tel: 020 8800 4091 fredericleris@virgin.net

Long & Ryle, 4 John Islip Street SW1P 4PX Tel: 020 7834 1434 gallery@long-and-ryle.com www.long-and-ryle.com

MacLean Fine Art, 10 Neville Street SW7 3AR Tel: 020 7589 4384 info@macleanfineart.com www.macleanfineart.com

Mall Galleries, 17 Carlton House Terrace SW1Y 5BD Tel: 020 7930 6844 johndeston@mallgalleries.com or brionychaplin@mallgalleries.com www.mallgalleries.org.uk

John Martin, 38 Albermarle Street W1S 4JG Tel: 020 7499 1314 info@jmlondon.com www.jmlondon.com

Menier Gallery, 51/53 Southwark Street SE11TE Tel: 020 7407 5388 admin@menier.org.uk www.menier.org.uk

Messum's Contemporary Gallery, 8 Cork Street W1X 1PB Tel: 020 7437 5545 enquiries@messums.com www.messums.com

Messum's Galleries, Duke Street, St James's SW1 Tel: 020 7839 5180 www.messums.com

Duncan R Miller Fine Arts, 17 Flask Walk, Hampstead NW3 1HJ Tel: 020 74355462 DMFineArts@aol.com www.duncan-miller.com

Sarah Myerscough Fine Art, 15–16 Brooks Mews, off Davies Street, Mayfair W1K 4DS Tel: 020 7495 0069 info@sarahmyerscough.com www.sarahmyerscough.com

Michael Naimski Gallery, 387 King Street W6 9NJ Tel: 020 8563 0078 enquiries@naimskigallery.com www.naimskigallery.com

New Grafton Gallery, 49 Church Road SW13 9HH Tel: 020 8748 8850

Oakham Gallery, 27 Bury Street, St James's SW1Y 6AL Tel: 020 7839 8800 asmith@oakhamgallery.fsnet.co.uk

Offer Waterman & Co, 11 Langton Street SW10 0JL Tel: 020 7351 0068 info@waterman.co.uk www.waterman.co.uk

Panter & Hall, 9 Shepherd Market, Mayfair W1J 9PF Tel: 020 7399 9999 enquiries@panterandhall.co.uk www.panterandhall.co.uk

Park Walk Gallery, 20 Park Walk, Chelsea SW10 0AQ Tel: 020 7351 0410 www.jonathancooper.co.uk

Michael Parkin Fine Art Ltd, Studio 4, Sedding Street SW1W 8EE Tel: 020 7730 9784

Piano Nobile Fine Paintings, 129 Portland Road W11 4LW Tel: 020 7229 1099 art@pianonobile.freeserve.co.uk www.piano-nobile.com

The Piccadilly Gallery, 43 Dover Street W1S 4NU Tel: 020 7629 2875 www.piccadillygall.demon.co.uk

Pollock Fine Art, 21 Beak Street, off Regent Street W1 Tel: 020 7434 9947 sjpollock@aol.com www.popmodart.com

Bryan Poole A.R.E., 30 Wilton Way E8 3EE Tel: 020 7254 1213 bryan@etchart.co.uk www.etchart.co.uk

Portal Gallery, 43 Dover Street, Piccadilly W1S 4NU Tel: 020 7493 0706 portalgallery@btinternet.com www.portal-gallery.com

The Red Mansion, 9 Park Square West NW1 4LJ Tel: 020 7486 8862 nk@redmansion.co.uk www.redmansion.co.uk

Rosenstiel's, Felix Rosenstiel's Widow & Son Ltd, 33–35 Markham Street, Chelsea Green SW3 3NR Tel: 020 7352 3551 sales@felixr.com www.felixr.com

Ryan Fine Art, 74 Vanbrugh Park SE3 7JQ Tel: 020 8305 0854 darrell@ryanfineart.com

Scolar Fine Art, 35 Bruton Place W1J 6NS Tel: 020 7629 4944 art@scolarfineart.com www.scolarfineart.com

The Sheridan Russell Gallery, 16 Crawford Street W1H 1BS Tel: 020 7935 0250

The Sladmore Gallery, 32 Bruton Place, Mayfair W1J 6NW Tel: 020 7499 0365 sculpture@sladmore.com www.sladmore.com

John Spink, 9 Richard Burbidge Mansions, 1 Brasenose Drive SW13 8RB Tel: 020 8741 6152

Timothy Taylor Gallery, 1 Bruton Place W1J 6LS Tel: 020 7409 3344 mail@ttgallery.com

Thompson's Marylebone, 76 Marylebone High Street W1U 5JU Tel: 020 7935 3595 enquiries@thompsonsgallery.co.uk www.thompsonsgallery.co.uk

Walton Gallery, 12 Gloucester Road SW7 4RB Tel: 020 7854 2097 matthewsfineart@aol.com ww.waltongallery.com

Whitford Fine Art, 6 Duke Street, St James's SW1Y 6BN Tel: 020 7930 9332

Will's Art Warehouse, Unit 3 Heathman's Road, Parson's Green, Fulham SW6 4TJ Tel: 020 7371 8787 will@wills-art.demon.co.uk www.wills-art.com

Wiseman Originals Ltd, 34 West Square SE11 4SP Tel: 020 7587 0747 wisemanoriginals@compuserve.com www.wisemanoriginals.com

Wolseley Fine Arts, 12 Needham Road W11 2RP Tel: 020 7792 2788 info@wolseleyfinearts.com www.wolseleyfinearts.com

Christopher Wood Gallery, 20 Georgian House, 10 Bury Street SW1Y 6AA Tel: 020 7839 3963 www.christopherwoodgallery.com

Wyllie Gallery, 44 Elvaston Place SW7 5NP Tel: 020 7584 6024

Merseyside
Boydell Galleries Tel: 0151 932 9220 www.boydellgalleries.co.uk

Middlesex
Footprints Studio, Footprints House, Upper Butts, Brentford TW8 8DF Tel: 020 8560 6965

Norfolk
The Fairhurst Gallery, Websdale Court, Bedford Street, Norwich NR2 1AR Tel: 01603 614214

Nottinghamshire
Sally Mitchell Fine Arts, Thornlea, Askham, Newark NG22 0RN Tel: 01777 838234 john@dogart.com www.dogart.com

Oxfordshire
4Impressions, 43 Oakthorpe Road, Oxford OX2 7BD Tel: 01865 516556 jessielee@fourimpressions.com

Brian Sinfield Gallery, 150 High Street, Burford OX18 4QU Tel: 01993 824 464 gallery@briansinfield.com www.briansinfield.com

Wiseman-Noble, 40/41 South Parade, Summertown, Oxford OX2 7JL Tel: 01865 515123 sarahjane@wisegal.com www.wisegal.com

Wren Gallery, Bear Court, 34 Lower High Street, Burford, Oxon OX18 4RR Tel: 01993 823495 enquiries@wrenfineart.com www.wrenfineart.com

SCOTLAND
Roger Billcliffe Fine Art, 134 Blythswood Street, Glasgow G2 4EL Tel: 0141 332 4027 roger@rbfa.demon.co.uk www.billcliffegallery.com

Carlton Gallery, 10 Royal Terrace, Edinburgh HU5 4JY Tel: 0131 556 1010 mail@carltongallery.co.uk www.carltongallery.co.uk

Cyril Gerber Fine Art, 148 West Regent Street, Glasgow G2 2RQ Tel: 0141 221 3095/204 0276 gerber@compassgallery.fsbusiness.co.uk

Glasgow Print Studio, 22 King Street, Glasgow G1 5QP Tel: 0141 552 0704

Ingleby Gallery, 6 Carlton Terrace, Edinburgh EH7 5DD Tel: 0131 556 4441 mail@inglebygallery.com www.inglebygallery.com

Kilmorack Gallery, By Beuly, Invernessshire IV4 7AL Tel: 01463 783230 art@kilmorackgallery.co.uk www.kilmorackgallery.co.uk

The Leith Gallery, 65 The Shore, Edinburgh EH7 5DD Tel: 0131 553 5525

info@the-leith-gallery.co.uk www.the-leith-gallery.co.uk

The Little Gallery, 20 High Street, Pittenween KY10 2LA Tel: 01333 311227

Mainhill Gallery, Ancrum, Jedburgh, Roxburghshire TD8 6XA Tel: 01835 830 518 mainhill@lineone.net www.mainhill.border.co.uk

The McEwan Gallery, Glengarden, Ballater, Aberdeenshire AB35 5UB Tel: 013397 55429 rhodmcewan@easynet.co.uk www.mcewangallery.com

The Scottish Gallery, 16 Dundas Street, Edinburgh EH3 6HZ Tel: 0131 558 1200 mail@scottish-gallery.co.uk www.scottish-gallery.co.uk

Shropshire
The Bridgegate Gallery, (Opening times by appointment), 46 Church Lane, Sheriffhales TF11 8RD Tel: 01952 461667 bridgegate.gallery@btinternet.co.uk

Mansers, 31 Wyle Cop, Shrewsbury SY1 1XF Tel: 01743 240328 info@fineartdealers.co.uk www.fineartdealers.co.uk

Wenlock Fine Art, 3 The Square, Much Wenlock TF13 6LX Tel: 01952 728232

Somerset
Adam Gallery, 13 John Street, Bath BA1 2JL Tel: 01225 480406 info@adamgallery.com

Staffordshire
Gordon-Craig Tel: 01785 660745 www.gordoncraig.com

Surrey
Peter Bennett, 88 Ennerdale Road, Kew Gardens TW9 2DL Tel: 020 83329164 bennett_fine_art@compuserve.com

Bourne Gallery Ltd, 31-33 Lesbourne Road, Reigate RH2 7JS Tel: 01737 241614 bournegallery@aol.com www.bournegallery.com

Henry Boxer, 98 Stuart Court, Richmond Hill, Richmond TW10 6RJ Tel: 020 8948 1633 henryboxer@aol.com www.outsiderart.co.uk

Pieroni Studios, Studio 1, Dickson House, 3 Grove Road, Richmond TW10 6SP Tel: 020 8948 8066

The Studio Art House, 16 Church Road, Leatherhead KT22 8AY Tel: 01372 361906 stuartstanleyart@aol.com

East Sussex
Rye Art Gallery, 107 High Street, Rye TN31 7JE Tel: 01797 222433

Louis Turpin, 19 Udimore Road, Rye TN31 7DS Tel: 01797 222307 www.louisturpin.co.uk

West Sussex
The Antique Print Shop, 11 Middle Row, East Grinstead RH19 3AX Tel: 01342 410501 www.theantiqueprintshop.com

The Canon Gallery, New Street, Petworth GU28 0AS Tel: 01798 344422

Folio Fine Art, High Seat, 1 High Street, Billingshurst RH14 9PJ Tel: 01403 782697

Peter's Barn Gallery, South Ambersham, Midhurst GU29 0BX Tel: 01798 861388 peters.barn@ic24.net www.petersbarngallery.co.uk

WALES
The Albany Gallery, 74b Albany Road, Cardiff CF2 3RS Tel: 029 2048 7158 albanygallery@btinternet.com

Warwickshire

The Stour Gallery, 10 High Street, Shipston-on-Stour CV36 4AJ
Tel: 01608 664411
stourgallery@dial.pipex.com

West Midlands

Driffold Gallery, 78 Birmingham Road, Sutton Coldfield B72 1QR
Tel: 0121 355 5433

Halcyon Gallery, 30 Marshall Street, Birmingham B1 1LE Tel: 0121 643 0906
marshallstreet@halcyongallery.com
www.halcyongallery.com

Number Nine the Gallery, 9 Brindleyplace, Birmingham B1 2JA
Tel: 00 44 121 643 9099
noninethegallery@btclick.com
www.numberninethegallery.com

Worcestershire

Broadway Modern Fine Art and Design (A division of John Noott Galleries, Broadway), 10 The Green, Broadway WR12 7AA Tel: 01386 858436
modern@john-noott.com
www.john-noott.com

Haynes Fine Art of Broadway, Picton House Galleries, 42 High Street, Broadway WR12 7AA Tel: 01386 852649
email@haynes-fine-art.co.uk
www.haynesfineart.com

John Noott Galleries Contemporary, 14 Cotswold Court, Broadway WR12 7AA Tel: 01386 858969
aj@john-noott.com www.john-noott.com

John Noott Galleries, 28 High Street, Broadway WR12 7DT Tel: 01386 854868
info@john-noott.com
www.john-noott.com

Priory Gallery, Forge House, 34 High Street, Broadway WR12 7DT
Tel: 01242 673226
rickjames@priorygallery.freeserve.co.uk

Yorkshire

M. Lawrence Antiques & Art, 40/44 High Street, Bridlington YO16 4PX
Tel: 01262 670281

Michael Pybus Fine Arts, 127 Church Street, Whitby YO22 4DE
Tel: 01947 820028
enquiries@mpybusfinearts.co.uk
www.mpybusfinearts.co.uk

Nautical Fine Arts, 16 The Close, Driffield YO25 5JS Tel: 01377 200071
michael@jwhitehand.fsnet.co.uk
www.nauticalfinearts.com

Sutcliffe Galleries, 5 Royal Parade, Harrogate HG1 2SZ Tel: 01423 562976

Walker Galleries, 6 Montpelier Gardens, Harrogate HG1 2TF Tel: 01423 567933
www.walkerfineart.co.uk

CANADA

Gallery Gora, 279 Sherbrooke Ouest, Suite 205, Montreal, Québec H3X 1Y2
Tel: 514 879 9694
art@gallerygora.com
www.gallerygora.com

Harbour Gallery, 1697 Lakeshore Road West, Mississauga, ON L5J 1J4
Tel: 905 822 5495
info@harbourgallery.com
www.harbourgallery.com

Loch Gallery, 306 St Mary's Road, Winnipeg, MB R2H 1J8 Tel: 204 235 1033 winnipeg@lochgallery.com
www.lochgallery.com

othergallery, #405–33 Kennedy Street, Winnipeg, MB R3C 1S5
Tel: 204 947 3551
info@othergallery.com
www.othergallery.com

DENMARK

Galleri Nicolai Wallner, Njalsgarde 21, Building 15, DK-2300 Copenhagen

Tel: +45 32 57 09 70
nw@nicolaiwallner.com
www.nicolaiwallner.com

ICELAND

Waage Arts, 1 Nupalind 4, 201 Kopavour Tel: +354 895 3013
hwaage@belugaarts.com
www.belugaarts.com

ITALY

Galleria del Leone, 597 Guidecca 30133, Venice Tel: 00 39041 5288001 info@galleriadelleone.com

REPUBLIC OF IRELAND

Apollo Gallery, 51C Dawson Street, Dublin 2 Tel: 00 353 1 671 2609
art@apollogallery.ie

Artistic License, The Old Coach House, Dundalk Street, Carlingford, Co Louth
Tel: 00 35393 4273745

Patrick F Brown, 28 Molesworth Street, Dublin 2 Tel: 00 353 1 661 9780

The Frederick Gallery, 24, South Frederick Street, Dublin 2 Tel: 670 7055
fredgal@aol.ie www.frederickgallery.net

Hugh Lane Gallery, Charlemont House, Parnell Square North, Dublin 1
Tel: 00 3531 874 1903
info@hughlane.ie www.hughlane.ie

Kerlin Gallery, 38 Dawson Street, Dublin 2 Tel: 353 677 9179

Cynthia O'Connor Gallery, 17 Duke Street, Dublin 2 Tel: 353 625 1317

Royal Hibernian Gallery, 15 Ely Place, Dublin 2 Tel: 353 1 661 2558
rhagallery@eircom.net
www.royalhibernianacademy.com

The Solomon Gallery, Powerscourt Townhouse Centre, South William Street, Dublin 2 Tel: 1679 4237

George Stacpoole, Main Street, Adare, Co. Limerick Tel: 6139 6409
stacpoole@iol.ie
www.georgestacpooleantiques.com

Taylor Galleries, 34 Kildare Street, Dublin 2 Tel: 676 6055

Russia

Alla Bulyanskaya Gallery, Hall 47, Central House of Artists, 10 Krymsky Val, Moscow 117049 Tel: 7 095 737 7392
info@allabulgallery.com
www.allabulgallery.com

South Africa

The Everard Read Gallery, 6 Jellicoe Avenue, Rosebank 2196, Johannesburg Tel: 00 27 11 788 4805
gallery@everard.co.za

Switzerland

Hauser & Wirth, Limmatstrasse 270, CH-8005 Zurich Tel: +41 1 446 65 28
info@ghw.ch
www.hauserwirth.com

U.S.A.

Aaron Galleries, 50E Oak, 2nd Floor, Chicago Il 60611
Tel: 001 312 943 0660
aarongal@interaccess.com

Adams Davidson Galleries, 27-29th Street NW, Suite 504, Washington DC 20008-5545
Tel: 001 202 965 3800
cooper@adgal.com

American Primitive Gallery, 594 Broadway, 205 New York NY 10012
Tel: 001 212-966-1530

Benedetto Arts LLC, 130 West 57 St., Ste. 9-D, New York NY 10019
Tel: 001 212 246 8126
www.benedettoarts.com

Roy Boyd Gallery, 739 N. Wells, Chicago IL 60610 Tel: 001 312.642.1606
roy.boyd@worldnet.att.net
www.royboydgallery.com

Bruce Gimelson, P.O. Box 440, Garrison, New York 10524-0440
Tel: 001 8454244689
bgimelson@aol.com
www.gimelson.com

Aldo Castillo Gallery, 233 W. Huron, Chicago IL 60610 Tel: 001 312 337 2536
info@artaldo.com www.artaldo.com

Jan Cicero Gallery, 835 W. Washington, Chicago IL 60607 Tel: 001.312.733.9551
cicero@concentric.net

Clark Art, 300 Glenwood Avenue, Raleigh, North Carolina 27603
Tel: 919 832 8319

Conner Contemporary Art Gallery, 1730 Connecticut Avenue NW, 2nd Floor, Washington DC 20009
Tel: 202 588 8750
info@connercontemporary.com
www.Connercontemporary.com

Cornell DeWitt Gallery, 521 W 26 St, New York 10001 Tel: 212 695 6845
cornell@dewittgallery.com
www.dewittgallery.com

Eastwick Art Gallery, 245 W. North Avenue, Chicago IL 60610
Tel: 312 440 2322

Kathleen Ewing Gallery, 1609 Connecticut Avenue NW, Washington DC 20009 Tel: 202 328 0955
ewingal@aol.com
www.kathleenewinggallery.com

Paco Filici, 411 West Monroe, Austin, Texas 78704 Tel: 512 326 5141
www.pacof.com

Richard Gray Gallery, 875 N. Michigan, Chicago IL 60611 Tel: 312 642 8877
info@richardgraygallery.com
www.richardgraygallery.com

Gruen Galleries, 226 W. Superior, Chicago IL 60610 Tel: 312 337 6262
lisa@gruengalleries.com
www.gruengalleries.com

Guarisco Gallery, Ltd., 2828 Pennsylvania Avenue NW, Washington DC 20007 Tel: 202 333 8533 guarisco@mindspring.com
artnet.com/guarisco.html

Anton Haardt Gallery, 2858 Magazine Street, New Orleans LA 705115
Tel: 504 891 9080 www.antonart.com

Jane Haslam Gallery, 2025 Hillyer Place NW, Washington DC 20009 Tel: 202 232 4644 haslem@artline.com
www.janehaslemgallery.com

F. B. Horowitz Fine Art Ltd Founded 1981, 830 Edgemoor Drive, Hopkins MN 55305 Tel: 952 935 2120
horow001@earthlink.net

Kenyon Oppenheimer Inc., 410 N Michigan Ave, Chicago IL 60611
Tel: 312 642 5300
joppen@audubonart.com
www.audubonart.com

Klein Art Works, 400 N. Morgan, Chicago IL 60622 Tel: 312 243 0400
art@kleinart.com www.kleinart.com

Matt Lamb, 13465 Quail Run Court, Lockport Illinois 60441 Tel: 708 301 8317
www.mattlamb.com

Rodger LaPelle Galleries, 122 N. Third St. (Old City), Philadelphia PA 19106
Tel: 215 592 0232
LaPelle@netreach.net
www.netreach.net/~lapelle/

Lindsay Gallery, 986 N.High Street, Columbus, Ohio 423201
Tel: 614 291 1973
www.lindsaygallery.homestead.com

Lyons Weir Gallery, 300 W. Superior, Chicago IL 60610 Tel: 312 654 0600
www.Lyonswiergallery.com

Ricco Maresca Gallery, Third Floor, 529 West 20th Street, New York NY 10011 Tel: 212 627 4819
csolomon@riccomaresca.com
www.riccomaresca.com

Marsha Mateyka Gallery, 2012 R Street NW, Washington DC 20009
Tel: 202 238 0088
www.marshamateykagallery.com

Thomas McCormick Gallery, 835 W. Washington, Chicago IL 60607
Tel: 312 226 6800
gallery@thomasmccormick.com
www.thomasmccormick.com

Richard Norton Gallery, 612 Merchandise Mart Plaza, Chicago IL 60654 Tel: 312 644 8855
NortonGallery@aol.com
ww.RichardNortonGallery.com

Okuda Gallery, 3112 M Street NW, Washington DC 20007 Tel: 202 625 1054 okudaint@bellatlantic.net
www.galleryokuda.com

Parish Gallery, 1054 31st Street NW, Wahington DC 20007
Tel: 202 944 2310
parishgallery@bigplanet.com
www.parishgallery.com

The Ralls Collection, 1516 31st Street NW, Washington DC 20007
Tel: 202 342 1754
maralls@aol.com
www.rallscollection.com

Alla Rogers Gallery, 1054 31st Street NW, Canal Square, Washington DC 20007 Tel: 202 333 8595
allarogers@cs.com
www.allarogers.com

Luise Ross Gallery, 568 Broadway, New York 10012 Tel: 212 343 2161
www.luiserossgallery.com

Judy A Saslow Gallery, 300 West Superior, Chicago Tel: 312 943 0530
jsaslow@corecomm.net
www.jsaslowgallery.com

William Secord Gallery, Inc., 52 East 76th Street, New York NY10221
Tel: 212 249 0075
www.dogpainting.com

Spanierman Gallery, LLC, 45 East 58th Street, New York NY 10022
Tel: 001 212 8340208
gavin@spanierman.com
www.spanierman.com

St. Luke's Gallery, 1715 Q Street NW, Washington DC 2009
Tel: 202 328 2424

Walnut Street Gallery, 217 Linden Street, Fort Collins Co 80524
Tel: 970 221 2383/800 562 3387
rockout@walnutst.com
www.walnutst.com

Wood Street Gallery, 1239 N. Wood, Chicago IL 6022
Tel: 001 773 227 3306
woodgall@aol.com
www.woodstreetgallery.com

Sonia Zaks Gallery, 311 W Superior, Suite 207, Chicago IL 60610
Tel: 001 312 943 8440

Zenith Gallery, 413 7th Street NW, Washington DC 20004 Tel: 001 202 783 2963 zenithga@rols.com
www.zenithgallery.com

Zolla/Lieberman Gallery, 325 W. Huron, Chicago IL 60610
Tel: 001 312 944 1990
zollaart@aol.com
www.zollaliebermangallery.com

Quester Gallery, 77 Main Street, PO Box 446, Stonington, Connecticut 06378 Tel: 860 535 3860

Directory of Specialists

If you wish to be included in next year's directory, or if you have a change of address or telephone number, please contact Miller's advertising department by January 2005. We advise readers to telephone first to check opening times before visiting.

Exhibition & Fair Organisers
West Sussex
Hodgson Events, Smithbrook,
Lodsworth GU28 9DG
Tel: 01798 861815
hodgsonevents@talk21.com
www.hodgsonevents.com

Framers
Cambridgeshire
The Cottage Gallery,
11/12 High Street,
Huntingdon PF18 6TE
Tel: 01480 411521

Greater Manchester
Dixon Bate Framing,
94–98 Fairfield Street,
Manchester M1 2WR
Tel: 0161 273 6974

Hampshire
Academy Arts Centre, Winton Road,
Petersfield GU32 3HA
Tel: 01730 261624
nixy@compuserve.com

Kent
Simon Beaugié Picture Frames, Manor
Farm Workshops, Kingsnorth, Ashford
TN26 1NL Tel: 01233 733353

London
Art & Soul, G14 Belgravia Workshops,
157 Marlborough Road N19 4NF
Tel: 020 7263 0421

John Campbell Master Frames,
164 Walton Street SW3 2JL
Tel: 020 7584 9268
www.campbellofwaltonstreet.co.uk

Chelsea Frame Works,
106 Finborough Road SW10
Tel: 020 7373 0180

Alec Drew Picture Frames Ltd,
5/7 Cale Street, Chelsea Green
SW3 3QT Tel: 020 7352 8716
adrew@hugill.demon.co.uk
www.hugill.demon.co.uk

Framework Picture Framing,
5–9 Creekside SE8 4SA
Tel: 020 8691 5140
enquiries@frameworkgallery.co.uk

Pendragon Fine Art Frames,
1–3 Yorkton Street, Shoreditch E2
8NH Tel: 020 7729 0608

Gallery Hire
Lincolnshire
Yarrow Gallery, Art Department,
Oundle School, Glapthorn Road,
Oundle, Peterborough PE8 4EN
Tel: 01832 274 034
www.oundleschool.org.uk./school/art
s/yarrow/html

London
Abbott & Holder,
30 Museum Street WC1A 1LH
Tel: 020 7637 3981
abbott.holder@virgin.net
www.artefact.co.uk/AaH.html

The Air Gallery, 32 Dover Street
W1X 3RA Tel: 020 7409 1255
admin@airgallery.co.uk
www.airgallery.co.uk

Alchemy Gallery,
157 Farringdon Road EC1R 3AD
Tel: 020 7278 5666

Art Connoisseur Gallery,
95–97 Crawford Street,
London W1H 1AN
Tel: 020 7258 3835

Artbank Gallery C,
114 Clerkenwell Road
EC1M 5SA Tel: 020 7608 3333
info@artbank.com www.artbank.com

Atrium Gallery, Whiteleys,
Queensway W2 4YN
Tel: 020 7229 8844

Charlotte Street Gallery, Charlotte
Street, Fitzrovia, London W1 2NA
Tel: 020 7255 2828
gallery@28charlottestreet.com
www.28charlottestreet.com

The Coningsby Gallery,
30 Tottenham Street W1 9PN
Tel: 020 7636 7478

Ebury Galleries,
200 Ebury Street SW1
Tel: 020 7730 8999

The Gallery in Cork Street,
28 Cork Street W1S 3NG
Tel: 020 7287 8408
enquiries@galleryincorkst.com
www.gallery27.com

Highgate Gallery, 11 South Grove,
Highgate N6 6BS
Tel: 020 8340 3343
admin@hlsi.demon.co.uk

Lauderdale House Arts & Education
Centre, Waterlow Park,
Highgate Hill N6 5HG
Tel: 020 8348 8716/8341 2032

Mall Galleries, 17 Carlton House
Terrace SW1Y 5BD
Tel: 020 7930 6844
johndeston@mallgalleries.com
www.mallgalleries.org.uk`

South London Gallery,
65 Peckham Road SE5 8UH
Tel: 020 7703 9799
mail@southlondonart.com
www.southlondonart.co.uk

Space Studios, 8 Hoxton Street
N1 6NG Tel: 020 7613 1925
mail@spacestudios.org.uk
www.spacestudios.org.uk

Westminster Gallery, Central Hall,
Storey's Gate SW1 9NH
Tel: 020 7222 8010
events@wch.co.uk
www.wch.co.uk

Merseyside
Hanover Galleries, 11–13 Hanover
Street, Liverpool L1 3DN
Tel: 0151 709 3073

Oxfordshire
Merriscourt Gallery, Sarsden,
Chipping Norton OX7 6QX
Tel: 01608 658 989
merriscourtpaintings@btinternet.com
www.merriscourt.com

Republic of Ireland
Royal Hibernian Academy, Gallagher
Gallery, 15 Ely Place, Dublin 2
Tel: 00 353 1 661 2558
rhgallery@eircom.net
www.royalhibernianacademy.com

Insurance
Dorset
Gwennap Stevenson Brown Ltd,
Kerris House,
12 Brickfields Business Park,
Gillingham
SP8 4PX Tel: 01747 821188
paulinegwennap@aol.com

London
Aon Ltd, 8 Devonshire Square EC2M
4PL Tel: 020 7882 0374

AXA Art Insurance
Tel: 020 7626 5001
helen.george@axa-art.co.uk
www.axa-art.co.uk

Blackwall Green (Jewellery and Fine
Art), Lambert Fenchurch House, Friary
Court, Crutched Friars EC3N 2NP
Tel: 020 7560 3381
cstephens@fgroup.co.uk

Byas Mosley & Co Ltd, International
Fine Art Division, William Byas House,
14–18 St Clare Street WC3N 1JX
Tel: 020 7481 0101

Crowley Colosso, Friary Court,
Crutched Friars EC3N 2NP
Tel: 020 7560 3000

Needham Jobson & Co,
Byron House,
102 Wimbledon Hill Road SW19 7PB
Tel: 020 8944 8870

Sedgwick Fine Art, Sedgwick House,
The Sedgwick Centre
E1 8DX Tel: 020 7377 3456

Lighting
Surrey
Acorn Lighting Products,
27 Marlyns Drive, Guildford
GU4 8JU Tel: 01483 564180

Packers & Shippers
Cornwall
3 Lanes Transport, 5 Albany Terrace,
St Ives TR26 2BS
Tel: 07970 896256 info@3lanes.com
www.3lanes.com

London
Art Move, Unit 3, Grant Road
SW11 2NU Tel: 020 7585 1801
artmove@dircon.co.uk

Momart Ltd, 199–205 Richmond Road
E8 3NJ Tel: 020 8986 3624
enquiries@momart.co.uk

Publications
London
Art Monthly, 4th Floor,
28 Charing Cross Road
WC2B 0DG
Tel: 020 7240 0389
artmonthly@compuserve.com
www.artmonthly.co.uk

The Art Newspaper,
70 South Lambeth Road
SW8 1RL
Tel: 020 7735 3331

West Midlands
Antiques Magazine, H.P. Publishing,
2 Hampton Court Road, Harborne,
Birmingham B17 9AE
Tel: 0121 681 8000
Subs 01562 701001
subs@antiquesmagazine.com
www.antiquesmagazine.com

Restoration
Hampshire
Association of British Picture Restorers,
P O Box 32,
Hayling Island PO11 9WE
Tel: 0239 2465115 abpr@lineone.net
www.bapcr.org.uk

The Conservation Studio,
Chandler's Ford SO53 2FX
Tel: 023 8026 8167
winstudio@aol.com
www.conservationstudio.org

London
Deborah Bates, 191 St John's Hill
SW11 1TH Tel: 020 7223 1629
deborah@deborahbates.com
www.deborahbates.com

Scotland
Alder Arts, 4 The Square, Beauly,
Invernesshire IV4 7BX
Tel: 01463 782247

Index to Advertisers

Glossary

academy: Group of artists meeting for teaching and/or discussion.

acrylic: Synthetic emulsion paint.

bodycolour: Opaque pigment made by mixing watercolour with white pigment. Same as gouache.

cartoon: Full size early design for a painting.

collage: Work of art in which pieces of paper, photographs and other materials are pasted to the surface of the picture.

Conté: Brand name for synthetic black, red or brown chalk.

counterproof: Mirror-image reproduction, achieved by wetting a drawing or engraving, laying a damp sheet of clean paper on it and then running both through a press.

drawing: Representation with line.

dry-point: The process of making a print by engraving directly on to a copper plate with a steel or diamond point.

edition: The run of a print published at any one time.

engraving: The process of cutting a design into a hard surface (metal or wood) so that the lines will retain the ink. Engravings can be roughly divided into three types: Relief, Intaglio and Surface. Each has its own special method of printing.

etching: Technique of print making developed in the 16th century, in which a metal plate is covered with an acid-resistant substance and the design scratched on it with a needle revealing the metal beneath. The plate is then immersed in acid, which bites into the lines, which will hold the ink.

genre: Art showing scenes from daily life.

gouache: Opaque watercolour paint.

grisaille: Painting in grey or greyish monochrome.

impression: Individual copy of a print or engraving.

lithograph: Print made by drawing with a wax crayon on a porous prepared stone which is then soaked in water. A grease-based ink is applied to the stone which adheres only to the design. Dampened paper is applied to the stone and is rubbed over with a special press to produce the print.

linocut: Design cut in relief on linoleum mounted on a wooden block.

measurements: Dimensions are given height before width.

mixed media: Art combining different types of material.

montage: The sticking of layers over each other, often done with photographs using an unusual background.

oil: Pigment bound with oil.

pastel: Dry pigment bound with gum into stick-form and used for drawing.

patina: Refers to the mellowing with age, which occurs to all works of art.

plate: The piece of metal etched or engraved with the design used to produce prints.

print: Image which exists in multiple copies, taken from an engraved plate, woodblock, etc.

proof: Print of an engraving usually made before lettering engraver worked on it adding title, dedication, etc.

provenance: The record of previous owners and locations of a work of art.

recto: Front of a picture.

remarque proofs: Proofs with some kind of mark in the margin to denote superiority to ordinary proofs.

silkscreen: Print-making process using a finely meshed screen, often silk, and stencils to apply the image.

state: Term applied to prints – to the different stages at which the artist has corrected or changed a plate – and the prints produced from these various 'states', which are numbered first state, second state, etc.

still life: Composition of inanimate objects.

tempera: Medium for pigment mostly made up of egg yolk and water, commonly used before the invention of oils.

verso: Back of a picture.

wash: Thin transparent tint applied over the surfaces of a work.

watercolour: Transparent, water soluble paint, usually applied on paper.

woodcut: Print made from a design cut into a block of wood.

Index to Abbreviations

A	Associate	**NEAC**	New English Art Club	**RGI**	Royal Glasgow Institute
AAA	Allied Artists' Association	**NG**	National Gallery	**RHA**	Royal Hibernian Academy, Dublin
b.	born	**NPG**	National Portrait Gallery	**RI**	Royal Institute of Painters
BWS	British Watercolour Society	**NGI**	National Gallery of Ireland		in Watercolours
CBE	Commander of the British Empire	**NSA**	New Society of Artists	**RIA**	Royal Irish Academy
CH	Companion of Honour	**NWS**	New Watercolour Society	**ROI**	Royal Institute of Oil Painters
cm	centimetre	**OBE**	Order of the British Empire	**RP**	Royal Institute of Portrait Painters
d.	died	**OM**	Order of Merit	**RSA**	Royal Scottish Academy
DBE	Dame Commander of the	**OSA**	Ontario Society of Artists	**RSMA**	Royal Society of Marine Artists
	British Empire	**OWS**	Old Watercolour Society, London	**RSW**	Royal Scottish
DCM	Distinguished Conduct Medal	**P**	President		Watercolour Academy
F	Fellow	**PS**	Pastel Society	**RUA**	Royal Ulster Academy of Arts
fl.	Flourished	**RA**	Royal Academy	**RWA**	Royal West of England
H	Honorary Member	**RBA**	Royal Society of British Artists		Academy, Bristol
ICA	Institute of Contemporary Arts	**RBC**	Royal British Colonial Society	**RWS**	Royal Society of Painters
in	Inch		of Artists		in Watercolours
IS	International Society of Sculptors,	**RBSA**	Royal Birmingham Society of Artists	**Snr**	Senior
	Painter and Gravers	**RCA**	Royal College of Art	**SS**	Suffolk Society
Jnr	Junior	**RCA**	Royal Canadian Academy of Arts	**SWA**	Society of Women Artists
LG	London Group	**RDS**	Royal Dublin Society	**VP**	Vice President
MM	Military Medal	**RE**	Royal Society of Etchers	**WCSI**	Watercolour Society of Ireland
NCA	National College of Art, Dublin		and Engravers	**WIAC**	Women's International Art Club

Bibliography

Archibald, E.H.H., *Dictionary of Sea Painters,* Antique Collectors' Club, 1980.

Arts Council of Great Britain, *British Sporting Painting, 1650–1850,* 1974.

Arts Council of Great Britain, *The Modern Spirit: American Painting 1908–1935,* 1977.

Baigell, Matthew, *A History of American Painting,* Thames and Hudson, 1971.

Baskett, John, *The Horse in Art,* Weidenfeld & Nicholson, 1980

Beetles, Chris, *The Illustrators, London,* 1991/92/93.

Benois, Alexandre, translated by Mary Britnieva, *Reminiscences of the Russian Ballet,* Putnam, 1947

Bernard, Denvir, *The Impressionists at First Hand,* Thames and Hudson, 1987.

Bindman, David, *Encyclopaedia of British Art,* Thames and Hudson, 1985.

Buckman, David, *The Dictionary of Artists in Britain since 1945,* Art Dictionaries, 1998.

de Goncourt, Edmond and Jules, *French Eighteenth Century Painters,* Oxford, Phaidon, 1981.

Fairley, John, *The Art of the Horse,* Abbeyville Press, 1995

Fielding, Mantle, *Dictionary of American Painters,* Connecticut, Modern Books and Crafts Inc, 1974.

Gaunt, William, *A Concise History of English Painting,* Thames and Hudson, 1973.

Hall, Donald and Corrington Wykes, Pat, *Anecdotes of Modern Art,* Oxford University Press, 1990.

Hall, James, *Dictionary of Subjects and Symbols in Art,* John Murray, 1979.

Hardie, William, *Scottish Painting 1837 to the Present,* Studio Vista, 1990.

Hassrick, Peter, *The Way West, Art of Frontier America,* Harry Abrams, 1977.

Hemming, Charles, *British Painters of the Coast and Sea,* Victor Gollancz, 1988.

Hislop, Duncan, *The Art Sales Index 2000/2001,* Art Sales Index, 2001.

Hook, Philip and Poltimore, Mark, *Popular 19th Century Painting,* Antique Collectors' Club, 1986.

Hubbard, R.H., *Canadian Landscape Painting 1670–1930,* University of Wisconsin Press, 1973.

Lucie-Smith, Edward, *The Thames and Hudson Dictionary of Art Terms,* Thames and Hudson, 1988.

Maas, Jeremy, *Victorian Painters,* Barrie and Jenkins, 1988.

McConkey, Kenneth, *A Free Spirit Irish Art 1860–1960,* Antiques Collectors' Club, 1990.

Mallalieu, H.L., *Understanding Watercolours,* Antique Collectors' Club, 1985.

Ottley, H., *Dictionary of Recent and Living Painters and Engravers,* Henry G. Bohn, 1866.

Oxford University Press, *Dictionary of National Biography,* 1975/81/86/90.

Osborne, Harold, *The Oxford Companion to Twentieth Century Art,* Oxford University Press, 1988.

Prendeville, Brendan, *Realism in 20th Century Paintings,* Thames and Hudson, 2000.

Redgrave, Richard and Samuel, *A Century of British Painters,* Oxford, Phaidon, 1981.

Rhodes, Cecil, *Outsider Art, Spontaneous Alternatives,* Thames and Hudson, 2000.

Rothenstein, John, *Modern English Painters,* Macdonald, 1984.

Secord, William, *Dog Painting 1840–1940: A Social History of the Dog in Art,* Antique Collectors' Club, 1992.

Spalding, Frances, *20th Century Painters and Sculptors,* Antique Collectors' Club, 1990.

Stewart, Brian and Cutten, Mervyn, *The Dictionary of Portrait Painters in Britain up to 1920,* Antique Collectors' Club, 1997.

Strong, Roy, *The British Portrait 1660–1960,* Antique Collectors' Club, 1990.

Taylor, Paul, *Dutch Flower Painting 1600–1750,* Yale University Press, 1995

Tooby, Michael, *True North Canadian Landscape Painting 1896–1939,* Barbican Art Gallery, 1991

Walpole, Josephine, *Art and Artists of the Norwich School,* Antique Collectors' Club, 1998.

Waterhouse, Ellis, *British 18th Century Paintings,* Antiques Collectors' Club, 1981.

Wingfield, Mary Ann, *A Dictionary of Sporting Artists 1650–1900,* Antique Collectors' Club, 1992.

Wood, Christopher, *The Dictionary of Victorian Painters,* Antique Collectors' Club, 1978.

Key to Illustrations

Each illustration and descriptive caption is accompanied by a letter code. By referring to the following list of auctioneers (denoted by ⚒) and galleries (⊞) the source of any item may be immediately determined. Inclusion in this edition in no way constitutes or implies a contract or binding offer on the part of any of our contributors to supply or sell the goods illustrated, or similar articles, at the prices stated. Advertisers in this year's directory are denoted by †.

If you require a valuation for an item, it is advisable to check whether the gallery or specialist will carry out this service and if there is a charge. Please mention Miller's when making an enquiry. Having found a specialist who will carry out your valuation it is best to send a photograph and description of the item to the specialist together with a stamped addressed envelope for the reply. A valuation by telephone is not possible.

Most galleries are only too happy to help you with your enquiry; however, they are very busy people and consideration of the above points would be welcomed.

AGN ⊞ Agnew's, 43 Old Bond Street, London W1S 4BA
Tel: 020 7290 9250
christopherkingzett@agnewsgallery.co.uk

AH ⚒† Andrew Hartley, Victoria Hall Salerooms, Little Lane, Ilkley, Yorkshire LS29 8EA Tel: 01943 816363
info@andrewhartleyfinearts.co.uk
www.andrewhartleyfinearts.co.uk

AHG ⊞ Alpha House Gallery, South Street, Sherborne, Dorset DT9 3LU Tel: 01935 814 944
artatalpha@aol.com
www.dorsetartweek.com/alphahouse

ALBE ⊞ Pat Albeck Tel: 01263 768439
albeckrice@waitrose.com

ArW ⊞ Art World Ltd, PO Box 6413, Leicester LE1 7YL
Tel: 0116 254 1902
info@artworldltd.com

B ⚒ Bonhams, 101 New Bond Street, London W1S 1SR
Tel: 020 7629 6602
www.bonhams.com

B(B) ⚒ Bonhams, 1 Old King Street, Bath, Somerset BA1 2JT Tel: 01225 788 988
www.bonhams.com

B(Ed) ⚒ Bonhams, 65 George Street, Edinburgh EH2 2JL, Scotland Tel: 0131 225 2266
www.bonhams.com

B(Kn) ⚒ Bonhams, Montpelier Street, Knightsbridge, London SW7 1HH Tel: 020 7393 3900
www.bonhams.com

B(L) ⚒ Bonhams, 17a East Parade, Leeds, Yorkshire LS1 2BH
Tel: 0113 2448011 www.bonhams.com

B(Nor) ⚒ Bonhams, The Market Place, Reepham, Norwich NR10 4JJ Tel: 01603 871443 www.bonhams.com

B(NW) ⚒ Bonhams, New House, 150 Christleton Road, Chester, Cheshire CH3 5TD Tel: 01244 313936
www.bonhams.com

B(O) ⚒ Bonhams, 39 Park End Street, Oxford OX1 1JD
Tel: 01865 723524 www.bonhams.com

B&L ⚒ Bonhams and Langlois, Westaway Chambers, 39 Don Street, St Helier, Jersey JE2 4TR, Channel Islands
Tel: 01534 722441 www.bonhams.com

BBA ⚒ Bloomsbury Auctions Ltd, Bloomsbury House, 24 Maddox Street, London W1S 1PP
Tel: 020 7495 9494 info@bloomsburyauctions.com
www.bloomsburyauctions.com

Bea ⚒ Bearnes, St Edmund's Court, Okehampton Street, Exeter, Devon EX4 1DU Tel: 01392 207000
enquiries@bearnes.co.uk www.bearnes.co.uk

Bel ⊞ Belgravia Gallery, 59 Ebury Street, London SW1W 0NZ
Tel: 020 7730 1511 laura@belgraviagallery.com
www.belgraviagallery.com

BENE ⊞ Benedetto Arts LLC, 130 West 57 St., Ste. 9-D, New York NY 10019, U.S.A. Tel: 001 212 246 8126
www.benedettoarts.com

BERN ⚒ Bernaerts, Verlatstraat 18-22, 2000 Antwerpen/Anvers, Belgium Tel: +32 (0)3 248 19 21
edmond.bernaerts@ping.be
www.auction-bernaerts.com

BM ⊞ Broadway Modern Fine Art and Design (A division of John Noott Galleries, Broadway), 10 The Green, Broadway, Worcestershire WR12 7AA
Tel: 01386 858436 modern@john-noott.com
www.john-noott.com

Bne ⊞ Bourne Gallery Ltd, 31-33 Lesbourne Road, Reigate, Surrey RH2 7JS Tel: 01737 241614
bournegallery@aol.com www.bournegallery.com

BOX ⊞ Henry Boxer, 98 Stuart Court, Richmond Hill, Richmond, Surrey TW10 6RJ Tel: 020 8948 1633
henryboxer@aol.com www.outsiderart.co.uk

BR ⚒ Dreweatt Neate formerly Bracketts Fine Art Auctioneers, The Auction Hall, The Pantiles, Tunbridge Wells, Kent TN2 5QL Tel: 01892 544500
tunbridgewells@dnfa.com
www.dnfa.com/tunbridgewells

BRID ⊞ The Bridgegate Gallery, 46 Church Lane, Sheriffhales, Shropshire TF11 8RD Tel: 01952 461667
bridgegate.gallery@btinternet.co.uk
Opening times by appointment

BrP ⊞ Bryan Poole A.R.E., 30 Wilton Way, London E8 3EE
Tel: 020 7254 1213 bryan@etchart.co.uk
www.etchart.co.uk

BSG ⊞ Brian Sinfield Gallery, 150 High Street, Burford, Oxfordshire OX18 4QU Tel: 01993 824 464
gallery@briansinfield.com www.briansinfield.com

BUK ⚒ Bukowskis, Arsenalsgatan 4, Stockholm, Sweden
Tel: +46 (8) 614 08 00 info@bukowskis.se
www.bukowskis.se

BuP ⊞ Burlington Paintings Ltd, 10 & 12 Burlington Gardens, London W1S 3EY Tel: 020 7734 9984
pictures@burlington.co.uk www.burlington.co.uk

BWL ⚒ Brightwells Fine Art, The Fine Art Saleroom, Easters Court, Leominster, Herefordshire HR6 0DE
Tel: 01568 611122 fineart@brightwells.com
www.brightwells.com

BYA ⊞ Byard Art, 4 St. Mary's Passage, Cambridge CB2 3PQ
Tel: 01223 464646 info@byardart.co.uk
www.byardart.co.uk

CAMB ⊞ Cambridge Contemporary Art, 6 Trinity Street, Cambridge CB2 1SU Tel: 01223 324 222
info@cambridgegallery.co.uk
www.cambridgegallery.co.uk

CARL ⊞ Carlyle Gallery, 62 Old Church Street, London SW3 6DP
Tel: 020 7352 8686 stephen.bartley@ukgateway.net

CCP ⊞ Coral Canyon Publishing, The Art of Jane Seymour,
23852 Pacific Coast Highway #313,
Malibu CA 90265, U.S.A. Tel: 310 456 9477
coralcanyon@mindspring.com www.janeseymour.com

CDBA ⊞ Camilla Davidson British Art, 57 Artesian Road, London
Tel: 020 72293828 camilla@davidsonpix.demon.co.uk

CDC ⚒ Capes Dunn & Co, The Auction Galleries,
38 Charles Street, Off Princess Street,
Greater Manchester M1 7DB Tel: 0161 273 6060/1911
capesdunn@yahoo.co.uk

CDW ⊞ Cornell DeWitt Gallery, 521 W 26 St, New York 10001,
U.S.A. Tel: 212 695 6845 cornell@dewittgallery.com
www.dewittgallery.com

CFAG ⊞† The Contemporary Fine Art Gallery, 31 High Street,
Eton, Windsor, Berkshire SL4 6AX Tel: 01753 854315
mail@cfag.co.uk www.cfag.co.uk

CGC ⚒ Cheffins, Clifton House, Clifton Road,
Cambridge CB1 7EA Tel: 01223 213343
www.cheffins.co.uk

CHTR ⚒ Charterhouse, The Long Street Salerooms, Sherborne,
Dorset DT9 3BS Tel: 01935 812277
enquiry@charterhouse-auctions.co.uk
www.charterhouse-auctions.co.uk

DB ⊞ Day Bowman Tel: 020 8960 5892
dayartbowman@hotmail.com
Photographer: Justin Piperger

DN ⚒ Dreweatt Neate, Donnington Priory, Donnington,
Newbury, Berkshire RG14 2JE Tel: 01635 553553
donnington@dnfa.com www.dnfa.com/donnington

DNY ⚒ Doyle New York, 175 East 87th Street, New York NY
10128, U.S.A. Tel: 212 427 2730
info@doylenewyork.com www.doylenewyork.com

DORO ⚒ Dorotheum, Palais Dorotheum, A-1010 Wien,
Dorotheergasse 17, 1010 Vienna, Austria
Tel: 515 60 229 client.services@dorotheum.at

Dr ⊞ Driffold Gallery, 78 Birmingham Road, Sutton Coldfield,
West Midlands B72 1QR Tel: 0121 355 5433

DW ⚒ Dominic Winter Book Auctions, The Old School,
Maxwell Street, Swindon, Wiltshire SN1 5DR
Tel: 01793 611340 info@dominicwinter.co.uk
www.dominicwinter.co.uk

FBH ⊞ F. B. Horowitz Fine Art Ltd, Founded 1981,
830 Edgemoor Drive, Hopkins MN 55305, U.S.A.
Tel: 952 935 2120 horow001@earthlink.net

FdeL ⊞ Fleur de Lys Gallery, 227A Westbourne Grove, London
W11 2SE Tel: 020 7727 8595
fleurdelysgallery@yahoo.com www.fleur-de-lys.com

FH ⊞ Felice Hodges Tel: 0207 261 0393 & 0208 891 5113

FHF ⚒ Fellows & Sons, Augusta House, 19 Augusta Street,
Hockley, Birmingham, West Midlands B18 6JA
Tel: 0121 212 2131
info@fellows.co.uk www.fellows.co.uk

G(L) ⚒ Gorringes Inc Julian Dawson, 15 North Street, Lewes,
East Sussex BN7 2PD Tel: 01273 478221
auctions@gorringes.co.uk www.gorringes.co.uk

GAK ⚒† Keys, Off Palmers Lane, Aylsham, Norfolk NR11 6JA
Tel: 01263 733195 www.aylshamsalerooms.co.uk

GALG ⊞ Gallery Gora, 279 Sherbrooke Ouest, Suite 205,
Montreal, Québec H3X 1Y2, Canada Tel: 514 879 9694
The President: Lyne Dubé The Director: Joseph Gora
art@gallerygora.com www.gallerygora.com

GC ⊞ Gordon-Craig Tel: 01785 660745
www.gordoncraig.com

GDC ⊞ Granville D. Clarke Tel: 01226 790860
g.danny.clarke@virgin.net www.granvilleclarke.com

GH ⚒ Gardiner Houlgate, The Bath Auction Rooms,
9 Leafield Way, Corsham, Nr Bath, Somerset SN13 9SW
Tel: 01225 812912 auctions@gardiner-houlgate.co.uk
www.invaluable.com/gardiner-houlgate

GNW ⊞ Galleri Nicolai Wallner, Njalsgarde 21 Building 15,
DK-2300 Copenhagen, Denmark Tel: +45 32 57 09 70
nw@nicolaiwallner.com www.nicolaiwallner.com

H&W ⊞ Hauser & Wirth, Limmatstrasse 270, CH-8005 Zurich,
Switzerland Tel: +41 1 446 65 28 info@ghw.ch
www.hauserwirth.com
(Andre Thomkins images courtesy of The Estate of
Andre Thomkins. Hauser & Wirth Zurich/London)

HFA ⊞† Haynes Fine Art of Broadway, Picton House Galleries,
42 High Street, Broadway, Worcestershire WR12 7DT
Tel: 01386 852649 email@haynes-fine-art.co.uk
www.haynesfineart.com

HG ⊞ Hart Gallery, 113 Upper Street, Islington,
London N1 1QN Tel: 020 7704 1131
www.hartgallery.co.uk

HN ⊞ Heather Newman Gallery, Milidduwa, Mill Lane,
Cranham, Nr Painswick, Gloucestershire GL6 6TX
Tel: 01452 812230 info@heathernewmangallery.co.uk
www.heathernewmangallery.co.uk

HnG ⊞ Halcyon Gallery, 30 Marshall Street, Birmingham,
West Midlands B1 1LE Tel: 0121 643 0906
marshallstreet@halcyongallery.com
www.halcyongallery.com

HUT ⊞ Sarah Hutton Tel: 01535 643882

HYD ⚒ Hy Duke & Son, The Dorchester Fine Art Salerooms,
Weymouth Avenue, Dorchester, Dorset DT1 1QS
Tel: 01305 265080 www.dukes-auctions.com

IN ⊞ Ingrid Nilson, Newenden, Kent TN18 5PL
Tel: 01797 252030 ingrid@ingridnilson.com
www.ingridnilson.com

JAA ⚒ Jackson's Auctioneers & Appraisers, 2229 Lincoln
Street, Cedar Falls IA 50613, U.S.A. Tel: 319 277 2256

JAd ⚒ James Adam & Sons, 26 St Stephen's Green, Dublin 2,
Republic of Ireland Tel: 00 353 1 6760261
www.jamesadam.ie/

JC ⊞ J. Collins & Son, The Studio, 28 High Street, Bideford,
Devon EX39 2AN Tel: 01237 473103
biggs@collinsantiques.co.uk www.collinsantiques.co.uk

JDG ⊞ John Denham Gallery, 50 Mill Lane, London NW6 1NJ
Tel: 020 7794 2635

JLx ⊞ Julian Lax, 37–39 Arkwright Road, Hampstead, London
NW3 6BJ Tel: 020 7794 9933

JN ⊞ John Noott Galleries, 28 High Street, Broadway,
Worcestershire WR12 7DT Tel: 01386 854868
info@john-noott.com www.john-noott.com

JNic ⚒ John Nicholson, The Auction Rooms, Longfield,
Midhurst Road, Fernhurst, Surrey GU27 3HA
Tel: 01428 653727

JS ⊞ James Starkey Fine Art International, Highgate,
Beverley, Yorkshire HU17 0DN Tel: 01482 881179

L ⚒ Lawrences Fine Art Auctioneers, South Street,
Crewkerne, Somerset TA18 8AB Tel: 01460 73041
www.lawrences.co.uk

L&T ⚒ Lyon & Turnbull, 33 Broughton Place, Edinburgh
EH1 3RR, Scotland Tel: 0131 557 8844
info@lyonandturnbull.com

LaP ⊞ Rodger LaPelle Galleries, 122 N. Third St. (Old City),
Philadelphia PA 19106, U.S.A. Tel: 215 592 0232
LaPelle@netreach.net www.netreach.net/~lapelle/

LAW ⊞ M. Lawrence Antiques & Art, 40/44 High Street, Bridlington, East Yorkshire YO16 4PX Tel: 01262 670281

LAY ⚒ David Lay (ASVA), Auction House, Alverton, Penzance, Cornwall TR18 4RE Tel: 01736 361414 david.lays@btopenworld.com

LCM ⚒ Galeria Louis C. Morton, GLC A7073L IYS, Monte Athos 179, Col. Lomas de Chapultepec CP11000, Mexico Tel: 52 5520 5005 glmorton@prodigy.net.mx www.lmorton.com

LHA ⚒ Leslie Hindman, Inc., 122 North Aberdeen Street, Chicago, Illinois 60607, U.S.A. Tel: 001 312 280 1212 www.lesliehindman.com

LJ ⚒ Leonard Joel Auctioneers, 333 Malvern Road, South Yarra, Victoria 3141, Australia Tel: 03 9826 4333 decarts@ljoel.com.au or jewellery@ljoel.com.au www.ljoel.com.au

LOCH ⊞ Loch Gallery, 306 St Mary's Road, Winnipeg MB R2H 1J8, Canada Tel: 204 235 1033 winnipeg@lochgallery.com www.lochgallery.com

M ⚒ Morphets of Harrogate, 6 Albert Street, Harrogate, Yorkshire HG1 1JL Tel: 01423 530030

Man ⊞ Mansers, 31 Wyle Cop, Shrewsbury, Shropshire S Y1 1XF Tel: 01743 240328 info@fineartdealers.co.uk www.fineartdealers.co.uk

MCA ⚒ Mervyn Carey, Twysden Cottage, Scullsgate, Benenden, Cranbrook, Kent TN17 4LD Tel: 01580 240283

MI ⊞ Mitofsky Antiques, 8 Rathfarnham Road, Terenure, Dublin 6, Republic of Ireland Tel: 00 353 1492 0033 info@mitofskyartdeco.com www.mitofskyartdeco.com

NFA ⊞† Nautical Fine Arts, 16 The Close, Driffield, East Yorkshire YO25 5JS Tel: 01377 200071 michael@jwhitehand.fsnet.co.uk www.nauticalfinearts.com

NNA ⊞ G. R. N'Namdi Gallery, 110 N. Peoria St, Chicago IL 60607, U.S.A. Tel: (001) 312 563 9240 grnnamdi@aol.com

No9 ⊞† Number Nine the Gallery, 9 Brindleyplace, Birmingham, West Midlands B1 2JA Tel: 00 44 (0)121 643 9099 noninethegallery@btclick.com www.numberninethegallery.com

OTG ⊞ othergallery, #405–33 Kennedy Street, Winnipeg MB, R3C 1S5, Canada Tel: 204 947 3551 info@othergallery.com www.othergallery.com

P&H ⊞ Panter & Hall, 9 Shepherd Market, Mayfair, London W1J 9PF Tel: 020 7399 9999 enquiries@panterandhall.co.uk www.panterandhall.co.uk

PEP ⊞ Peter Phillips Collection c/o 07770 418466

PFY ⊞ Patricia Fyfe, 187 Minto Place, Ottawa, Ontario K1M 0B6, Canada Tel: 001 (613) 749-6951

PGB ⊞ Priory Gallery, Forge House, 34 High Street, Broadway, Worcestershire WR12 7DT Tel: 01242 673226 rickjames@priorygallery.freeserve.co.uk

PY ⊞† Michael Pybus Fine Arts, 127 Church Street, Whitby, Yorkshire YO22 4DE Tel: 01947 820028 enquiries@mpybusfinearts.co.uk mpybusfinearts.co.uk

RSW ⊞ Rosemary Sarah Welch Tel: 01590 681392 rosemarywelch@talk21.com www.rosemarysarahwelch.com

RTo ⚒ Rupert Toovey & Co Ltd, Spring Gardens, Washington, West Sussex RH20 3BS Tel: 01903 891955 auctions@rupert-toovey.com www.rupert-toovey.com

S ⚒ Sotheby's, 34-35 New Bond Street, London W1A 2AA Tel: 020 7293 5000 www.sothebys.com

S(HK) ⚒ Sotheby's, 5/F Standard Chartered Bank Building, 4–4A Des Voeux Road, Central Hong Kong, China Tel: 852 2524 8121 www.sothebys.com

S(NY) ⚒ Sotheby's, 1334 York Avenue at 72nd St, New York NY 10021, U.S.A. Tel: 212 606 7000 www.sothebys.com

S(O) ⚒† Sotheby's Olympia, Hammersmith Road, London W14 8UX Tel: 020 7293 5555 www.sothebys.com

S(P) ⚒ Sotheby's France SA, 76 rue du Faubourg, Saint Honore, Paris 75008, France Tel: 33 1 53 05 53 05 www.sothebys.com

S(SI) ⚒ Sotheby's (Singapore) Pte Ltd, 1 Cuscaden Road, 01-01 The Regent, Singapore 249715 Tel: 65 6732 8239 www.sothebys.com

SCAN ⚒ Sotheby's, 9 Hazelton Avenue, Toronto, Ontario M5R 2EI, Canada Tel: 416 926 1774 www.sothebys.com

SHSY ⚒ Shapiro Auctioneers, 162 Queen Street, Woollahra, Sydney NSW 2025, Australia Tel: 612 9326 1588

SK ⚒ Skinner Inc., The Heritage On The Garden, 63 Park Plaza, Boston MA 02116, U.S.A. Tel: 617 350 5400

SMi ⊞ Sally Mitchell Fine Arts, Thornlea, Askham, Newark, Nottinghamshire NG22 ORN Tel: 01777 838234 john@dogart.com www.dogart.com

SMy ⊞ Sarah Myerscough Fine Art, 15–16 Brooks Mews, off Davies Street, Mayfair, London W1K 4DS Tel: 020 7495 0069 info@sarahmyerscough.com www.sarahmyerscough.com

ST ⊞ The Studio Art House, 16 Church Road, Leatherhead, Surrey KT22 8AY Tel: 01372 361906 stuartstanleyart@aol.com

StI ⊞ St Ives Society of Artists, Norway Gallery, Norway Square, St Ives, Cornwall TR26 1NA Tel: 01736 795582 www.stivessocietyofartists.com

TEN ⚒ Tennants, The Auction Centre, Harmby Road, Leyburn, Yorkshire DL8 5SG Tel: 01969 623780 enquiry@tennants-ltd.co.uk www.tennants.co.uk

TGG ⊞ The Graham Gallery, Highwoods, Burfield Common, Reading, Berkshire RG7 3BG Tel: 0118 983 1070

TR ⊞ Tracks, PO Box 117, Chorley, Lancashire PR6 0UU Tel: 01257 269726 sales@tracks.co.uk www.tracks.co.uk

TREA ⚒ Treadway Gallery, Inc., 2029 Madison Road, Cincinnati, Ohio 45208, U.S.A. Tel: 001 513 321 6742 www.treadwaygallery.com

TTCG ⊞ Thompson's The City, 26 Copthall Avenue, London EC2R 7DN Tel: 020 7256 5815 enquiries@citygallery.co.uk www.citygallery.co.uk

WA ⚒† Whyte's Auctioneers, 38 Molesworth Street, Dublin 2, Republic of Ireland Tel: 00 353 1 676 2888 info@whytes.ie www.whytes.ie

Waa ⊞ Waage Arts, 1 Nupalind 4, 201 Kopavour, Iceland Tel: +354 895 3013 hwaage@belugaarts.com www.belugaarts.com

WoF ⊞ Wolseley Fine Arts, 12 Needham Road, London W11 2RP Tel: 020 7792 2788 info@wolseleyfinearts.com www.wolseleyfinearts.com

WrG ⊞ Wren Gallery, Bear Court, 34 Lower High Street, Burford, Oxon OX18 4RR Tel: 01993 823495 enquiries@wrenfineart.com www.wrenfineart.com

WW ⚒ Woolley & Wallis, Salisbury Salerooms, 51-61 Castle Street, Salisbury, Wiltshire SP1 3SU Tel: 01722 424500/411854 junebarrett@woolleyandwallis.co.uk www.woolleyandwallis.co.uk

Index

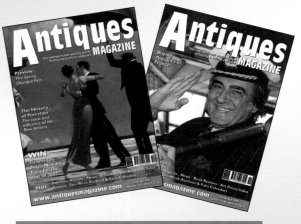